A WAR-TORN CHESTER PARISH

A War-Torn Chester Parish

St. Werburgh's before,
during and after the Great War

Contents

Acknowledgements	ix
Preface St. Werburgh's and the Great War *Fr. Paul Shaw*	xi
Chester and St. Werburgh's in 1914 *G. Tighe*	1
The King of Spain and St. Werburgh's *Ann Marie Curtis*	12
Building a Church St. Werburgh's Chester *John W. Curtis*	19
St. Patrick's Day Concerts 1913–20 *Alan Mapp*	27
"Our Birkenhead Friend" Arthur Killingworth Bourne Brandreth *John W. Curtis*	33
Benedict Williamson WW1 Priest and St. Werburgh's Forgotten Baldaquin *John W. Curtis*	46
A Rather Special Chalice *G. Tighe*	51
No Men Left at St. Werburgh's The Impact of the Great War on St. Werburgh's Parish *Great War Group*	53
Schools in Wartime *Great War Group*	58
Wartime Clergy Changes *Ann Marie Curtis*	66
A Chester Hero Returns The Great War Experiences of Walter Keating *Angela Clark*	71
Sergeant Major Patrick Currivan A True Irish Hero, but not in the Great War *John W. Curtis*	74
Canon Hugh Welch Parish Priest of St. Werburgh's and Prisoner of War *Fr. Paul Shaw*	83
A Family of Priests – The Welch Family *Ann Marie and John Curtis*	91

Australian Influences in Chester
Matthew Clayson 1887–1916 *Harper Wright* 98

A Tale of Two Architects
John Douglas (1830–1911) and
Edmund Kirby (1838–1920) *Ann Marie Curtis* 103

An Irish Childhood in Chester *Walter Cunniff* 116

The Belgian Connection *Stella Pleass* 120

Father Joseph Loos
A Belgian Priest at St. Werburgh's *Stella Pleass* 128

Belgians at Deeside Cottage *Ann Marie Curtis* 134

Memories of Steven Street, Boughton, Chester
Margaret Murray and Tony Jones 140

The Easter Rising and St. Werburgh's, Chester *Celia Murphy* 146

The Enigma of Roger David Casement 1864–1916 *John R. Caley* 151

Missionaries in Chester *Celia Murphy* 155

The Wallis Family and St. Werburgh's
Recusant Family Connections joining Cheshire and Yorkshire
John W. Curtis 163

The Tragedy of the Vickers Family *Harper Wright* 169

Racehorses and Altars
Donations of the Topham-Hall Family *John W. Curtis* 176

The Nelson Cup *Ann Marie Curtis and G. Tighe* 181

The Hunt for Lieutenant A. F. Hughes
How Fortune occasionally Favours Persistence *John Curtis* 185

From Shoes to Sparks to Shells
Gunner Charles Henry Creighton *Ann Marie Curtis* 198

A Night Ride *C. H. Creighton* 200

The Ears of the Guns *C. H. Creighton*	202
The Sky Pilot *Gunner C. H. Creighton, 72012*	204
Two Brothers and Two Wars *Stella Pleass*	205
The Duke's Dash through the Desert *Ann Marie Curtis*	207
Third Time Lucky at St. Werburgh's *Ann Marie Curtis*	212
The History and Mystery of the War Memorial Chapel St. Werburgh's Catholic Church, Chester *Ann Marie Curtis*	216

Copyright © St. Werburgh's Great War Study Group

Authors retain copyright of individual articles

First published in 2017 on behalf of the authors by
Scotforth Books

ISBN   978-1-909817-36-4

Typesetting and design by Carnegie Book Production, Lancaster.

Printed in the UK by Jellyfish Solutions

Acknowledgements

St. Werburgh's Great War Study Group would like to acknowledge the following persons and institutions, without whose help, this book would not have been brought to completion and publication:

Fr. Paul Shaw, parish priest of St. Werburgh's Catholic Church, Chester, for his support, encouragement and enthusiasm
St. Werburgh's parishioners who gave pictures and information
James Cashman for his legal expertise
John Clark for his expert enhancing of often originally very poor quality, pictures
John Curtis for photographs taken during the research period
Dr. Hannah Ewence and Dr. Jessica van Horssen for support with work concerning Belgian refugees
Brian Webster for the collation of material for publication

Staff at the following institutions:-
Beaumont College Archives
Cheshire Archives and Local Studies, Duke Street, Chester
Chester History and Heritage, Bridge Street, Chester
Diocese Catholique d'Amiens, Archives, France
Diocese Catholique de Malines, Archives, Belgium
Eaton Estate Archives
Friends of Flaybrick Cemetery, Birkenhead
Great War Forum
Military Museum, Chester
National Archives, Kew (TNA)
Pembroke College Oxford, Archives
Shrewsbury R.C. Diocesan Archives
St. Cuthbert's College, Ushaw, Archives
St. Ignatius' R.C. Parish, Sunbury-on-Thames
St. Mary's R.C. Parish, Crewe
Stonyhurst College Archives
University of Chester, Dept. of History and Archaeology

Sources

Army Service Records accessed via "Ancestry"
Cheshire Trade Directories, Cheshire Archives and Local Studies, Chester (CALS)
Local Newspapers covering the Great War period, held at CALS
Naval Records held at the National Archives, Kew
Royal Flying Corps Records held at the National Archives, Kew
Parishioners of St. Werburgh's, Chester
Records of Edmund Kirby and Sons, held at Liverpool Archives
Records of Hardman held at Birmingham Archives
Records of H.M.S. Conway School, Liverpool Maritime Museum
Records of Overleigh Cemetery, held at CALS
Regimental Diary of the Cheshire Regiment, held at the Military Museum, Chester
Registers of St. Werburgh's and St. Francis' Parishes, and an assortment of Anglican Parish registers, held at CALS
Pembroke College Oxford, student records, held at the college
St. Ignatius' R.C. Church, Sunbury-on-Thames, registers
St. Werburgh's Schools' logbooks and registers, held at CALS Studies, Chester
St. Werburgh's Parish Magazines 1904-1917, held at St. Werburgh's Church, Chester

Photographs

All non-attributed photographs are believed to be either in the public domain, or have been taken by John W. Curtis over the last five years. He waives copyright for this volume.

Preface
St. Werburgh's and the Great War

The fascination of historical research is that you never know what you are going to find. You start on a journey: sometimes it leads nowhere, sometimes to just where you want to be, but most often it takes you off in fascinating by-ways and side-roads that you had no idea existed. Rarely do you end up where you expected to be.

When we as a Parish decided we wanted to commemorate the centenary of the Great War in 1914, we were far from sure how we should go about it. One approach was to research the lives of the Parishioners and friends of St. Werburgh's who'd lost their lives in that conflict. That proved to be a gold-mine. We realised how little we knew: how incomplete existing records were and how much there was to discover. *We Shall Remember Them* was published in 2015, full biographies – or as full as we could possibly make them – of all our 120 or so Great War Dead.

But the road did not end there. The success of that first book – over 500 copies were sold – encouraged us to keep going. Our Great War Memorial disappeared from church in the 1970's, and clearly needed replacing. But saying what? Placed where? Erected when? In what medium? All vital questions with which our indefatigable Great War Study Group are wrestling as I write, October 2017. We have a firm target date of November 2018 for the installation and blessing of this new Memorial by our Bishop. We hope the City of Chester will also be represented by our Civic Leaders on that proud occasion. The work goes on.

As those more than 120 lives were researched and the biographies written, so many members of our Group realised there were other aspects of the life of St. Werburgh's during those Great War years that they would like to explore further. And so this present volume of essays has come about, and I am delighted to welcome its publication, almost forty essays and articles about so many different aspects of our life together, as Church and City, a hundred years ago.

What was Chester like in 1914 and the Edwardian period beforehand? Why did King Alfonso XIII of Spain visit? What's the story behind some of our most intriguing War Dead, men such as Brandreth, Currivan, Creighton and Keating? What were our Church and School like at this period, not to mention our Priests? Our army Chaplains? How international a city did Chester become in the war, welcoming the Belgians and Australians, St. Werburgh's still being a predominantly Irish part of the City? How conscious were we of the Easter Uprising of 1916? St. Patrick's Day

Concerts, Tontine, Choir, how far did the ordinary peace-time life of any busy parish continue despite the war? So many of the family names of the time continue to resonate with us: the Dodsworth, Vickers, Hall and Hughes families. What did they mean to us then, and how have they fared in the century since? We hope you will find the answers to some of these questions in these pages.

The War Memorial Chapel today is back in use, the fine chalice of that period still very much in evidence: this is a living Parish, proud of its past and determined to take its rich heritage forward into the future. We hope you enjoy reading these articles as much as we have all relished writing them.

(Fr.) Paul Shaw

October 2017

Chester and St. Werburgh's in 1914

"The past is a foreign country; they do things differently there"

This striking opening line in L.P. Hartley's novel "The Go Between" provides an evocative backcloth to any study of a bygone age. For those of more senior years and for long standing Parishioners there will be vivid memories of past events and characters. For others much of what is written here may be new information. As far as possible I have tried to base this account on contemporary sources although shades of colour and opinion no doubt show through.

The Chester of 1914 was considerably smaller in both land area and population than the present City. With a population in the region of 50,000 according to the 1911 census it was under half the size of the present community. There was little to be found in the present suburbs of Blacon, Lache, Huntington or Upton and Newton. Parts of central Chester were densely populated with low quality housing which contained no bathroom or indoor toilet. Adjacent to the Town Hall could be found cramped and crowded dwellings which were only removed in the 1930's. Off Boughton, close to the Shropshire Union Canal could be found Steven Street in which some 80% to 90% of the inhabitants were descendents of migrants from Ireland who had fled to this country in the years after the famine of the 1840's. To see what a courtyard dwelling area looked like make the journey up the steps from Lower Bridge Street into Gamull Place. Today these houses offer comfortable living accommodation but in 1914 it would have been very different.

Davis Court off Steam Mill Street
Reproduced by kind permission of
Chester History and Heritage

Chester was and is a mixed community with people of different social strata and wealth living at close quarters with one another. There were luxury and opulent dwellings in Queens Park, Curzon Park and parts of Hoole, in close proximity to much humbler abodes. It is worth considering the current debates into plans for student accommodation in the Garden Lane area and the controversy that surrounded the former Western Command Bank Building in Queens Park; now home to the Business Management Campus of the University of Chester.

In 1914 the two largest employers in Chester were the Leadworks and the Railways. The former (Walker, Parker and Co.) dated from 1800 and was built adjacent to the Canal and the latter arrived in Chester in the 1840's. There were three stations serving our area; Chester General (our current station) at the bottom of City Road, Northgate on the site of the Leisure Centre and Liverpool Road on the site of Total Fitness which one passes on the way to the Countess of Chester Hospital. The 1911 Census reveals 698 railway workers and of this number there were 200 platform staff alone at Chester General at the time of a railway strike in that same year. In addition there were two engine sheds and also wagon works providing additional employment. Chester was served by trains of the Great Western, London North Western and Cheshire Lines Committee Railways. Other Cestrians were employed in corn mills along the Canal (think of Frosts at the Steam Mill), in retailing and in brewing. In 1910 there were also five snuff mills including a famous one overlooking the Dee Weir in Handbridge. Chester had two breweries within the City Walls. The Lion Brewery on Pepper Street (you can still see the statue of the Lion on the Car Park lift shaft above Dawsons Music Shop) and the Northgate Brewery. It is interesting to note that until 1830 there had been 200 stage coaches leaving Chester per week.

Chester Leadworks

Chester Steam Mill, now converted to apartments 2015

In 1914 there was no inner ring road or A55 and all traffic heading to and from North Wales had to pass through the City Centre and over the Grosvenor Bridge.

Between 1870 and the early 1900's Chester had horse drawn trams but these had been replaced by electric trams in 1903. These ran up City Road, from the depot which is currently being re-developed behind the Westminster Hotel, to Saltney and as far as the Bridge Inn on Tarvin Road. There would have been clanging bells and rattles caused by these trams as they made their way round the Bars and along Foregate and Eastgate Street. All would have been familiar to the Parishioners of St. Werburgh's in 1914.

4 A War-Torn Chester Parish

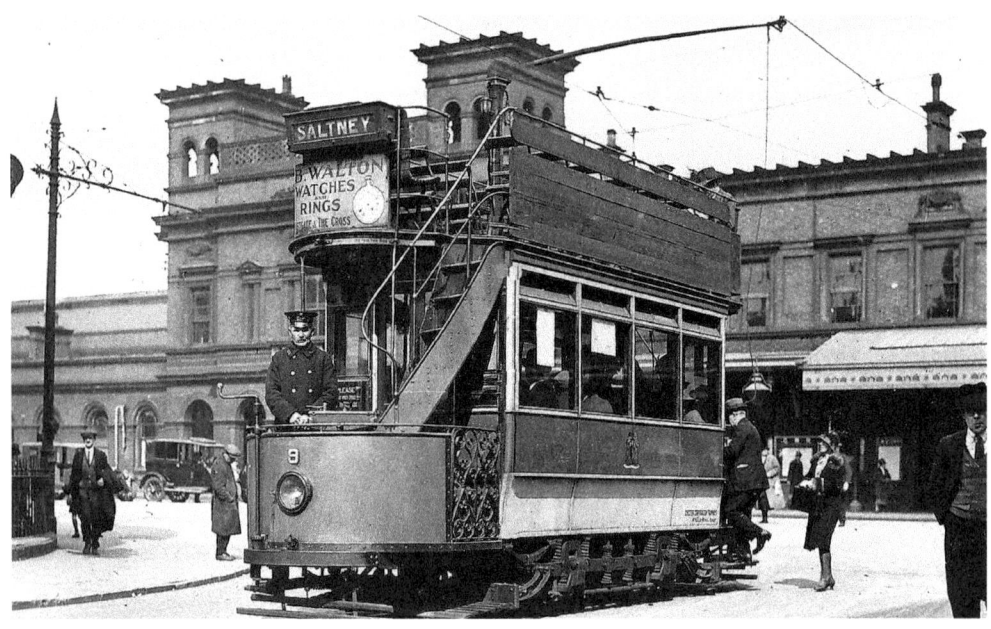

Electric Tram outside Chester Railway Station ca 1930's

Chester Town Hall and Market ca 1900

Chester has been the centre for a market since at least 1139. It was also an important military centre. Many will recall the imposing Victorian Market Hall next to the Town Hall which was sadly demolished in the early 1970's. There are just small traces of this building remaining over the archway leading to a passage by the side of The Dublin Packet pub. By 1914 Browns (Debenhams) was clearly Chester's leading department store but there were others of note such as Richard Jones in Bridge Street and Burrells on Foregate Street. By 1910 Boots and Marks and Spencers had arrived. Most grocery shopping would have been carried out at the Market or at local independent stores. There were, however, chains of stores starting to appear and older readers may recall Liptons, Home and Colonial, Maypole and Peagrams. Kelly's Street Directory for 1914 shows there being eight butchers, one fishmonger and six grocers Shops on the ground level of Bridge Street between The Cross and Pepper Street; a marked contrast to the number of coffee shops and eateries there today. There will be some of you who will recall your Co-Op Divi. No! Puzzled by this reference? The Divi. Number was used by shoppers in the days before we had loyalty cards or even Green Shield and Pink Stamps! I remember our family number as being 26653. I jest not.

Much could be said about Education in 1914. Suffice to say that the period we are covering was a time of great Social Change. There were still no votes for women but the Suffragette movement was active. The Old Age Pensions Act of 1908 had introduced for the first time a pension for the elderly (5 shillings a week) and from 1902 onwards Local Authorities had become active in the provision of additional Elementary and Secondary Education. There were of course prestigious independent schools in Chester such as Kings founded in 1541 and Queen's in 1878. The Catholic population for the most part would have supported their own schools. Dee House Convent, offering day and boarding accommodation, overlooking today's Amphitheatre, opened in 1854. This survived until 1972 when comprehensive secondary re – organisation led to the closure of St. Bede's, a Secondary Modern School and the creation of the Catholic High School in buildings formerly occupied by Overleigh Secondary Modern School.

It is easy to forget that in 1914 most children only ever attended one all age school and that the majority left school at 13 (at the end of the current Year 8)! School Leaving Age did not rise to 14 until the 1918 Education Act. St. Werburgh's School had been established in 1854 in Queen Street and survived there until its relocation to the current buildings in Lightfoot Street in the 1960's. St. Francis also had its own school in Cuppin Street. This was opened in 1883 and closed in 1972. The nuns who staffed both Dee House and St. Werburgh's were initially members of the F.C.J. Order (Faithful Companions of Jesus). They were replaced by the Ursuline sisters in 1925.

Life was undoubtedly hard for many people in Chester in 1914 but one has to remember that all is relative to the time in which one lives. Opposite St. Werburgh's Church was the main entrance to the wonderful Grosvenor Park given as a gift to Cestrians by the Second Marquis of Westminster in 1867. At the corner of Bath Street and Union Street was and is the City Baths opened in 1901 – a magnificent building for its day which has recently received a welcome facelift. Two swimming pools are here, one called the Pacific and the other the Atlantic. The Baths also had public washing facilities for those who did not have a bathroom. Clothes washing could also be carried out here. Chester Football Club had been founded in 1885 on a ground which was originally in Hoole. I must not forget to mention the Racecourse at the Little Roodee which has the distinction of being the oldest in England, having been established in 1539. There were also venues for live music, variety and theatrical events. One such building was the Music Hall (now Superdrug) in St. Werburgh Street and the Royalty Theatre in City Road (the site of today's Premier Inn). The Royalty Theatre could accommodate 2,000 people. The programme for the 27th June 1914 comprised:-

1) The Five Sollies in Mad Moments of Vaudeville
2) The Lanedale Trio
3) Little Zaza who is described as The Last Word in Thought Translation
4) Dick Trubb – The Grotesque Comedian

There were two shows every night! How would these folk fare on the talent shows of today?

There were two cinemas in Chester in 1914. At the Picturedrome on Eastgate Street the 27 June offering was the silent film of "An Officer and a Man" described as a stirring military story. The Glynn in Foregate Street was showing "The Midnight Wedding" followed by a very early version of the classic Frances Hodgson Burnett story, "Little Lord Fauntleroy".

The Parish of St. Werburgh's is a huge and fascinating subject and so I have decided to look at the buildings, people and activities of 1914 as separate but interlinked topics.

The Church

The current building was designed by Edmund Kirby who had started his professional career working with the much acclaimed John Douglas. The land was acquired thanks to the generosity of two brothers, a Michael and John Harnett. The first Mass was celebrated on Christmas Day 1875 with the official opening on the 13 July 1876. The Church was of a Gothic style with stonework from Yorkshire. The interior was smaller than the building with which we are familiar today since the last 2 bays and porch had not yet been built.

In 1904 two sacristies connected by an ambulacrum were erected, while during 1913 and 1914 two bays, a front porch and façade were added. Grey quarried stone from Stourton near Birkenhead was used on this extension. The magnificent High Altar of onyx and marble which has recently (2012/2013) been restored was not to be added until 1926. The Centenary Handbook for the Diocese of Shrewsbury produced in 1951 states that St. Werburgh's at that time could accommodate 800.

Canon Joseph Chambers

The Rector of the Parish in 1914 was Canon Joseph Chambers and he was assisted by two Curates, Fr. Maurice Hayes and Fr. O'Hara. Joseph Chambers was born in Reading in 1864 and after ordination served in a number of parishes as a curate. For two years (1897–99) he was a curate in Chester at St. Werburgh's before being appointed Parish Priest of St. Edward's in Runcorn. On the death of Canon Lynch in 1903 he was re-appointed to St. Werburgh's as Rector of the Parish. He was still in his late thirties and was to remain as Rector for 21 years. Canon Chambers died in harness on the 30 November 1924 and is buried in Overleigh Cemetery in Handbridge. A statue of St. Joseph (near the organ console) was presented in his memory by the children of St. Werburgh's School and he is also commemorated in one of our beautiful stained glass windows.

Canon Chambers worked tirelessly for the Parish of St. Werburgh's. He comes across as a "can do" person who represented St. Werburgh's in every possible manner on the local scene. He was appointed to the Education Committee for the City and County Borough of Chester. He commissioned extensions to the Church, had leaded light windows installed, replaced gas lighting with electricity in 1906 and saw to it that considerable improvements took place at the School and Club in Queen Street. New vestments were purchased and in 1909 a Mission was given by the Redemptorist Fathers. He arranged for a Parish Chalice dating back to 1867 to be restored and enlarged in 1913. The provenance of this Chalice has been carried out as part of this Project. It bears two Birmingham assay marks and is again being used when Holy Mass is celebrated on major Feast Days. Bishop Mark used it when he celebrated Mass for the re-dedication of the High Altar Tabernacle in 2013 and also when he came to confer the Sacrament of Confirmation in December of the same year. This Chalice has probably been used by every priest who has served in the current Church.

On Sunday, 1 December 1907 Canon Chambers celebrated a Low Mass at which the then 21 year old King of Spain attended, accompanied by other Spanish nobles. The King was staying at Eaton Hall as a guest of the 2nd Duke of Westminster. In 1909 the S.V.P was established and in the previous year the Archconfraternity of St. Stephen had been set up. In this year the Bishop visited St. Werburgh's to administer the

Canon Joseph Chambers

Sacrament of Confirmation. The 1910 Diocesan Year Book states that 274 Candidates were confirmed! In 1911, at the invitation of Canon Chambers, the Little Sisters of the Assumption came to Chester. They lived first of all at 45, Queen Street but moved in 1913 to a purpose built convent on Union Street (today the site is a block of flats known as Knightsbridge Court). The work of the Sisters is described as "the nursing of the sick of the working classes of all denominations and to assist them both spiritually and corporally". The July edition of Parish Magazine for 1913 records the Sisters as having made 200 home visits and that 160 children had visited the dispensary. This certainly was another world before the advent of the National Health System.

Canon Chambers worked hard to reduce the Parish debt. He was concerned not to take on more than the parish could afford. The structural works of 1913/14 cost £4,000.00. There were calls on the Parishioners to raise this money by Sales of Work and various Fundraising Events. Yes, the pennies of the poor were important but there were also some generous personal donations. Some donors are mentioned on the magnificent windows that adorn the Church, as is the name of Pat Collins on the base of the Pulpit.

The Chester Chronicle of 27 June 1914 records the solemn re-opening of St. Werburgh's on 21 June and describes it as having been accompanied by "much rejoicing and religious ceremony". The account goes on to comment that, "Canon Chambers has been not the Moses but the Joshua of his people: he has led them into the Promised Land". On the morning of the re-opening Pontifical High Mass took place and among those present were the Mayor (Ald. J.M. Frost) the Sheriff (Mr. J. Dodd) and the Town Clerk. The Celebrant was Dr. Hugh Singleton, Bishop of Shrewsbury and the Preacher was Dr. Keating, the Bishop of Northampton. Interestingly tickets were sold for admission to this Mass; 2 shillings (10p) for a nave seat and 1 shilling (5p) for an aisle seat. There was no charge for the Evening Service which took the form of Vespers, Sermon by Bishop Singleton and Procession of the Blessed Sacrament.

At some stage during 1913 Canon Chambers visited Rome, Assisi, Venice and Turin. The Canon speaks of his travels in the Parish Magazines of the time which include a picture of the then Pope, Pius X. The Pope was to die on the 20 August 1914 shortly after the outbreak of the First World War. In May 1914 Canon Chambers represented the Catholics of Chester and was presented to King George V and Queen Mary at a Stand erected in front of the Town Hall. On this visit the King consented to the title of "Royal" being added to the Infirmary which was sited on Nuns Road next to Queen's School and dated back to 1761. The original building can still be seen. The Canon seems to have been a good mixer with all ages and on 19 July 1913 there is mention of him accompanying 88 youngsters on a Sunday School trip to the Overton Hills accompanied by nuns and assistant teachers. He was also Chaplain to the Tarvin Union; a name for one of the Workhouses of the area and a regular parish visitor. In the April 1913 Parish Magazine the Canon gives a tip for the forthcoming Chester May Meeting Races:

"Put your money on St. Werburgh's Church and you'll not fail"

Canon Chambers served for 21 years as Parish Priest of St. Werburgh's during turbulent and changing times.

Services and Activities within St. Werburgh's in 1914

The times of services were different to those of today. Sunday Masses were celebrated at 8.00; 9.00; 10.00; and 11.00a.m. the last being a High Mass with Celebrant, Deacon and Sub-Deacon. There was a Sunday Evening Service at 6.30p.m. It took various forms according to the Sunday of the month. i. e.

- 1st Sunday Sacred Heart Devotions
- 2nd Sunday Votive Vespers of the Blessed Virgin Mary
- 3rd Sunday Rosary and English Hymns
- 4th Sunday Compline
- 5th Sunday Vespers B.V.M.

Weekday Mass was celebrated at 8.00 a.m. There were no doubt Masses also celebrated daily for the Sisters in their convents at Dee House and in Union Street.

In addition Benediction was held on Thursday evenings at 7.30 p.m. and the Rosary was recited in Church every other evening at the same time. Confessions were heard on Saturday evenings between 6.00 p.m. and 9.00 p.m.

As for other activities there were a good number of Guilds and Sodalities. These included The Children of Mary; Guild of St. Stephen; Catholic Young Men's Society; Tontine Society; Clothing Club; Protection and Rescue Society; The Altar Society; Ladies of Charity and the S.V.P. There was also a flourishing Parish Choir which is mentioned as having a summer seaside day trip into North Wales followed by a "Meat Tea".

August 1914

It is said that Sir Edward Grey, Britain's longest serving Foreign Secretary was standing at a window in the Foreign Office on the 3 August when he uttered the immortal lines:-

"The lamps are going out all over Europe. We shall not see them lit again in our time"

On the following day Britain declared war on Germany after it had invaded France and Belgium, which at that time was a neutral country. The First World War was to change forever the map of Europe and caused great suffering, death and countless personal stories of heroism and tragedy. Chester and the people of St. Werburgh's Parish were not immune from this catastrophe. One gets some idea by reading letters and poetry of the period and of how families were torn apart by death and injury to loved ones. Canon Chambers wrote movingly in the Parish Magazine of this time.

At the beginning of August the weather was cool and cloudy with temperatures below average. By the middle of the month the country was experiencing a heatwave with temperatures in the mid 80'sF. There was much activity at the Castle and by the 22 August recruits were enlisting at the rate of 100 a day. Since the commencement of hostilities 2250 had already volunteered in Chester alone. The Duke of Westminster offered all the horses on the Eaton Estate for military service and stated that Eaton Hall and Grosvenor House in London could be used as hospitals. Belgians were nursed at the convent in Union Street, in recognition of which the Medelle de la Reine Elizabeth was awarded to the Superior by the King of the Belgians.

In the December 1914 issue of the Parish Magazine it was stated that 190 Parishioners had already joined the army and that in that month alone 3 deaths were recorded. The total number of casualties during the First World War was to exceed 16 million.

"They shall grow not old as we that are left grow old:
Age shall not weary them nor the years condemn.
At the going down of the sun and in the morning
We will remember them"

An extract from Lawrence Binyon's poem "For The Fallen" first published in The Times in September 1914

G. Tighe　　　　　　　　　　　　　　　　　　　　　　　　　　　　　　**February 2017**

The King of Spain and St. Werburgh's

The autumn of 1907 proved very unsettling for Canon Chambers. Since October the Royal Family of Spain had been resident in this country. Nothing to do with us, you might think. But you would be wrong. The Canon had been advised that there was some likelihood that during the hunting season, the King might stay at Eaton Hall, as a guest of the Duke and Duchess of Westminster. If that stay should include a Sunday, then the King might come to St. Werburgh's Church to Mass. Whilst it would be an honour to have the monarch at Mass, Canon Chambers was only too aware of how poor St. Werburgh's Church must appear to a monarch more used to the most opulent of Spanish Cathedrals. Nevertheless, the Canon would hold himself in readiness, should this unsettling event ever come to pass[1].

Who was this monarch who had the power to so discompose the Canon? He was a very unusual monarch indeed. King Alfonso XIII of Spain was a King even before he was born! His father, King Alfonso XII, had died a few months before his birth and the young King was brought up by his mother, Queen Christina (formerly of Austria) who acted as his Regent until he reached the age of sixteen. Then he formally acceded to the throne. His education had been somewhat restricted but he had been thoroughly schooled in Spanish law, the rights and duties of the monarchy and he was a good linguist. The young King, unsurprisingly, had a taste for adventure and a certain amount of rebelliousness.

Queen Christina was anxious for Alfonso to marry and start a family, in order to stabilise the succession, at what was a rather tumultuous time in Spanish

King Alfonso XIII of Spain and his mother Queen Maria Christina

affairs, with anarchists always a threat to governments of any persuasion. She had been considering princesses of different European countries but had not thought to overly concern herself with British princesses, as marriage with one of them could lead to too many complications.

Alfonso was not particularly interested in his mother's searches, but in 1905 he accepted the invitation to visit the Court of King Edward VII. It was whilst here that he met Princess Ena, the daughter of King Edward's youngest sister, Princess Beatrice and the late Prince Henry of Battenburg. There seemed to be a spark between them immediately.

They were both of similar age and found they enjoyed each other's company. Ena had been born at Balmoral and had been used to much more freedom of action than Alfonso. She may not have been quite as formal as the Spanish ladies he was used to meeting. The couple talked about the problems concerning their possible union and worked out the answers to the three main problems themselves, before Alfonso returned to Spain and had to confront his mother.

The first problem was the religion of Princess Ena. A Spanish Queen was Catholic almost by definition, which Ena was not. This did not seem to bother Princess Ena. She had already informed Alfonso that she had no objection to converting to Catholicism and would take steps to set that in train. The second problem concerned her status. Princess Ena was the granddaughter of Queen Victoria but her father had not been a King and she was referred to as Her Highness, Princess Victoria Eugenie (her full name) not, Her Royal Highness. This seemed to give her a rather inferior status compared with

King Alfonso XIII of Spain in uniform

some other European princesses and moreover, Queen Christina did not consider the Battenburg family to be a dynasty. Princess Ena partly solved this problem by getting her uncle, King Edward, to promise to change her title to Her Royal Highness and King Alfonso undertook to talk his mother around.

The third problem was one which could not be settled in advance, nor one which the couple could alter at all: the problem of haemophilia. This condition was known to run in Queen Victoria's family. Prince Leopold, one of Queen Victoria's sons had died at a very young age, due to this condition, for which there was no effective treatment at that time. One of Ena's brothers, also called Leopold, was also affected, (though he did not die until 1922 age 32). This meant that Ena's mother was a carrier for the disease and also that there was a 50% chance that Ena herself could be a carrier. There was no way of finding out if Ena was a carrier, until she had a baby boy. The couple decided to take the chance that Ena would not be a carrier and the Queen soon dropped her objections to the match, as her son was so insistent upon it.

The couple were married in Madrid on 31 May 1906. Unfortunately their celebrations were disturbed by the action of an anarchist, who threw a bomb at the wedding party as they were proceeding from the marriage service to the reception. The couple were not killed or injured but several surrounding persons were and the scene became one of carnage and terror. This was not a very auspicious start to their married life. However, they recovered from the shattering experience and their son, Prince Alfonso of Asturias, heir to the throne, was born on 10 May 1907.

Later that year the couple decided to spend some time in this country and show the heir to the Spanish throne to his British relations. It was a private, not a state visit. HMS Renown carried the Spanish Royal Family from Cherbourg to Portsmouth on 29 October 1907. The Royal party then went by train to London, where they proceeded to Kensington Palace, home of Queen Victoria Eugenie's mother[2]. They stayed with her for a few days, going to St. James' Catholic Church, Spanish Place, for Mass on Sunday 3 November[3]. Later they visited Sandringham to stay with King Edward[4] calling at Cambridge, where the Queen's brother, Prince Leopold of Battenburg was a student[5]. They returned to London from whence they made several excursions, though it was noticeable that the Queen did not accompany King Alfonso on hunting or shooting expeditions[6].

It was not surprising therefore, that the Queen did not accompany King Alfonso when he visited Eaton Hall for a hunting and shooting weekend at Eaton, hosted by the Duke and Duchess of Westminster. On the evening of Thursday 28 November, King Alfonso, with four Spanish noblemen, arrived by train at Crewe Station, from Euston. Here the King transferred to a special train ordered by the Duke of Westminster, which

King Alfonso and Queen Victoria Eugenie of Spain

took the party as far as Waverton Station, arriving around 6.00pm. The King was then whisked off to Eaton Hall in the Duke's motorcade, where he was graciously received by the Duchess. Security was paramount and four young Spanish men, who had made the journey from Liverpool, where they were employed, to see their Sovereign, were detained by police as a precaution. They were released when they proved to be of no threat and were even allowed to watch the King's arrival through the waiting room window. This would have given them a much better view than other members of the public, who had gathered at Waverton. They were then allowed to return to Chester in the special train which had carried the King!

The following day, Friday, the party rode to hounds, the King being mainly accompanied by the Duchess of Westminster and on Saturday there was a shooting party, which took place in dense fog! The Chester newspapers reported practically every shot and chase. King Alfonso apparently both rode well and also bagged a good number of game[7]. On Saturday Canon Chambers received the message from Eaton, which he was both anticipating and dreading. The King of Spain would be attending the 11.00am Mass the following day. I do not think that the Canon slept much that night. However, he had Fr. Maurice Hayes to help him and between them a welcome was prepared which was hopefully suitable for a King.

According to the Chester Chronicle of 7 December 1907, the motorcade carrying the King arrived at 2 minutes before 11.00am. on Sunday 1 December. The King and his entourage entered St. Werburgh's Church along a red carpet, and were conducted to the altar. The King was placed in a special chair on the altar and the nobles seated on a choir stall. The mass was said by Canon Chambers with Rev. Fr. Hayes in attendance. There was no sermon and the visitors left the church to the strains of the Spanish National Anthem, played by the organist, Mr. Massa. The party was cheered by the congregation, as the members entered the motor cavalcade to return to Eaton and Canon Chambers could now relax!

King Alfonso XIII of Spain leaving St. Werburgh's Church, 1 Dec 1907

St. Werburgh's Church, Chester, the Sacred Heart side Chapel with King Alfonso's Chair

Canon Chambers described the occasion in the December issue of St. Werburgh's Parish Magazine, stating that the King had left a donation of £5 for the church completion fund. He also took issue with some persons in the crowd who had cast aspersions on the poor entry to the unfinished church. He hoped that money would be forthcoming soon to complete the church and that in future, the entry would be suitable for the reception of any Monarch of any country.

On Sunday evening the King's party returned to London and on the evening of Tuesday 3 December the Spanish Royal Family took the train to Portsmouth. Here they once more embarked on HMS Renown and the following morning left for La Rochelle[8]. Whilst the Spanish Royal Family may have enjoyed a pleasant stay in this country in 1907, they were to lead a rather unfortunate life thereafter. Their infant son, who was with them on their visit, proved to be a haemophiliac, had many bouts of illness and died at a comparatively early age. Another son, Fernando was stillborn and a third son, Gonzalo was also a haemophilia sufferer. Their two daughters, Princesses Beatriz and Cristina proved not to be carriers, and two other sons proved unaffected, though one of them had other health issues. Their hosts in Chester, the Duke and Duchess of Westminster also experienced family problems during subsequent years, as mentioned in the essay "The Duke's Dash."

By summer 1914, the narthex entry of St. Werburgh's was completed, the Great War had started and King Alfonso and Queen Victoria Eugenie began to lead separate lives.

Their marriage was not strong enough to withstand the pressure of so many children with health problems, which were apparently regarded as the Queen's fault. Later, the Queen returned to Britain but eventually settled in Switzerland, where she died in 1969.

Alfonso had a very difficult reign post WW1, with five attempts made upon his life. He took several mistresses and fathered five illegitimate children. There were political problems, which are far too complex to describe in this essay and these resulted in his having to leave Spain and abdicate his throne. Alfonso died in Rome in 1941.

Spain itself, though remaining neutral during both World Wars, went through several turbulent administrations but is now a modern, democratic state. The present Spanish Royal Family is descended from Prince Juan Carlos, the only prince of the Royal Anglo-Spanish marriage, who had no health problems.

Meanwhile, the narthex entry of St. Werburgh's, to which King Alfonso contributed, has not received any other Monarchs visiting Chester. However, it has sheltered numerous parishioners and wedding parties, as they make their way into or out of the church and the chair occupied by King Alfonso is at present in the Sacred Heart side Chapel.

Ann Marie Curtis   **July 2017**

References

1. St. Werburgh's Parish Magazine December 1907
2. Western Daily Press 30 October 1907
3. Leeds Mercury 4 November 1907
4. Norfolk News 9 November 1907
5. London Evening Standard 12 November 1907
6. Grantham Journal 23 November 1907
7. Chester Chronicle of Sat. 7 December 1907 and Chester Courant of Wed. 4 December 1907
8. London Daily News 4 December 1907 and Morning Post 5 December 1907

Building a Church

St. Werburgh's Chester

It was during the Rectorship of Provost Buquet (1868–1882) that the construction of this handsome building was undertaken, as the old Chapel in Queen Street was totally inadequate for the numbers now in the parish. The foundation stone was laid on 15 October 1873 and the Church opened for Divine Worship in December, 1875. The Debt then on the Mission (£6,000 for the church and £1,400 for the conversion of the original Queen Street Chapel to a school) prevented its completion. The main part of the church was of stone but a 'temporary' west wall of brick faced Grosvenor Park Road as shown in the photograph.

The majority of the parishioners were Irish immigrants living in Boughton who worked in the nearby Flour Mills, railway works, tobacco, snuff works or the local plant nurseries. The 1911 census shows the houses in the nearby streets, such as Steven Street in Boughton to contain 3 rooms including the kitchen. The 1861 and 1871 censuses show these same houses occupied by up to 14 people from 3 different families, such was the poverty of the recently arrived immigrants. With such an inauspicious background there must have been more than an element of luck that Chester should be endowed with such a handsome building as St. Werburgh's Church.

It may be argued that there was fortunate timing. John Douglas, the Chester based architect to the Duke of Westminster, had been employed just before the turn of the century by Chester Council to draw up plans for the redevelopment of the area of Chester close by the Grosvenor Park. His work today is still in evidence in the Victorian buildings opposite St. Werburgh's entrance, City Baths and a terrace of houses in Bath Street. His assistant, Edmund Kirby, previously articled to E. W. Pugin, had left Chester to set up his own practice in Liverpool in 1867. Kirby would have come to Provost Buquet's attention, as in 1867 he had designed a wing containing a chapel, that was added to Dee House Convent. The choice of Edmund Kirby as the architect for St. Werburgh's Church was inspired and led to a long term working relationship with his firm that lasted for more than 90 years.

If the choice of Edmund Kirby was inspired, St. Werburgh's was also most fortunate in the rectors who succeeded Provost Buquet. When Canon Lynch became Rector in 1882, he had to face a debt close on £7,000. Individuals both from Chester and elsewhere came forward with donations to help reduce the debt but unfortunately none of these was sufficient to pay it off. As a result Canon Lynch and later Canon Chambers had to take the lead with their parishioners in finding ways to generate income to pay off debts. This they did through a variety of fund raising events or direct calls on their impoverished parishioners. Fund raising events included Sales of Work, bazaars, charity sermons, concerts, Saturday collections, even "The One Day's Wage for the Church Building Fund". Canon Lynch managed to reduce the debt to £3,750 and by 1899 legacies from the Tatlock family (Chester Solicitors) enabled the debts at both St. Francis and St. Werburgh's Churches to be cleared completely.

Canon Lynch then strove his utmost to raise funds for the completion of the church. He left at his death in November 1902, £1,500 which he had collected for this purpose. This Fund was considerably increased in 1903 by the efforts of Canon Chambers. There was then sufficient in hand to start building towards completion. Two handsome Sacristies were added to the Chancel end and a new wall enclosing the Church property was built in Bath Street. After completing this end of the Church, about £500 was left towards building the Grosvenor Park Road West Front. In all these endeavors,

St. Werburgh's was supported by the citizens of Chester and the City Council who permitted free use of the Town Hall for fund raising events. Successive Mayors, council appointed school managers, and many interested Cestrians, lent their aid.

Over the next few years a number of different plans were drawn up by the architect, Edmund Kirby, as the difficulties of raising money for the completion became apparent. Canon Chambers' efforts to complete the church were thwarted by the poverty of his parishioners and the need for significant expenditure to raise the standards of the schools buildings to an acceptable level. Canon Chamber's own words best sum up the situation over the following years as he attempts to find sufficient funds to complete the Church, a daunting task. Appendix 1 describes Canon Chambers' personal marathon to raise funds for the Mission to pay off the debt on the School and the Church, as shown by extracts from St. Werburgh's Parish Magazine.

Though the sacrifices of the parishioners were extraordinary to help fund the ever growing mission debt, one year Canon Chambers had to use money donated for his Jubilee, to pay off the interest of the debt when it fell due. Even so, the efforts of the clergy and the parishioners and the donations from supporters of St. Werburgh's external to the parish, enabled the work of improving the internal beauty of our Church to continue. Individual families donated money to provide memorial windows in the Apse and Chancel, other windows were provided as memorial windows by public subscription, e.g. Canon Lynch, Mother Elizabeth. Other persons donated Sanctuary lamps, vestments, candle sticks, electric lighting for the church, etc. However, actions towards raising funds for the completion of the Church were making little progress.

It was at this point that the weather took an intervening hand. The terrible winter storms of 1911/12 caused the de-stabilisation of the "temporary west wall" of the Church. By March 1913 the situation of the Church west brick wall was becoming desperate. Tiles on the wall were falling off and netting had to be put in place to protect parishioners entering the Church. Canon Chambers then had two alternatives, to rebuild another temporary wall at great cost or to go for completion of the Church, at astronomical cost. Canon Chambers then embarked on a great act of faith. He decided to go for the completion of the church, rather than rebuilding another temporary wall. To complete the Church, would cost £4,000. The Church Building fund had £2,000 so an additional £2,000 would be needed. To raise £2,000 in 12 months would be impossible. With the Bishop's permission, Canon Chambers was able to announce that if one half of the amount still needed was forthcoming, the Bishop would guarantee that the church would be finished. So unless another £1,000 could be found, it would be necessary to spend the existing money on a temporary wall and porch. So in April 1913 the great race to gather funds for the church completion began. Notices on the Church Door Stated £3,000 wanted to complete the Church (£2,000 already obtained). It was promoted as the chance of a lifetime, the privilege of helping to build one's church may not, will not, be offered again to many parishioners.

On 14 April 1913 work on the new foundations started and the task of raising additional funds ran in parallel with the work. With the benefit of hindsight, including the knowledge that World War 1 would begin later in 1914, it is questionable whether St. Werburgh's would ever have been completed, if the first and somewhat easier alternative had been taken.

By July 1913, £250 had been raised and a further £750 was required. Concerts etc. were planned to raise funds. The people of Chester rallied to the event, the proprietor of the Royalty Theatre permitting its use without charge. Even so the half yearly interest on the Mission debt, in excess of £100, still had to be paid.

Building work continued through the winter of 1913/14 and plans put in place for the Dedication of the additions and the re-opening of St. Werburgh's were set for 10 May. Unfortunately delay in completing the building resulted in the opening being delayed until 21 June. The solemn re-opening of the Church was truly a high point, attended by Civic Dignitaries and parishioners joyful at their achievements. Pontifical High Mass was held at 11 a.m. Celebrant: The Right Reverend, The Bishop of the Diocese of Shrewsbury, Dr. Hugh Singleton, Preacher: The Right Reverend, The Bishop of Northampton, Dr. Keating. Charges for admission were 2/- for the Nave, 1/- for the side Aisles. Amongst those present were the Mayor, (Ald. J. M. Frost), the Sheriff (Mr. J. Dodd), the Town Clerk (Mr. G. N. S. Hull (clerk to the Chester Guardians), Ald. McCabe (the Lord Mayor of Manchester) etc.[1]

The Church was resplendent, having the form which we recognize today. The gift of a statue of St. Werburgh (carved in Portland Stone) for the porch had been donated by Mr. and Mrs. William Evans. The Font, a previous gift from Mrs. Barker of Heron Bridge, was refurbished and moved to a different location, at her expense. The Memorial Window to Mother Elizabeth and the window to the memory of John McGeever, first president of the Young Men's Society had been installed.

The additions to the Church consisted of two more bays, a facade and a narthex (porch). With the new extension the total amount spent on the building of St. Werburgh's Church, had been altogether about £16,000. By the extension and the re-arrangement inside, the accommodation had been about doubled, the Church being spacious enough to comfortably seat 800 people.[1] However, a great debt had been incurred and much had still to be done. A new High Altar of stone or marble, new Communion Rails, Choir Stalls etc., were all needed to complete the interior of the church.

However, in the August 1914 edition of St. Werburgh's Parish Magazine, Canon Chambers was able to have printed the photograph below showing the West Front of the Church exactly as it appears today.

The same month as the photograph below was printed, Britain's entry into World War 1 was announced by the Prime Minister in London. It is truly fortunate that St. Werburgh's Church was completed before this cataclysmic event began. Many of the families who strove to pay for this church lost their lives or loved ones over the next four years. Current day parishioners may perhaps reflect that they also are the lucky ones, that the sacrifices of their forebears endowed us with this truly wonderful church, that benefits all who visit Chester. The dedication of the completed church was on Sunday, 21 June 1914, and so we celebrate its centenary in the same year as we also commemorate the start of the Great War.

St. Werburgh's Church, Chester.
Completed in June 1914.

Appendix 1 – A Selection of Extracts from Canon Chambers' Monthly Appeals in St. Werburgh's Magazines.

St. Werburgh's Magazine 1905 November

The Church's completion, alas, seems very distant. Fancy an attendance of 600 and the offertories to come, in the total, to an average of less than 1 penny each! 'Charity Sermons' in most parishes realize about £30; in St. Werburgh's, beyond the extra expense, £5 cannot be obtained. It is evident that these appeals are in vain. We hope in some other ways funds may be secured.

St. Werburgh's Magazine 1907 November
THE CHURCH COMPLETION

The great debt soon to be incurred in connection with our schools will naturally draw our attention away from the Church completion Fund. We must not lose sight of it all together – and why should we? Have we not £1,200 toward it already? This is very true. To complete the church will cost £4,000, and before the work is started we must have in hand two thirds of the amount. To put it briefly, before the Church Completion can be started, £1,500 are required; and to pay for it, £2,800 are required.

St. Werburgh's Magazine 1908 May
THE PLAN FOR THE CHURCH FRONT

The Plan, as given in our last issue, has been admired generally, and by many favourably spoken of, whilst by a few a little severely criticised. For each of the parishioners the question to the point is not will it ever be realised? Will St. Werburgh's church ever be finished in that particular form? What have I given to increase the necessary fund towards the Completion? What am I doing now; am I giving what I can and collecting from my friends and acquaintances? It is strange how few cards have been applied for; strange how little real enthusiasm there is in the completion of the Church. O would that some benefactors be forthcoming to help us in this work! We must beseech Heaven, we must pray that God will raise up some kind friends. Frequently one reads in the papers of gifts and bequests to various Churches and Charities, but no one thinks of St. Werburgh's, the old mission of Chester. Perhaps we don't "shout" enough – certainly no parish needs outside assistance more. Perhaps, however, we may not be doing all we might ourselves: there are surely some of us who could do more. Remember, God helps them who help themselves, and duty begins at home.

St. Werburgh's Magazine April 1912

The position we are in at present has been already explained from the pulpit by Canon Chambers. We must, however, try to enlist the sympathy of all our friends, far and near, for if the Church is ever to be finished help from outside the parish – as well as from within – must be obtained.

To put our school premises in good condition, acceptable alike to the Board of Education and the Local Education Authority, has cost about £6,000 in the past few years, and about £5,000 of this is still upon us – a heavy crushing debt, to meet the interest of which is more than the Congregation can do at present. It may be natural to ask then; why should we attempt to complete the Church, and thus add to the burden?

In reply we would remind such enquires the Church was started in 1873!!! It was opened for divine worship at Christmas 1875. At the time of opening it was incomplete at both ends, i.e. it had no Sacristies, was not its full length, and had no Façade, Porch or Baptistry. In 1905 the Sacristries were added, and have proved a boon to the Clergy and congregation, in their use as vestries and for choir practice, and confraternity meetings.

The addition and the front of the church could not then be attempted owing to the lack of funds and the school difficulties already mentioned. Since 1905, we have been waiting patiently for the Completion fund to increase, or some benefactor to come forward and complete the church. The latter has not been found and the church building Fund is now at £1,600.

This statement, our friendly critics will say, only proves the more how foolish it would be to attempt the completion which according to the most economic plan must cost at least £5,000.

We reply: the brick front wall put up in 1875, and intended for only a few years (it has stood for nearly 40 years) in place of a proper 'West Front'. The heavy snow storms of the past winter have told much upon it, and we ask 'are we going to waste money by taking it down and rebuilding it?'

Something must be done, but we say something **better** must be done. The Bishop has decided this question for us. The architect has received instructions to devise a plan that can be proceeded with and partly if not wholly carried out at once, provided the necessary amount of cost can be obtained.

St. Werburgh's Magazine March 1913
THE CHURCH'S COMPLETION

We have progressed a step further in the work of completing, or at least adding to the Church and doing away with the ugly wall which faces the Church, and is fast falling to pieces. The Architect's plans, approved by the Bishop, have been placed in the hands of several contractors who are, at the moment we go to press, preparing their estimates for the work. We have £1,900 in hand. It is perfectly certain that the work cannot be done for that amount. If the work is to be started – it will be started with hope and on the understanding that more money is gathered in whilst the work proceeds.

To our parishioners generally we give the stirring motto "Be up and at it".
N.B. – The Mission cannot "stand" any more debt. £5,000 for Schools is too great a burden already.

St. Werburgh's Magazine April 1913

The notices on the Church Door have not been far out in calculation: £3,000 wanted to start the completion of this Church.
A list of subscribers is hung at the Church Door, and week by week new names are added, and the amount received in the Out-Door.

John W. Curtis   **June 2014**

References

1. Chester Chronicle 27 June 1914

Primary Sources

St. Werburgh's Parish Magazines 1904–1914

Secondary Sources

Census data accessed via Ancestry

St. Patrick's Day Concerts 1913–20

The St. Patrick's Day Concerts were an established feature of the church's year for both St. Werburgh's and for St. Francis' parishes during the period before the First World War. They were a celebration of the faith of their predominantly Irish populations and served as one of the main fund-raisers to help pay off the churches' debts. Typical concert fare was a mixture of singing, dancing and comedic turns, performed by well-known regional entertainers, supplemented, especially as the war progressed, by the staff and children of the schools. Even in times of hardship these concerts were well-attended and enthusiastically received. Looked at in detail they provide some small insights into the life of the two parishes, and how the war affected them during this period.

The St. Werburgh's Concerts took place on St. Patrick's Eve, and were usually staged in The Music Hall Theatre in St. Werburgh St. the site of the present-day Superdrug.

The front page advertisement in the Chester Chronicle for 14 March 1914 proclaims "A grand Concert in aid of St. Werburgh's Building Fund", staged almost entirely by entertainer Will Horabin from Crewe and "The Merrie Sextette" and described in the following week's review as "a musical event of no ordinary kind". This indicates its status as a feature of the church's entertainment calendar, while that week's parish

Music Hall Theatre Exterior

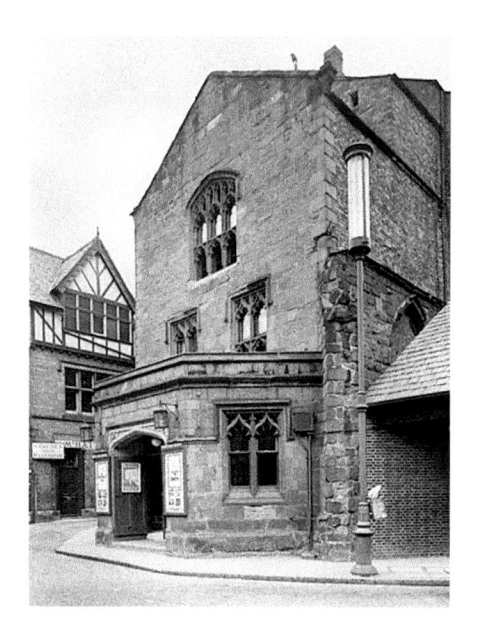

Music Hall Theatre Interior

magazine points to its other function of providing debt-relief, in its exhortation to parishioners to attend at all costs, jocularly chiding those "yet without tickets" even those too old or cranky, to go for it!

The press reports show a concert based mainly around popular Irish songs such as "Sweet County Clare" and "Dear Little Shamrock" and broadly humorous sketches and monologues, all performed, according to the Chronicle "to a very high standard". It singles out J.W.Cottrell for praise: a "tenor of exceptional purity and range" whose performance provoked "demands for an encore that would brook no disappointment" and commends "that widely-known figure Mr. Louis Towneley" for his equally well-known routine "PC 40", while the concert culminated in "an hilarious ensemble farce."

The concert given at St. Francis' was on broadly similar lines, with a more pronounced Irish tone, and, possibly reflecting its smaller size, a more localised approach. It had a greater contribution from the schoolchildren – though, like St.Werburgh's effort, it was very well attended and received. Again, from the Chester Chronicle: "the infants with their Irish jig delighted all present. Florrie Parry, a young girl who appeared unabashed dressed in top hat and frock-coat, sang "Sing Me an Irish Song" to great effect."

The year 1915 saw this pattern repeated, but with two slight changes attributable to the onset of war. The St. Werburgh's parish newsletter (3/15) enjoins with more urgency the need to attend the concert and help towards paying off the debt interest (particularly important now that the church building has been completed). The newsletter also acknowledged the concerns and hardship beginning to be felt due to the war, particularly with regard to the decrease in parish numbers. In the concert itself, though as the Chronicle (20 March) reports "old favourites were included and approved" there starts to appear more topical, nationalistic material:" The Green Isle of Erin" and "My Irish Lad" now performed alongside "The Belgian Cross" and the children singing "A Hymn to the Soldiers and Sailors". The same edition draws attention to Father Hayes' interval speech in which he refers to "the suffering of the Belgian people" and reminds people of the strong response made by Irish parishioners "to the call of Empire".

While there was uncertainty and ambivalence over the Irish response to the war, in society, and probably the parish at large, the church backed the British position. The parish magazine of 3/15 describes the concert as "Ireland's reply to the Kaiser" and refers to the Belgian people as a "sister soul in Faith, Valour and Art". The slightly smaller bill and greater participation by the school's children could also be seen as an effect of the war, though it is still a great success, both artistically, "... the children charmingly dressed in national costume gave a splendid exhibition of singing and dancing"- Chronicle (20 March) and financially, managing to raise almost its target of half of the half-yearly debt repayment (£55, an increase on the previous year).

A similar effect can be seen at St.Francis' concert, again heavily reliant on the contribution of the schoolchildren, guided by the school staff, (Mr. Dring, the choirmaster is often given honourable mention in the press). It also expressed concern for the effect on the health of the young performers that the constant demands for encores would have! The Chronicle (20 March) praises their opening choruses, "Hail Glorious St. Patrick" and "Men of the West", and is delighted at the dance display of "little harpists" during a harp recital. The Irish element is present, George Moore's recital "Shamus O'Brien" is greeted with "frequent applause" though tellingly this is followed by Miss H. Williams (soprano) with "By Order of the Queen", a topical rewriting of "The Wearing of The Green" and Blanche Cottier (contralto) with the now popular "When You Come Home". Likewise, the parish priest Fr. Vincent makes reference to the affirmative Irish response to the war.

These two aspects in regard to the St.Patrick's Day Concerts become more evident the following year. St. Werburgh's could still afford to employ the talents of outside performers such as Will Horabin, Liverpool's Eva Warren and Manchester's Arthur Wilkes but there is more involvement from the schools' staff and children. This can be attributed to the lack of resources caused by the war, and there is a detectable sense of anxiety now regarding the parish debt. In the parish newsletter, the church stresses the

HELP ST. WERBURGH'S
♣ ♣ DEBT (£7000) ♣ ♣
—— By taking Tickets for the ——
ST PATRICK'S CONCERT,
THURSDAY MARCH 16th.

STAR PROGRAMME.

THE CHILDREN OF THE GIRLS AND INFANTS' SCHOOLS, assisted by
Madame EVA WARREN (Liverpool).   Miss BEATRICE WALLEY (Crewe).
Mr. ARTHUR WILKES (Tenor, Manchester Cathedral).   Mr. WILL HORABIN (Crewe).
HILL and TAYLOR (Irish Comedians).

Tickets: 2/-, 1/-, and 6d.

The 2/- tickets may be booked at Messrs. Ellis' Piano Warehouse, Foregate Street, Chester.
Commence at 7-45 p.m.   Early doors, 3d. extra.
YOUR HELP IS URGENTLY NEEDED.

need to keep servicing this, placing it on an equal footing with any service for the war effort, no doubt becoming aware of the challenge posed by the war on parishioners' ability and inclination to support a fixture, which by the same token, it was beginning to rely on ever more. This is well illustrated by that month's parish magazine advertisement: (3/16).

Secondly, the following week's review again shows a consciousness of the doubt apparent at the time about the Irish position on the war, adopting a slightly re-assuring tone with its description of the concert as fit for "Royal approval". Likewise, the Chronicle review of the concert (18 March 1916) reveals an increase in topical war-related material. It describes "tiny laddies in khaki" being marched onto the stage and doing military drills, while the seniors and juniors from the Girl's school performed " two action songs- "Our Khaki Daddy" and "We Red Cross Nurses" It must have been a touching moment when James McCleary stepped onto the stage to take part. The family had only recently heard that one of their menfolk had been killed at the front. Irish material is still evident though, "Mother Machree" for example, by Miss Beatrice Whalley, who then "brought down the house" with "When Irish Eyes are Smiling", and Messrs Taylor and Evans' song and dance sketch "Two Irish Swells" was "very cleverly done".

Despite the hardships now being felt, the concert was a success in almost meeting its debt-relief target, and, though stern in its reminders about their duties, the church always showed gratitude for their response, and likewise paid tribute in the magazine to those who contributed to the staging of the concerts. Another indication of the drain on parish resources now was the fact that St. Francis' was seemingly unable to put on a concert that year.

James McCleary age 5, St. Patrick's Concert 1916 Reproduced by kind permission of Mary Powell nee McCleary, James' daughter

Royalty Theatre,
City Road

A change in venue occurred for St. Werburgh's in 1917, with The Royalty Theatre replacing The Music Hall, but again there is a noticeable further reduction in scale. Though still carrying a front-page advert in the Chronicle (3/17) it is now "A Grand Variety Entertainment" by "the children of St. Werburgh's school", with the few outside entertainers being mostly female singers. Attention is drawn to dances in "Old English, Oriental and Dutch national costumes" and to "character songs and dances" (Parish Newsletter 4/17)

Although it was a reduced, quieter affair it still raised nearly half the debt interest, which reflects well on the spirit and determination of the parish at what must have been a period of severe privation. A similar state was apparent over at St. Francis' but it too managed a lively dance-oriented celebration, directed by the school staff once again and accompanied by the Chester Catholic Chorale, and was again well attended.

This pattern held true in the final year of the war, with small concerts at both parishes, both consisting of school-centred features. As well as a shortage of personnel it's probable too that a lot of resources that were available were now being directed to war related efforts, such as Hospital Fundraisers and Concerts for Injured Soldiers. For 1919 St. Francis' managed to repeat this, but St. Werburgh's failed to produce any concert. However, by 1920 it had recovered enough to again begin re-staging celebrations for St. Patrick's Day. Though still basically "a children's concert", there are signs of renewal. It drew praise for the "admirable scenery and costumes and clever rhythmical dancing" (Chronicle 13/3/20), and featured some optimistic-sounding music, typical of the time: "Glimmer, Glimmer, Little Nightlight", and "Have a Smile". More importantly, perhaps, they were very well attended and received.

Through the Great War, both St. Werburgh's and St. Francis' parishes continued to stage concerts in honour of St. Patrick, as a demonstration of their faith and background and to raise funds to help pay off onerous church debts. They reveal a church that was largely supportive of the war effort. Despite the difficulties and hardships stemming from the war which affected the concerts most notably in terms of their scale and content, the two parishes were successful in achieving those aims, which shows, albeit in a minor way, a noteworthy spirit in the church during this period.

Alan Mapp 2015

Sources

St. Werburgh's Parish Magazines 1904–1917
Chester Chronicle, Cheshire Observer 1913–1919

Photographs

Three views of Chester Theatres were reproduced by kind permission of Chester History and Heritage.

"Our Birkenhead Friend"

Arthur Killingworth Bourne Brandreth

Arthur Killingworth Bourne Brandreth, was obviously "upstairs" in Victorian and Edwardian England. He was born at Malpas, Cheshire on 15 February 1880, only child of Joseph Pilkington Brandreth and Eva Jane nee Hedges[1]. Eva Jane's father, Killingworth Hedges, was a solicitor from Sunbury on Thames. Joseph Pilkington Brandreth was the grandson of a Liverpool doctor who had acquired land around Shocklach in South Cheshire. Both Joseph Pilkington Brandreth, Arthur's father and his grandfather William Harper Brandreth had been educated at Eton and Christ Church Oxford, before entering the Anglican Ministry. At the time of Arthur's birth, Joseph Pilkington Brandreth was a newly appointed curate at St. Oswald's, Malpas, Cheshire and the family lived at nearby Cuddington Lodge. St. Oswald's is recognised as one of the best examples in Cheshire of a late 15th to early 16th-century church. The internal fitments are very ornate, having been bequeathed by the Cholmondeley and Brereton families who owned large estates in south Cheshire. After appointments at Tilstone and Shocklach, in 1885, Joseph Pilkington then served as Vicar of Standish, Wigan after the death of his father who had been the resident Vicar of Standish for 44 years. After only one year in this appointment, Joseph Pilkington moved to Hove in Sussex and became a "licenced preacher" of the Diocese of Winchester[2]. Joseph was not attached to a specific church and therefore it is unlikely he undertook an active role in the routine duties of a parish. This less onerous position seems well-suited to a gentleman, living on his own means. Arthur's parents continued to live in Hove for nearly twenty more years, census returns showing that Brandreth and Hedges cousins visited them during this period, maintaining family contacts.

Little is known of Arthur's education at this time. It must have been an unusual, possibly lonely upbringing, as Arthur had no siblings and would have spent much of his early formative years in adult company. It is possible that for his early education, his parents tutored him at home. Typically at the age of about 8 a boy child would then be sent away to a preparatory school. It is possible that Arthur attended one until he was about 13 years of age.

Surprisingly Arthur did not then go to Eton but on the 1 September 1893, was enrolled as a cadet on the School Ship Conway. This was a converted sailing ship, moored in the River Mersey, near Rockferry. Arthur's entrance details show that his previous school was St. Kenelm's, Brighton[3]. No such school exists or has existed. It is likely that the Brighton reference relates to his parents' address and that St. Kenelm's

*Cuddington Lodge 2015
Built on the ruined site of
the original Lodge where the
Brandreth family lived in 1880
Photograph by John Curtis with
permission of the present owner*

College, Oxford, a school founded in 1880 which catered particularly for the sons of clergymen who desired an Anglican High Church education for their children, was the school which Arthur attended.

At School Ship Conway, young men from a mainly middle class background, were educated to provide the officer class of the Mercantile Marine service, who would also be potential officers in an enlarged Royal Navy in a time of war. Arthur stayed at Conway until the end of 1895, two to three years being the average period of tuition at this time. In his naval and academic reports Brandreth is described as 'Good' or 'Fair' but he seems to have maintained rather a low profile, not being a member of any school teams or societies. He was appointed Petty Officer (a type of cadet prefect) for the Armoury at the beginning of the Autumn Term of 1894 and maintained this position until he left Conway. On Wed 19 June 1895 Arthur Brandreth was confirmed by the Anglican Bishop of Birkenhead, Bishop Royston[4].

Typically there would be around 75 young men aged between 13 and 15 years of age being trained at Conway at any one time. Some of them would be from large families where they would have been exposed to sibling rivalry. For others, single children, this would possibly be their first occasion away from the security of home. Living in close proximity to each other, this would be an opportunity for friendships to be formed, with the opportunity to visit each others homes during vacations or weekends, if the family lived close by. In such circumstances it is anticipated that friendships would be made by people with similar interests or backgrounds.

Two of Brandreth's contemporaries at Conway were John Masefield and Hugh Laurence Kirby. Masefield, like Brandreth, was also an only child but also an orphan. He was being brought up by an elderly spinster aunt, at Cheadle in Staffordshire. He was sent to Conway to meet other boys of his own age. Hugh Laurence Kirby was the orphaned son of Daniel Kirby, brother of the Liverpool architect Edmund Kirby, who acted as his guardian and who was also the architect of St. Werburgh's, Chester[5]. None of the three boys appear to have excelled in sport, but appear to have been quiet, potentially introverted boys. Later, John Masefield wrote many poems about the sea and eventually became Poet Laureate. Hugh Laurence Kirby spent only 6 months at Conway in 1894 before being sent to Stonyhurst College, where his cousins were at school. However, he did later join the Merchant Navy and served in the Royal Naval Reserve during World War 1. As cadets at SS Conway, this is the first occasion where A. K. B. Brandreth and a member of the Kirby family are known to have met. It is likely that Brandreth could have been invited to meet the Kirby family who lived locally at Birkenhead.

Exercising his penchant for doing the unexpected, after he left Conway, Arthur became an apprenticed engineer at Messrs. Laird of Birkenhead[6]. Arthur's joining Laird's as an apprentice is surprising, as cadets typically left Conway to join a merchant marine line. Laird's shipyard is adjacent to the location where SS Conway was moored. Unfortunately within 18 months of starting his apprenticeship the 48 Hours Dispute occurred. This prolonged dispute started in July 1897 and continued until January 1898. It is likely that Arthur, as a newly apprenticed engineering draughtsman, would have been laid off from work during this period. Laird was one of 702 firms in the engineering industry to successfully resist the attempt to force a reduction of the working hours from 54 to 48 hours. At the end of the dispute the employers declared they were vindicated, as they had maintained the Employers right to "Freedom of Management."

Arthur is next found working as a draughtsman for the London and North Western Railway, from August. 1903 to December 1904, in Crewe.[7] His railway records state that he had been given a reference by Messrs. Vickers, Sons and Maxim, Barrow-in-Furness. He had worked for Vickers from June 1902, so presumably he had gone to this firm after leaving Laird's.

The first evidence of Arthur's interest in the Catholic Church, rather than the church of his father, came in 1901. Arthur was in lodgings at 10 Charlecombe Street, Birkenhead. During this year he wrote a letter to The Tablet, 30 October on the subject of Plain Chant, which he had heard sung at Holy Trinity, Bermondsey, London. In 1904 he wrote an article on the history of Plain Chant and it was included in the March 1904 edition of St. Werburgh's Parish Magazine.

Plain Chant, or the Gregorian Chant was the complete collection of music for Church services produced by Pope St. Gregory First in the 7th Century. He established a college of choristers, consisting of Benedictine monks, who when proficient, were sent over the whole of Europe to teach and disseminate the Roman Chant. Over time the original purity of the chant had been lost. In 1843, the Abbot of Solesmes, who had recently restored the Benedictine Order to France following their revolutions, anxious that the original chant of St. Gregory be sung in his monastery, sent out monks to scour the libraries and archives of Europe to try and discover the original chant. As a result of their efforts, they were able to publish, in 1880, a treatise, "les melodies gregoriennes". Over a period of time, this restored understanding of the Chant became more widely accepted and popular and on the 22 November, 1903, Pope Pius X issued a "moto proprio", directing that a prominent position in church services be occupied by "the ancient traditional Gregorian Chant". On 19 January 1904, the choir of St. Joseph's Liverpool gave a public performance of the Gregorian Chant in Chester Town Hall and returned to Chester in February, on the Feast of St. Werburgh to sing the Chant in St. Werburgh's Church[8].

In May 1904, Arthur's uncle, Henry Pilkington Brandreth died in Ormskirk, Lancashire. In his will he left £35,851 – 9s – 1d. It is possible that Arthur was a beneficiary of this will, as later that year, in December Arthur left the railway drawing offices, and subsequently lived on his own means. It is apparent that by this time Arthur's interests in Church music and architecture were fully developed, most likely through a strong link with Edmund Kirby the Liverpool architect and his family. He sang at High Mass in many Catholic Churches and in 1905 was choirmaster at St. Ignatius R.C. Church in Sunbury-on-Thames, the area from which his mother's family had originated. By 1906 he was a resident of Lowestoft[9]. In the 1911 census he is described as a retired engineering draughtsman, living on private means.

It is believed that Arthur made frequent donations to the Catholic Church, but this is difficult to verify, as many of his donations were given anonymously. The first possibly recorded, was a gift to St. Joseph's Parish, Birkenhead in 1901. The Lady Altar and statue were erected after a special appeal (and through the generosity of a "non-Catholic gentleman"). St. Joseph's Church was built in just two years. The foundation stone was laid in March 1899 at a large gathering at which it is recorded representatives of the Young Men's Societies of St. Werburgh's, St. Laurence's and Our Lady's Church were present. The church was opened on the 19 August 1900. It was designed by Edmund Kirby and is in his characteristic style, its striking height compensating for the lack of a tower. So similar was the design of the lancet windows that on the demolition of the church in 1996, a triptych of windows, The Birth, The Death and The Resurrection of Christ were removed from the church and re-installed at St. Werburgh's Chester, above the main entrance.

From 1904 onwards it is clear that Arthur Brandreth has converted to Catholicism. There is no evidence that Arthur ever lived in Chester, but it is certain that he took a close interest in St. Werburgh's church and its progress towards completion, presumably through receipt of St. Werburgh's Parish Magazine. In many issues Fr. Chambers would list those "gifts" most urgently needed by St. Werburgh's to aid progress towards the church's completion. Most of these gifts were donated anonymously and are recorded as gifts from "Our Birkenhead friend". (Arthur maintained a small house in Birkenhead.) It is certain that he donated the Sanctuary Lectern and some vestments to St. Werburgh's, Chester. It is also probable that he donated a cope, further sets of vestments, four small stained glass windows and a large (Assumption) window, in gratitude for his reception into the Catholic Church. Provost Buquet's Memorial Window was indicated as the gift of a friend, also very likely to be Brandreth. Canon Buquet was the Rector of St. Werburgh's, Chester and had commissioned Edmund Kirby to design St. Werburgh's Church, the main body of which was completed in 1875. In 1882, Canon Buquet left Chester, to become the Rector of St. Werburgh's, Birkenhead, the leading Catholic Mission in Birkenhead at the time.

By 1909 Arthur was resident in Parkfield Avenue, Birkenhead. In February 1910, Arthur Brandreth sang from the lectern in St. Werburgh's Church, Chester at the High Mass celebrated here by the Bishop of Shrewsbury, on the occasion of St. Werburgh's Feastday. In 1911 he was living in Price Street, Birkenhead.

In 1907 Joseph Pilkington Brandreth, Arthur's father, had been appointed licensed preacher in the Diocese of Oxford, though he had taken a house in Kintbury, Hungerford, Berkshire, where he lived until his death in 1941[10]. It may not be a coincidence that also in 1907 Arthur matriculated to Pembroke College, Oxford. However, as shown by the above, Arthur did not display the slavish devotion to his set studies as might be expected of a more normal student. He continued to study Church architecture and music in his own inimitable fashion. He was also a member of Pembroke College O.T.C. during his time at Oxford[11].

Unsurprisingly, given the range and depth of his extra-curricular activities, it was not until 8 February 1913 that Arthur obtained his B.A. and 30 April 1914 his M.A. His B.A. was gained by the pass school examinations. These examinations were taken by those students who were deemed unlikely to achieve an honours degree. Arthur took examinations in Political Economy, History, English Literature, and French[12].

In 1915 Arthur Brandreth was elected a life member of the Manx Society. This was an organisation which published a magazine "Mannin" to provide Manx countrymen at home and abroad with details of matters of interest to all Manxmen, and so keep them in closer touch with each other. However, other than this membership of the Manx

Quad and Chapel of Pembroke College, Oxford

Society, there is no other observable connection between Brandreth and the Isle of Man. His election was noted in the 1915 issue of Mannin. His enlistment was noted later in 1915 and afterwards his death in 1916.

Arthur drew up his will in 1910 at the age of 30, well before the start of the Great War, leaving the bulk of his estate to building and other projects in Catholic Churches[13]. This would indicate that he did not contemplate marriage and possibly had in mind joining the priesthood. He left drawings and instructions concerning these projects. Many aspects of work at St. Werburgh's, including his ideas for a High Church Altar were to be carried out by Benedict Williamson, if he were available. Benedict Williamson, like Brandreth was a convert, and he had trained as a church architect before entering the priesthood. If he were not available, then Edmund Kirby or someone recommended by him was to complete the work.

When war broke out Arthur enlisted as a private soldier. Again, a person of Arthur's background, who had army officers within his family, and had also trained with Pembroke College O.T.C. might himself have been expected to join as an officer. This was not the case. Arthur doubtless had his own reasons for enlisting in this manner but they were not made public. Even when he was preparing to enlist, it is obvious that St. Werburgh's, Chester was in Brandreth's thoughts. The July 1915 copy of St. Werburgh's

St. Nicholas Church, Raincheval, Amiens

Magazine indicates that even though he had recently joined His Majesties Forces, "our old Birkenhead friend" had presented a new green frontal, tabernacle curtains, vestment and cope. As the article states these were necessary to cover the poor wooden altar which needed dressing up to make it presentable.

Arthur's enlistment papers have not survived, so we have few details of his army career. According to St. Werburgh's Parish Magazine of January 1917, Arthur Brandreth first enlisted at the beginning of the war, with the Welsh Fusiliers. This is not supported by the Army Medal Roll records. These reveal he joined the Royal Fusiliers, City of London Regiment, enlisting at Liverpool. (PS2492). It seems that though Arthur had not enlisted as an officer, he had certainly joined an elite unit[14].

Arthur first entered France on 14 November 1915 and from September to the end of October 1916, Brandreth's Battalion was stationed at or near Raincheval, near Amiens. This area came under heavy German mortar attack due to its situation near a railhead and other logistical factors. Arthur knew that he would be going into the front firing line trenches in a few days time. He had already added five codicils to his will, as and when further inspirational ideas had occurred to him. On 24 October 1916 Brandreth added his sixth and last codicil. He greatly admired the spire at the church in Raincheval. His codicil asked that his previous plans for a spire at St. Mary's R.C. Church, Crewe should be ignored and a spire similar to the one on the French Church, substituted. He described a spire as progressing gradually, by small steps, towards heaven.

He also altered his previous plans for St. Werburgh's. He directed that a statue of St. Werburgh in red sandstone, 5ft. high be placed in the niche on the south side of the church, adjacent to the pulpit. The codicil was written on a leaf of paper torn from a notebook, witnessed and proved later to be quite legal, though, like Arthur himself, rather unusual. Arthur's unit took its place in the front trenches on 30 October 1916 and Arthur was killed there, at the Battle of Ancre, on 1 November 1916[15].

His obituary was printed in the January 1917 edition of St. Werburgh's Parish Magazine and his name is on the WW1 Memorial Boards of the School Ship Conway, Pembroke College Oxford, St. Ignatius' R.C. Church, Sunbury-on-Thames and St. Mary's Catholic Church, Crewe. He is also commemorated on the Thiepval Memorial, Departement de la Somme, Picardie, France. Arthur was entitled to the 1914–15 Star, the British War Medal and the Allied Victory Medal.

There is also a memorial tablet to Arthur Killingworth Bourne Brandreth in St. Giles R.C. Church, Cheadle, Staffordshire, the "Pugin Gem" which Brandreth particularly admired. He left £2,000 in his will for the support of a priest at this church and also requested that on his death his body be buried in the graveyard there. In the Fifth Codicil to his will, dated 6 October 1914, enacted following the outbreak of the Great War, Arthur indicated that in the event of his dying and being buried outside the United Kingdom, a memorial tablet bearing a Latin inscription should instead be erected at St. Giles. The designing of the tablet was to be entrusted to the Reverend Benedict Williamson. A photograph of the memorial and a translation of the Latin, are shown below.

"Let him lie honoured, Arthur Killingworth Bourne Brandreth. Master of Arts of Oxford and soldier of the royal cohort armed with balls of fire (London Royal Fusiliers) who, in battle at Ancre on the Feast of All Saints in 1916, fulfilling the duties of his station, fell for his fatherland. Hail, soldier of Christ and farewell. May you rest well in peace, veteran."

Translation by James Aglio

Summary of the Last Will and Testament of A. K. B. Brandreth, noting his legacy to St. Werburgh's

The last remaining part of Brandreth land in Cheshire, Round House Farm, Leese near Middlewich was left to Colvin Brandreth, a distant cousin, son of the late Admiral Sir Thomas Brandreth.

Then, apart from the St. Giles bequests mentioned in his biography, four bequests for Church Towers and some minor personal items to individuals, the remainder of Arthur's estate was left to finance projects at St. Werburgh's Chester.

The sum of £450 to be used to erect a high altar of oak or red sandstone and surmounted by a baldaquin with four columns of oak and of two statues five feet in height carved in sandstone placed in the sandstone niches near the entrance to the sanctuary. The altar baldaquin and statues to be entrusted to Benedict Williamson, with his fees paid out of the legacy. Any fees left after £450 to go to the completion of St. Werburgh's church. The fee of £450 can be increased by 30% of the original legacy if the original amount will not suffice for the proper carrying out of the works, provided that a certificate of Benedict Williamson or other architect stating the necessity and amount of increase is supplied.

£100 for the erection of choir stalls in the sanctuary or chancel and designed by Benedict Williamson with his fees paid out of the legacy. If Williamson be unavailable, the fee of £100 for the choir stalls can be increased to £150 and Edmund Kirby & Sons design the choir stalls. The choir stalls should be placed behind the high altar and around a wall of the apse of the church. Edmund Kirby & Sons' fees to be paid out of the legacy.

£350 in providing and putting in two stained glass windows representing scenes in the life of St. Plegmund and the completion of the seven stained glass windows in the apse of the church. The designing of the stained glass windows to be entrusted to Edmund Kirby & Sons and execution entrusted to Messrs Hardman Powell & Co of Birmingham. The fees to be paid out of the legacy.

£2,000 to erect at the south east angle of the church a tower or steeple in the style of a gothic campanile to be surmounted by a bronze weathercock poised on an agate, the weathercock to be not less than 110 feet above the ground.

Extract from the 6th and last Codicil dated 24 October 1916, 8 days before his death on 1 November 1916 "Statue of St. Werburgh, Virgin Abbess, in red standstone and five feet in height placed in the niche on the south side of the church adjacent to the

Brandreth Window in St. Werburgh's Apse. St. Plegmund baptising at his well.

Brandreth window in St. Werburgh's apse St. Plegmund consecrates seven Bishops at Canterbury.

pulpit instead of in wood on the baldaquin which shall be substituted by one of St. George, Martyr."

Records of the England and Wales National Probate Calendar show that when his will was published 29 September 1917, Arthur owned two small houses, 52 Price Street and 41 Parkfield Avenue, Birkenhead. In his will he left £17,566 10s with probate to the Public Trustee. It is understandable that in the midst of war, execution of the will would be delayed. Arthur's grandiose plans for church building projects also proved in many cases, too expensive to be carried out using the allotted funds. Some were indicated to be dependent on trust funds that would come to Arthur on the death of his father, which did not occur until 1941. For whatever reason, delays occurred in the release of his legacy for his stated bequests. St. Werburgh's Parish Magazine, No.

109 June 1936 was issued as a Souvenir of the Consecration and Diamond Jubilee of St. Werburgh's, Chester. In his article on St. Werburgh's and its development, Father Hayes indicates the High Altar and the Altar Rails were erected from money left by Canon Chambers and Miss Margaret Collins. There is no mention that the design for the altar, and a bequest to cover its cost, had been made by Arthur Brandreth, nor is he listed in the names of outstanding benefactors that had supported the Church and its construction.

Letters in the Kirby Files in Liverpool Archives, written in mid 1939, indicate Father Hayes' frustration with the Public Trustee that no money from any of the legacies had yet been received. However, later that same year, 2 November 1939 just after the commencement of World War 2, came a letter from John Hardman Studios, indicating that the remaining 2 Sanctuary windows (Arthur Brandreth bequests) were now completed but were of different design to the other chancel windows since the funds available did not allow for such detailed work. Later letters also indicated that the glass had been forwarded to Chester prior to fitting, as retention here was better than in Birmingham, which was an important industrial city (and likely to be bombed). The Brandreth stained glass windows were therefore stored at St. Werburgh's but not fitted until after the end of WW2.

The onset of the World War 2 could also have prevented further execution of the Brandreth legacy, the value of which would have been eroded with time. Arthur's father, Joseph Pilkington Brandreth died 3 May 1941, leaving an estate of £24,343 8s 10d, some of which may have accrued to his son's legacy.

The final chapter of the legacy is recorded in the setting up of the Charity of Arthur Killingworth Bourne Brandreth for Churches, registered 20 July 1965, removed 27 August 1997.

> Charitable objects!
> Completion of Towers to the following churches:-
> St. Werburgh's Roman Catholic Church: Chester
> St. Joseph's Roman Catholic Church: Stockport
> St. Anne's Roman Catholic Church: Rock Ferry Birkenhead
> Our Lady's Roman Catholic Church: Price Street Birkenhead

No evidence has been found that any of these towers were ever built. Inflation would likely have rendered the cost of such building far greater than anticipated when the bequests were first made. However, here in St. Werburgh's we are particularly fortunate to have in the apse of our church, the lovely altar, the carved woodwork and two stained glass windows, all carried out according to Arthur's directions and ultimately paid for using his bequest. Truly these are a fitting memorial to this unusual man. As a long term, thoughtful benefactor of this Church, the name of Arthur Brandreth, "Our Birkenhead Friend," should be added to any new memorial at St. Werburgh's.

John W. Curtis   April 2017

The author is grateful for the help of James Cashman who gave extremely useful advice about obtaining copies of Arthur Brandreth's will and other legal matters.

References

1. Baptism records of Parish Church of St. Oswald, Malpas, Cheshire Archives and Local Studies
2. Records of graduates of Christchurch College, Oxford, kept at the college
3. Register of SS Conway Cadets, Maritime Museum Liverpool, D/CON/13/11 Cadet No. 86
4. "The Cadet" issue 9 July 1895, Maritime Museum, Liverpool D/CON/14/2
5. Register of SS Conway Cadets, Maritime Museum Liverpool, D/CON/13/11 Cadet No. 144
6. Register of SS Conway Cadets, Maritime Museum Liverpool, D/CON/13/11 Cadet No. 86
7. UK Railway Employment Records, London and North Western Railway Company, RAIL 410 Piece 1941 pp 61 and 142 TNA, Employee number 2866
8. St. Werburgh's Parish Magazine, issue March 1904, kept at St. Werburgh's
9. "*The Tablet*," 19 June 1906 – News from the Dioceses – Westminster, Sunbury-On Whitsunday votive Vespers were rendered by the male-voice choir, under the leadership of Mr. A. K. B. Brandreth, of Lowestoft, the late choirmaster.
10. Records of graduates of Christchurch College, Oxford, kept at the college
11. OTC records – ask archivist at Pembroke
12. Records of graduates of Pembroke College, Oxford, kept at the college
13. Obtainable at the District Probate Registry, Derby Square, Liverpool
14. Arthur is listed as being a member of the 23rd (Service) Battalion Royal Fusiliers, (First Sportsman's). Ref *The 23rd (Service) Battalion Royal Fusiliers, (First Sportsman's) Printed 1920*
    Mrs. Cunliffe-Owen conceived the idea of a battalion formed of men over the then enlistment age who, by reason of their life as sportsmen, were fit and hard. Approaching the War Office, she obtained permission to raise a special battalion of men up to the age of forty-five. Although called the Sportsman's Battalion, its personnel included scullers, footballers, boxers, runners, wrestlers, actors,

musicians, artists. Quoting from the Battalion memoirs, "With the formation of the Sportsman's battalion it will be admitted a new type of man was brought into the British Army. Public School's battalions, the Chums, the Footballers, and other battalions were formed. But to the First Sportsman's belongs the honour of introducing an actually new type (of Battalion). To begin with it was cosmopolitan. Practically every grade of life was represented, from peer to the peasant; class distinctions were swept away, every man turned to and pulled his bit." The people who joined the First Sportsmen's came from all walks of life, trappers from the Canadian woods, railway engineers from Argentina, big game hunters from Africa etc. What marked them out was their enthusiasm to do their "bit" as just common or garden Tommies. Hard work and plain but plentiful food soon made the battalion as hard as nails, a phrase coined by the London Evening News, and a phrase that stuck.
15. Commonwealth War Graves Commission site, accessed online

Benedict Williamson WW1 Priest and St. Werburgh's Forgotten Baldaquin

In the will of A. K. B. Brandreth, 14 Jan 1910, various legacies were left for additions to St. Werburgh's Church, Chester. Brandreth bequeathed £450 for the erection of a High Altar in St. Werburgh's, the said altar to be of Oak or Red Sandstone and surmounted by a baldaquin supported by four columns of oak. Two statues five feet in height, carved in red sandstone, were also to be placed in the sandstone niches near the entrance to the sanctuary.

To undertake these bequests Brandreth stipulated that Benedict Williamson was his preferred architect. Williamson had already undertaken design work for the baldeqin (a stone canopy supported by four pillars, surmounting the altar) at St. Werburgh's in 1907. One can only assume that it was due to a request from Brandreth that this work was undertaken, as Canon Chambers, the rector at the time, had as preferred architect Edmund Kirby, who had designed the church and extensions since it was built in 1873.

Then in the first codicil to the above will, dated 26 September 1910, Brandreth left a further legacy of £100 to be devoted to the fitting of choir stalls in the sanctuary or chancel of St. Werburgh's. Although not a member of St. Werburgh's Parish, Brandreth continued to take a great interest in the church and the improvement of its internal fittings. This is shown by the provision in a 2nd codicil to his will, dated 7 February 1912. Brandreth now declared he wished the altar to be of red sandstone and to stand on the chord of the apse. The baldaquin and the columns should be of oak and the columns should contain four decorated guilded statues, representing St. Werburgh, St. Patrick, St. Oswald and St. Chad. He also stated that the two sandstone statues to be placed in the niches near the entrance to the sanctuary should represent St. Plegmund of Plemstall, Archbishop of Canterbury and the other St. Joseph, Foster Father of Christ. He still indicated a preference to use Benedict Williamson as architect for this work but if he was unable to do so, then Edmund Kirby and Sons should be requested to undertake the commission. Brandreth's attention to detail concerning the design of the altar was such that he stipulated that the altar should have no reredos (ornamental screen behind the altar) or Halpas, though it could have gradines (shelves at the back of an altar on which candlesticks and flowers could be placed) if the architect so desired. Arthur Brandreth was killed on 1 November 1916, towards the end of the second Battle of the Somme. (See essay "Our Birkenhead Friend" and entry for Brandreth in "We Shall Remember Them") Needless to say, Brandreth's legacy later proved insufficient to install all his desired artefacts at St. Werburgh's, including the baldequin previously described in such detail.

So who was Benedict Williamson, what were the qualities in the man that had so enthused Brandreth that he desired him, rather than the resident architect, to undertake his bequests? It is assumed that Brandreth must have met Williamson and found in him a kindred spirit. Both came from a high Anglican background. They were both only children and had become converts to Catholicism. Benedict Williamson was born, William Williamson and had taken the name Benedict following his reception by the Jesuits at Farm Street, Mayfair in 1896. He had trained as an architect in the office of Newman & Jacques, architects and surveyors in Stratford, London. The 1891 census shows Williamson as an architect's assistant. As a fully trained architect he later set up his own business in partnership with John Henry Foss, calling the business Williamson & Foss.

In 1896, Williamson was appointed as a new architect to continue work at Farnborough Hill, Hampshire for Empress Eugenie, wife of Emperor Napoleon III of France. The Emperor had been exiled to England in 1870. Following the deaths of her husband in 1873 and her son in 1879, she commissioned a French Architect, Destailleur to build St. Michael's Abbey at Farnborough and to include a chapel, to house the bodies of her husband and son. Originally the Abbey and church were administered by Premonstratensian Canons but in 1895[1], the Empress replaced them with French Benedictine monks from St. Peter's Abbey, Solesmes.[2] However, it is recorded that Williamson's additions, started in 1903, which replicated the neo-Romanesque architecture of the Abbey at Solesmes, so displeased the Empress that she withheld further financial support for the project.[3]

In 1907 Williamson went to Rome to enter the Beda College, where he studied for the priesthood and was ordained in 1909 for the Archdiocese of Southwark. Following his ordination to the priesthood, he still continued to do architectural work and was advisor to Southwark Diocese on building work. He was appointed Rector of St. Gregory's, Earlsfield, Wandsworth, an appointment he retained into the 1920's, except for a period when he served as an army chaplain on the Western Front.

Very early in the morning of 22 May 1917, Benedict Williamson said his last mass at St. Gregory's and at just under 50 years of age set off to serve with the army. His army papers indicate he served as a Lieutenant, in the London Regiment, 9th (County of London) Battalion (Queen Victoria's Rifles). His first appointment was to attend the wounded during the attack on the Messines Ridge. This attack was a prelude to the Battle of Passchendaele which lasted from July to November 1917. Williamson recounted his wartime experiences in a book published in 1921 titled ""Happy Days" in France and Flanders with the 47th and 49th Divisions".

It is not known when Brandreth and Williamson first met, but it is possible that it was through the Solesmes Benedictine connection that they found a shared interest. The Abbott of Solesmes had commissioned monks to re-establish the early purity of the Chant, in 1843. As a result of their efforts, they were able to publish, in 1880, a treatise, 'les melodies gregoriennes'. Brandreth had shown a great interest in the Gregorian Plain Chant and had written a letter to the Tablet in 1901, describing plain chant sung at Holy Trinity, Dockhead, Bermondsey.[4] He also submitted an article on plain chant, to the first St. Werburgh's Parish Magazine, in 1904. In Williamson, Brandreth would also have found someone who could expand his knowledge of Church architecture. Perhaps Brandreth also saw something else, the inner quality of Benedict Williamson that would cause him to volunteer to serve on the Western Front with such distinction. This quality is best described by quoting the words of Lieutenant – Colonel R.C. Fielding, D.S.O., who wrote the introduction to Williamson's book on his wartime experiences:

"The life of a British Army chaplain on the Western Front was almost what he himself chose to make it, but to succeed in the role required a superman. A true vocation, coupled with rare insensibility, courage, and almost inhuman tact, could alone carry him through.

He wore the insignia of an officer, but, as no place was assigned to him either in the line or out of it, he was, in a sense, Pariah among the officers of the battalions which he served. From the men he was separated by the official barrier which his commissioned rank entailed.

Being without status, our padres were usually relegated to a Field Ambulance, whence – according to temperament- they could pursue their vocation assiduously, as they generally did, in spite of the handicap of the distance which divided them from their flock, or live a life of comparative ease at a comfortable distance behind the line.

Father Benedict, the writer of the following pages, possessed a personality which will ever remain a happy memory to those who knew him in the War. The most zealous of priests, the most human of men, he rejoiced in the atmosphere of the trenches – in the proximity of the forward troops. For there he found a selflessness supreme. There, on a scale so grand as perhaps to surpass anything experienced before in the history of mankind, he saw the spirit of self-sacrifice incarnate – the essence of Christ's teaching made practical. Such is the influence of the shells!

He was known in the 47th Division – in which the writer of this preface served with him – by the nickname of "Happy Days," on account of his unquenchable optimism. He seemed to live in a world of sunshine, destitute of shadows. He carried out his duties as he faced the sordid horrors of the battlefields, with a child-like simplicity, inspiring the living, and comforting with his faith the parting moments of many a dying soldier.

His diary, which is printed practically as it was written, contributes further first-hand evidence as to the wonderful qualities of our men – their never-failing cheerfulness under the most appalling circumstances; their bravery; the complete absence of rancour with which they fought. As Father Benedict says, 'During all my experience on the front, even when the enemy was raining his shells on us, I have never heard an expression of hatred uttered by our boys'.

He tells how the British soldier took his medicine. Indeed, poor fellow, is he still not doing so – in many cases half starving in our streets – in the same quiet way he took it in the trenches?

May the publication of this book awaken, in those of its readers who may still need a reminder, a true sense of their responsibilities – that the debt which England has contracted may be redeemed in full."

Rowland C. Fielding D.S.O.
Twyford, Hants.

It is only fitting to end this story of Benedict Williamson by quoting his own words written in the final paragraph of his book. In this chapter, entitled "Afterwards", he recounts his disappointment in the way life in England was being conducted after the Great War.

"It is the third year since the Armistice. I had written more, but had not the heart to print it, so tear it up instead.

The England to which we have returned is so different from the England of our hopes and dreams; and when the boys say to me, 'I am sorry I came back; I would be happier lying under a little white cross in France,' what can I say, when I know it is true. If only the wonderful spirit of the trenches had been brought to England – but it is not. The world is more sordid and self-seeking than ever before . . . 'And we hoped that this had been He that should have redeemed Israel, and besides it is the third day since these things were done.' But no sacrifice can be in vain, and we trust where we cannot trace that 'All is well, and we shall be well, and He shall make all to be well,'

EXPECTO RESURRECTIONEM MORTUORUM ET VITAM VENTURI SAECULI."

John W. Curtis   July 2017

References

1. McQueen, A., Empress Eugénie and the Arts: Politics and Visual Culture in the Nineteenth Century
2. St. Michael's Abbey, Farnborough From Wikipedia, the free encyclopedia https://en.wikipedia.org/wiki/St_Michael%27s_Abbey,_Farnborough August 2017
3. ibid
4. The Tablet Page 19, 2 November 1901

A Rather Special Chalice

A chalice (from the Latin *calyx,* mug borrowed from Greek *kalyx*, shell, husk) is a goblet or footed cup intended to hold a drink. In religious terms it is intended for drinking during a ceremony. As Catholics we are familiar with a Chalice being used during the celebration of Holy Mass at the Consecration, when wine mixed with a little water becomes the Precious Blood of Our Lord, Jesus Christ. Since Vatican II it has also become more common for Holy Communion to be available under both species, the Sacred Host and the Precious Blood. Both forms represent in their entirety the Real Presence.

At St. Werburgh's you will notice four Administration Chalices brought to the altar from the Credence Table just before the Offertory part of the Mass. These Chalices are modern and simple in design and are engraved on their base with the date 2012. However, they are not the only Chalices that our Church possesses. This is where the story becomes interesting. When it was decided to sort out the archives kept within the Parish it was noted in the bound copies of the Parish Magazines for 1912 and 1913 there was mention of repairs being carried out to a Chalice. Could this be the one which had not been used for many years? After cleaning certain hallmarks were noted but not being experts in such matters it was decided to seek external advice. The staff in Lowe's on Bridge Street Row were very helpful, as were those in Boodle and Dunthorne in Eastgate Street. The hallmarks were those of the Birmingham Assay Office but they were not of the same date. The comment of "curiouser and curiouser" from Lewis Carrol's Alice's Adventures in Wonderland springs to mind and the only way of solving the problem was to visit the Birmingham Assay Office. This was done in January 2014.

It seems that our Special Chalice is a marriage of two separate pieces. The base and stem were made by a firm called Thomas Brawn and Joses Weaver Downing (hence BD) and have a date mark of 1876. The firm was only registered with the Birmingham Assay Office on 8 October 1867 and hence must have been a very early piece. The cup of the chalice was made by Hardman and Powell (hence HP) and has a date mark of 1912/13. The style of the cup is that which was made famous at an earlier date by A.W. Pugin, who did much work in design for Hardman and Powell and is thought to be an excellent example.

Having established the provenance of the special Chalice it has been cleaned and it will once again be used by the celebrant at Mass on major Feast Days. Bishop Mark used the Chalice when he conferred the Sacrament of Confirmation during Mass in late 2013 and Fr. Paul used it when we celebrated the Feast of St. Werburgh in February 2014.

The Chalice is undoubtedly that about which Canon Chambers wrote in the monthly Magazines leading up to the outbreak of the First World War. It is something to be treasured as part of the history of our Parish.

G. Tighe   **2014**

St. Werburgh's Chalice

No Men Left at St. Werburgh's

The Impact of the Great War on St. Werburgh's Parish

The impact of the Great War on individual persons and families was of course both profound and personal. No-one can adequately describe the effects of bereavement on these families, nor the daily support of a family member who has been altered almost beyond recognition, by actually surviving this conflict. Here we make no attempt to do so. Instead we aim to describe what life was like for the people of this parish during the years 1914–1919. Almost every aspect of their lives was altered by the Great War and we have picked out some aspects for further scrutiny. The first area of perusal is that of the men who were actually living in the parish at the start of the war.

Young Men's Society

Before the Great War, from about 1905, there had been a Young Men's Society within the parish. It had premises in Queen Street and in 1914 was possibly the most thriving society within the parish. In the club premises could be found a range of comforts and activities, leading Canon Chambers to describe it as a "home from home." Although

St. Werburgh's Football Team ca1890

the establishment was completely teetotal, non-alcoholic refreshment was available. There was heating, a blessing indeed in winter, when many families in the Boughton area of Chester could ill afford coal. Newspapers were available and there was also a library. Whist was very popular, with St. Werburgh's winning the Yerburgh Cup for Whist Competition, several times. Debates took place and there were often visits by local dignitaries, who would address the young men on current national or local affairs. Many parishes had similar clubs, which were promoted by the City Council, as they addressed the two main problems of civic order, i.e. drunkenness and providing cheap recreational activities to the young men of the city, who might otherwise put their energy into more nefarious activities.

Members played football on a field in Hoole and another very popular offshoot was the Swimming Club, held at the City Baths. The average attendance at the baths in 1914 was around 54 visits per week by members. The club paid £5 per year for use of the swimming bath and so at the end of 1914 there was a profit of £2.2.0d.

From 1909 onwards the Nelson Cup formed a focus for other sporting activities. (See separate essay) Thomas Cormac Nelson J.P., who had moved to the Mollington Banastre in 1905, donated this competition cup in 1909, to be awarded annually, for competition between the young men of St. Francis' and St. Werburgh's parishes. There

Chester Baths built by John Douglas 1901

were three sports involved in the competition, football, boxing and shooting and the competition was as intensely contested as only a local Derby can be. To the chagrin of St. Werburgh's men, all pre-war competitions were won by St. Francis' parish.

There had been talk during the whole of the Edwardian period, that there would be a European War and that when it came, Britain and Germany would be on opposite sides of the conflict. By 1914 people had got used to living in this shadow. They no longer expected war to erupt at any minute and did not let the possibility seriously affect their lives.

The first intimation in the parish that something unusual really could be about to happen, was at the beginning of July, when Peter Beatty received an official looking letter. Peter was one of the many members of the Young Men's Society, who had been in the armed forces, usually enlisting around the age of 18. Peter had served in the Royal Navy for a "five and a seven." That is to say, he had spent five years before the mast and was now almost at the end of his seven years in the reserves. As a reservist, he lived at home in Beaconsfield Street, and trained with the Royal Fleet Reserve at Devonport, when asked to do so. Peter now had a job in Chester as a machine engineer and was in hot pursuit of a female parishioner, Alice McCleary. However, the letter recalled Peter to service and by 14 July he was aboard H.M.S. Drake[1]. What did the Admiralty know that the population at large did not?

Peter Beatty may have been the first to be recalled but he was not of course the only member of the Young Men's Society to enlist. By December 1914 over 190 from St. Werburgh's Parish had enlisted, many of them members of the Young Men's Society. The men mainly joined the Cheshire Regiment and the Royal Welsh Fusiliers. Some were regular army reservists who had been recalled at the beginning of the war. Others were no longer on the list of reservists but enlisted with their old units anyway. Their faces will be somewhere on the famous photograph of the Cheshires and Royal Welsh Fusiliers going to Mons.

In the September 1914 issue of the Parish Magazine, the Young Men's Society announced that the annual trip had been cancelled, as most members had already been called to training or were waiting to be so. By Christmas 1914, ten of them had already died. The Nelson Cup was not contested during the war but some younger men still went to Mollington, to drill with the Citizen Volunteers. This was the first Citizen Volunteer unit in the country and served as a model for other Volunteer units, which sprang up later, throughout the whole country[2].

The President of the Young Men's Society later stated that 24 members of the swimming club were now in different units of His Majesty's Forces. During the course of the war the membership fell considerably and eventually the swimming club ceased to be a viable organisation.

During the war, the president of the Young Men's Society was James Beatty, elder brother of the aforementioned Peter. James was overage for conscription and was deployed on war-related industrial work. James died in 1916, because of an illness contracted during this wartime service. His brother Hugh died in France, later in 1916. Peter, who had managed to marry Alice McCleary when on leave in 1915, died in 1917, as the result of a tragic accident, whilst in service. In 1918 their brother Richard Beatty died of a tropical illness, contracted whilst on service in the Middle East. There are other examples of families within the parish of St. Werburgh's, who made similar sacrifices, including several examples of fathers and sons who were killed during active service in the Great War. There were also numerous men, of a particularly unfortunate age, who were just old enough to serve in WW1, survived it and were still young enough to serve in WW2 when it broke out, twenty years later.

Tontine Club

This was an important parish association, which provided a kind of social security insurance provision for the families of the parish. Remember that health and social security were not at this time considered appropriate matters for national or local governments to concern themselves with. These Tontine Societies existed in many parishes and St. Werburgh's Tontine Society was fairly typical of most. Every male member paid a weekly sum of 6 pence. If the member became ill and could not work, he received 5 shillings per week for 8 weeks. (This compares with a purported average weekly wage of £5. However, £1 per week was more usual for unskilled labourers and gardeners, many of whom were employed in Chester.) There was also a death grant of £5. If there was money over at the end of the year, a dividend was distributed between the members.

During the Great War the number of men contributing, fell significantly. It was then decided to accept younger men into the scheme, at half the former contribution rate and they would receive half the benefits. These would have been boys who had left school at 13 but were not yet old enough to enlist. The rules were also altered to make allowance for the high number of serving men. Service men who kept up contributions, would receive full sickness and death benefit. However, soldiers who ceased to contribute would have to wait 3 months after re-joining before becoming eligible for benefits. As time went on, the continuation of this society was also threatened. Nevertheless, it managed to remain in existence, though in a slightly different form, throughout the war.

Church Choir

This was a male choir, which sang Gregorian chant at High Mass and a range of music at other Masses. The lead singers in the choir either enlisted or were called up and so the standard of the singing was adversely affected. The choir master also appears to have volunteered for war-related service and was not able to continue his musical work. One of the curates undertook choir practice. Choir numbers were much reduced and Canon Chambers had reason to ask mothers, via the parish magazine, to stress the appropriate behaviour expected of the choir boys, whilst they were on the altar. It seems that without the presence of the older choir members, the standard of behaviour was certainly slipping!

Pre-war, choir boys' outings had been to interesting resorts such as Rhyl or West Kirby. This involved an exciting journey by train, followed by a midday dinner. An afternoon of games on the sands and a noisy progress through the town, where no doubt locals were tormented by the behaviour of the lads, was then followed by a substantial high tea. A train journey back to Chester completed the day in fine style. During the war, the choir boys were glad to go to Eccleston Ferry by horse and cart, or simply to the Convent gardens, to play football and devour such sustenance as was available!

Research for the above article was carried out by John Broadhurst, Norah Clewes, Celia Murphy, Stella Pleass and Mary Powell. The material was edited by Ann Marie Curtis.

Bibliography

St. Werburgh's Parish Magazines, 1904–1917, held at St. Werburgh's
St. Werburgh's Registers held at Chester Archives and Local Studies (CALS)

References

1. Service record of Peter Beatty held at the National Archives, Ref ADM 188/1094/970
2. Cheshire Observer 28 Oct. 1916 held at CALS

Schools in Wartime

St. Werburgh's Schools broke up for the summer holidays on 24 July 1914. By the time they re-opened on 24 August, two tragedies had occurred, one national and one local. The local tragedy took place on 31 July when Mr. James Leonard Pearce, a young teacher at the Boys' School, died due to the after effects of typhoid fever. Typhoid stalked the country relentlessly during the summer months, when the bacillus bred quickly and was then carried to the population in general. The national tragedy was the outbreak of the Great War on 4 August. In such circumstances the schools re-opened, with a depleted number of staff and much gossip and conjecture about forthcoming events.

In 1914 St. Werburgh's Schools were in Queen Street, near the present back entrance of Tesco. The schools were a mish-mash of buildings, consisting of the original Catholic Chapel and presbytery, which had been built in Queen Street in 1799, together with the schoolroom, which had been attached to it around 1850. The front lawn of the Chapel was then built over by Edmund Kirby in 1875, (whilst he was building St. Werburgh's Church), and then attached to these older buildings. There is a lithograph of the original Chapel, designed by Thomas Harrison and a photograph of the St. Werburgh's Schools before they were demolished in the 1960's, which shows the Kirby additions and modifications. The cross, which was originally on the Chapel and later the school façade, now hangs over the bar in the Catholic Social Centre on Brook Street!

In 1914 most children attended school from the age of 5 until the age of 13 and usually the schools attended were on the same site. St. Werburgh's Schools consisted of mixed infants' school, with pupils ages 5–7, then separate boys' and girls' schools, ages 7–13. The 3 schools had separate head teachers and staff, though in St. Werburgh's case they were all housed within the same building. Pupils normally left school on their 13th birthday. This was pedantically adhered to in one particular family, where a boy told the headmaster "Please Sir, I shall not be coming to school this afternoon. I shall be thirteen at dinnertime"![1]

In 1882 a young teacher, Philip Lane had arrived in Chester to take over as Headmaster of the Boys' School. He was a fully trained teacher, with a couple of years' experience in the Pro-Cathedral School at Clifton. Lane stayed at St. Werburgh's for the rest of his career and celebrated 25 years as headmaster in 1907[2]. This event was marked by a presentation evening in the Club premises in Queen Street. Fr. Maurice Hayes presided, with Fr. Edward Kirby in attendance. A concert was followed by eulogistic speeches, and then Mr. Lane was presented by five of his ex-pupils, with an inscribed

Schools in Wartime 59

Catholic Chapel, Queen Street, Chester, 1799
Reproduced by kind permission of CALS

St. Werburgh's Schools, Queen Street 1950's
Reproduced by kind permission of CALS

silver bowl. For the finale, all the past pupils "lined up" shoulder to shoulder around the room, to sing "Auld Lang Syne" and "He's a Jolly Good Fellow". The event showed the high esteem in which Philip Lane was held by his ex-students, though it is of course, remarkably easy to think well of a person who no longer has the authority to place one in detention or prescribe extra homework!

Most teachers became certified, after finishing their 5 year apprenticeship as pupil teachers. In 1914 pupil teachers had to be at least 16 years of age and they assisted regular class teachers, taking on more and more responsibility for a class as time went on. They were themselves taught, after school hours, by the head teacher (1.5 hours each evening) and took annual exams set by the local council. After they had passed a sufficient number of examinations and received good reports about their teaching ability from their school and demonstrated this during Council inspections, they became Certified Teachers. Some were awarded full time scholarships to the few Teacher Training Colleges which were being founded but most, particularly women, gained Certified Teacher Status via the pupil-teacher route. Women teachers always left employment if or when they married.

Headmaster Philip Lane and pupils 1883
Reproduced by kind permission of CALS

In August 1914 the staff at the Boys' School consisted of Mr. Philip Lane (Headmaster), Miss Mary Hargrove, Mrs. Alice Isabel McWalter nee Embrey (temporary supply for the late Mr. Pearce) and Mr. Charles Roger Sinclair. Mr. Harold Wilfrid Hartland arrived on 1 October to permanently replace the late Mr. Pearce[3]. At that time there were 212 boys on register and an average attendance of 184. There were no half term holidays but as usual, throughout the war, school still closed for three days in October and May, for the Chester Races! This was taken as an opportunity by the children certainly to enjoy a holiday but more importantly, to earn some money by running errands around the race course.

There was no set uniform at most schools, though standard grey short trousers and soft round-collared shirts for boys, dark dresses and white pinafores for girls, was the norm. Shirts and pinafores were often made by ladies of the parish and distributed to needy families. Boots were worn by both sexes.

Parents paid 1 penny per week for each child's education. This was then matched by the City Council, provided that the school was housed in sound buildings and could show good attendance figures and good academic progress by the children, during Council inspections. Unfortunately St. Werburgh's struggled to meet some of these requirements, as older children could be kept from school to look after younger ones, particularly if the mother was ill. In these times, when there were no vaccinations, infectious diseases also spread like wild fire, exacerbating the attendance problem and requiring governors to close the school on public health grounds, to help prevent the spread of an epidemic. Poor attendance was also sometimes caused by lack of suitable clothing, such as lack of boots in winter or lack of funds, particularly if the father was an unskilled labourer. His normal income would have been the equivalent of today's minimum wage and he could easily lose work during bad weather. In consequence he would be unable to pay the penny per child per week.

City Council inspectors arrived annually and informed the school managers (governors) and the City Council, of the strengths and failures of the school. In addition, school managers were always visiting to check on school matters. St. Werburgh's was fortunate in that it never lost its Council contribution but the same could not be said of its sister schools at St. Francis. Unfortunately their overcrowded buildings were not of sufficiently high quality and they received no Government or rates contribution between 1913 and 1922[4]. This created a knock-on effect, as pupils who would normally have enrolled at St. Francis, enrolled at St. Werburgh's instead. This threatened to cause untenable overcrowding at St. Werburgh's and Edmund Kirby was brought in to devise alterations and additions which would ensure that the school buildings were suitable. These had just been finished in 1914, leaving the parish with excessive debt, when war broke out.

Philip Lane, headmaster of the Boys' School continued as such throughout the war and had to make many alterations to normal practice as the war extended beyond Christmas and became thought of as an almost permanent feature. As early as November 1914 drawing lessons had been cancelled and lessons moved to earlier in the day, for greater energy conservation. However, I am sure that there was joy among the pupils when Christmas examinations had to be cancelled, "owing to pressure of other matters recently."

Mr. Sinclair and Mr. Hartland who enlisted in 1915 and 1916 respectively, were replaced by female teachers. Mr. Lane was then the only male teacher in the three schools. Mr. Hartland's temporary supply teacher was once again Mrs. Alice Isabel McWalter (nee Embrey), who started on 2 February. She was however absent due to sickness from 11 – 28 February and no supply teacher could be found. She resigned on 19 April. The reason was to be found in the Parish Baptism Register – a daughter, Jane Emily McWalter had been born on 5 October to Richard Patrick and Alice Isobel McWalter, nee Embrey. She was baptised on 20 November 1916. I am sure that Philip Lane had never had to put up with this sort of thing before in his professional career – the sooner that this odious war was over, the better! However, married women continued to be recalled to teaching, either permanently or on a temporary basis, throughout the war. Classes were often 'doubled up' and teachers had to take on classes such as art, P.E. or technical subjects, which they had not taught before.

In 1916 woodwork classes, formerly held in premises at the rear of the Grosvenor Museum, were cancelled, as Mr. Morris, the instructor, had been relocated for War Service and there was no-one else to instruct the lads. Swimming lessons had already been cancelled, as the City Baths were closed in an effort to conserve fuel. (This would also have greatly penalised the women of the parish, who relied on the slipper baths there for family bathing and the hot water provided for their laundry.) The school curriculum, particularly for boys, appears to have narrowed considerably.

Unfortunately, Mother Monica, headmistress of the Girls' School, did not keep a very detailed log book. Entries mainly consisted simply of noting attendance and the start and end dates of each term! This makes it difficult to analyse the effects of the war on the Girls' School[5]. Dee House Convent School was run by the Faithful Companions of Jesus, until 1925. Few records of Dee House in those times have survived, though the order's archivist in Salford has given us whatever references to Dee House or St. Werburgh's Girls' School, (in which two of the nuns taught), that she has been able to find. On the whole, the war is not specifically mentioned in the school log books. An impression is given that the teachers' energy is being spent on trying to cope with an increasingly adverse situation and to provide as good an education as possible, under such difficult circumstances.

Dee House, FCJ Convent, later Ursuline Convent, Chester
Reproduced by kind permission of CALS

Different activities began to replace the lost ones. The children were always taking part in charity concerts to raise money for war charities, or to provide entertainment in hospital for convalescing soldiers. They also co-operated with non-catholic schools in concerts to raise funds for Belgian refugees and war wounded. In addition Dee House Convent School produced an endless supply of knitted garments for troops. There would have been no trench foot or frostbite if all had reached their destination!

In May 1917 King George V and Queen Mary visited Chester[6] and the St. Werburgh's boys formed a line at the front of the castle to witness the ceremony held there. In July a school nurse arrived to weigh the older boys and compare their weights with those of the previous year, to see if these had been affected by food shortages during the war. The results were not recorded in the school logs. In November, Christopher McCleary was presented with a silver medal and certificate for saving two persons from drowning in the Chester Canal. He had actually saved the lives almost a year previously, presumably whilst still able to enjoy swimming lessons.

On the night of 27–28 November 1917 a strange event occurred in Chester. The nuns in Dee House Convent were warned by a telephone message that there was the possibility of a Zeppelin raid on Chester[7]. In the middle of the night the nuns and boarders were roused and made their way in complete darkness and allegedly in good order, to the chapel in the lowest part of the house. Fortunately the raid did not materialise and the ladies later returned to bed. The boarders were allowed an extra long sleep the following morning, to make up for their night time revelry!

In January 1918 school re-opened accompanied by bad weather and illness. By July influenza was running riot and the local council ordered schools to close on 8 July for one week. They re-opened 15–26 July and then closed for the summer holidays! By October, influenza was again running uncontrollably through the city and school attendance figures hit an all time low.

However, the Dee House annals contain the information that "On November 11th we hailed the news of Victory; the town did honour to the occasion, according to its immemorial wont. The whole country resounded with the symphony of joy-bells, as we proceeded to chapel with our Catholics and non-Catholics alike, to thank God for the great final success... recognizing that we owe Peace and victory primarily to the protection of the Sacred Heart over our Navy and our Allied Armies."

The entry of Mr. Philip Lane in the Boys' School log book was more succinct and was written in red ink.

11 November

"An armistice was signed this morning. A holiday for the rest of the week was given the boys in celebration of the joyous occasion."

Research for the above article was carried out by John Broadhurst, Norah Clewes, Ann Marie Curtis, Jill Devine, Celia Murphy, Stella Pleass and Mary Powell. The material was edited by Ann Marie Curtis.

References

1. M.W. Sturman OSU, Catholicism in Chester, A Double Centenary 1875–1975, p75
2. Cheshire Observer Saturday, 30 November 1907 Mf 225/30
3. Details of St. Werburgh's Boys' School from the log book held in Chester Archives and Local Studies (CALS) Z DES 46/2
4. A History of the County of Chester: Volume 5 Part 2, the City of Chester: Culture, Buildings, Institutions. Originally published by Victoria County History, London, 2005. Leisure and culture: Education Pages 277–291.

5. Details of St. Werburgh's Girls' School from the log book held in CALS Z DES 47/3
6. Chester Chronicle Saturday, 19 May 1917
7. Details of Dee House Convent from the deposits held by the Archivist of the Faithful Companions of Jesus, Salford

Bibliography

M.W. Sturman OSU, Catholicism in Chester, A Double Centenary 1875–1975
St. Werburgh's Parish Magazines, 1904–1917 held at St. Werburgh's

Wartime Clergy Changes

The clergy of St. Werburgh's had been fairly static in the years leading up to the Great War. Canon Joseph Chambers was rector and his senior curate was Fr. Maurice Hayes. The two priests were complete opposites of each other. Canon Chambers was short and somewhat portly, whilst Fr. Hayes was tall and rangy. Chambers was elderly and English, Hayes was still young and Irish. He had arrived at St. Werburgh's straight from his ordination in 1899, "on loan" from his Irish diocese, for a few years. He was formally incardinated (transferred to the Catholic Diocese of Shrewsbury) in 1907, whilst still at St. Werburgh's. The two priests worked tirelessly, each in their own way, for the good of their parishioners and that of the wider Chester population. They raised the profile of Chester Catholics, which had been rather low key for obvious reasons, since penal times. The two men regularly represented the Catholic community on local committees and Canon Chambers was presented to their Majesties King George V and Queen Mary, as the representative of the Catholic community of Chester, when they visited Chester in 1917[1]. Fr. Hayes was elected to the Board of Guardians of the Poor Law Institutions of Cheshire and made his mark on all sections of society, as an inveterate fighter for those Cestrians who had no effective voice. Normally, Chambers and Hayes were assisted by a younger curate. In 1914 this curate was Fr. Edward O'Hara. He had arrived as a newly-ordained priest, at the start of September 1913 and was also probably on loan from an Irish diocese.

As the war progressed the complement of clergy altered considerably. In October 1914 they were joined by Fr. Joseph Loos, a Belgian refugee, who lived at St. Werburgh's and who looked after the spiritual and temporal welfare of his fellow countrymen, scattered throughout Cheshire and North Wales. (See essay on Fr. Loos). After sterling work with fellow refugees and injured Belgian soldiers who had been evacuated to Chester hospitals, Loos himself was called up to serve in the Belgian Army Red Cross and left St. Werburgh's in September 1915, for training in France.

The Great War was the first armed conflict in which Catholic Chaplains were officially allowed to serve in the British Forces. All the chaplains were volunteers but their bishops rarely refused to allow them to go, indeed they were anxious for them to do so. They felt that the large number of Catholic servicemen warranted having Catholic Chaplains but it also meant that bishops often had to stretch the remaining clergy between competing parishes and duties. So it was that clergy back home were often moved, by bishops trying to keep all parishes supplied with suitable priests. In August 1915 Fr. Edward O'Hara transferred to the Liverpool Archdiocese, where he remained until 1920 and the newly ordained Fr. Henry E.G. Rope arrived to replace him at St. Werburgh's.

Fr. Maurice Hayes was the next to move, going as parish priest to Northenden, in early 1917. He was greatly missed. The Parish, Mayor and Corporation organised an event in the Town Hall, at which Hayes was presented with a cheque and an illuminated address. Many speeches of appreciation for his work were delivered by different civic dignitaries. Later he received thanks and a pair of handsome silver candlesticks from representatives of the National Union of Railwaymen, Chester Branch[2]. The Chester Guardians[3] were the last group to pay their tributes to Fr. Hayes, at a special meeting in the Town Hall in March 1918. After several complimentary speeches, Fr. Hayes was presented with a handsome clock. Hayes was visibly moved by these unsolicited demonstrations of the affection with which he was regarded by all Cestrians, not simply those of St. Werburgh's parish.

All were sad to see Hayes leave Chester but all would have been pleased to know that he was to return to St. Werburgh's as Rector, ten years later. The Irishman, whose suitability for a post in Chester had been called into question and who was only expected to stay in this country for about 5 years, instead spent the whole of his ministry in the Diocese of Shrewsbury and all but ten years of it at St. Werburgh's Chester. He died in 1948 and was buried in his native Tralee.

Back in September 1917 Fr. Maurice Hayes was replaced by Fr. John Porter and the newly ordained Fr. Cuthbert Joseph James arrived to replace Fr. Henry Rope. Porter and James remained with Canon Chambers at St. Werburgh's until after the end of the Great War. The curates who served at St. Werburgh's during the Great War proved to be quite a mixed bag and I suspect that Canon Chambers spent many hours addressing the problems which they unwittingly presented.

Fr. Porter was the least controversial of the curates. He had been born in Dukinfield in 1880, educated at Oscott College and the English College in Rome and then ordained in Rome in 1909. He had served at New Brighton and St.

Canon Maurice Hayes

Werburgh Birkenhead before coming to St. Werburgh's Chester. His final posting was as parish priest at Church Stretton, where he died in 1957. He was an ascetic character and a conscientious pastor. Though the income at Church Stretton was minute, he never touched any part of £5,000 left to him in a legacy and in his turn, left the whole of it to the diocese, when he died. He was buried in Dukinfield.

Fr. Henry Rope was a unique character in the annals of the Diocese of Shrewsbury. He was born in Shrewsbury into an Anglican family and was educated at Shrewsbury School and Christ Church, Oxford. After his father's premature death, his mother became a Catholic. Henry and four of his five siblings followed suite. Rope detested industrialisation and hated machinery. He was a founder member of the "Back to the Land" movement, and refused to use either the railway or a motor car. Many of his family were artistic, his aunt being a sculptor and his sister and his cousin, both called Margaret, were artists in stained glass. Rope himself was a poet and it was whilst he was a curate at St. Werburgh's Chester, that his first book of poetry was published[4].

As was usual, Fr. Rope, as the most recently arrived curate, was put in charge of the choir. This involved his taking the choir boys on their annual outing, which event evolved into an unmitigated disaster. Instead of going by rail to Rhyl or West Kirby, the party went by open horse and cart to Eccleston Ferry. The boys could not help but feel that they had been short-changed. Rain apparently soaked them on the way back, sealing the end of a perfect day! The following year Canon Chambers took the

Fr. Henry Rope in County Wicklow September 1929 Reproduced by kind permission of Shrewsbury Diocesan Archives

unusual step of leading the choir boys' outing himself – they were taken to the convent gardens, where they were allowed to play football and other raucous games!

Obviously, Rope's writing took up much of his time and Canon Chambers was probably relieved when Rope was transferred to Crewe in 1917. Whether this suited the violently anti-railway cleric is debatable. What is certain is that it did not suit his new rector, who was moved to write to the bishop to complain about Rope's unusual behaviour, which involved minimal parish involvement and maximum time spent in his room, presumably "scribbling"[5]. Rope passed only one year at Crewe, leaving in August 1918. He was then transferred as rector to the rural community of Plowden. His time at Plowden is remembered mainly for two events – his first sermon, which consisted of a tirade against the evils of the tractor and in 1919 the publication of his second book of poems![6]

For the next twenty years it was to prove difficult for the bishop of the day to find suitable postings for Fr. Henry Rope. Eventually, when WW2 broke out, he was posted as archivist to the English College in Rome, which was located at Stonyhurst "for the duration." He went with the College when it transferred back to Rome after WW2 and enjoyed this period of his life enormously. Rope retired from his position at the College in 1959 and returned to this country. He was posted as chaplain at Palotti Hall, until he was relieved of these duties in 1969. From this time onwards he was dogged by ill-health and increasingly confused by the developments set in train by the Second Vatican Council. He died in 1978.

Before training for the priesthood, Henry Rope had been employed on the Oxford English Dictionary project and for the whole of his life he continued to send in slips (definitions), some written on the back of lists or grocery papers, to the OED headquarters in Oxford. By the time of his death in 1978, shelves were allegedly groaning under the weight of his contributions[7].

By contrast, Fr. Cuthbert James had been born in Birkenhead, educated at Oscott College and ordained at Seacombe in March 1917. St. Werburgh's was his first curacy. After the end of the war he moved to Birkenhead, then Stockport. In 1923 he was received into the Church of England. He then followed his clerical vocation in the Anglican Church, until his death, as Rector of Pilton with Wing (Diocese of Peterborough) in 1968. No doubt Fr. James led a fulfilled life as an Anglican cleric but I feel sure that Canon Chambers would have felt somewhat alarmed, if he had known what path his Great War curate would eventually follow!

Ann Marie Curtis   **June 2017**

References

1. Chester Chronicle Saturday, 19 May 1917
2. Chester Chronicle Saturday, 13 October 1917
3. Chester Chronicle 23 March 1918
4. Rope, H.E.G. Religionis ancilla and other poems, Heath, Cranton, London 1916
5. September 1917 Letter from the Rector of St. Mary's Crewe to the bishop, held at Shrewsbury Diocesan Archives
6. Rope, H.E.G. Soul's belfry and other verses, Stretton Press, Church Stretton, 1919
7. Winchester, S. The Meaning of Everything: The Story of the Oxford English Dictionary p.209

Bibliography

Abbott, E. M. *To Preserve Their Memory* gives clergy postings and some biographical details.
Winchester, S. *The Meaning of Everything: The Story of the Oxford English Dictionary*
Gilliver, P. *The Making of the Oxford English Dictionary*

A Chester Hero Returns

The Great War Experiences of Walter Keating

18570 9th Bn. Cheshire Regiment and 64776 South Lancashire Regiment

Walter Keating, my grandfather, was born in Chester in 1881 and lived with his family in William Street, Newtown, Chester. He was one of eight children, the three eldest born in County Mayo, Ireland, the remaining five born in Chester.

Along with thousands of men of his generation, Walter Keating volunteered near the beginning of WW1. This was a very difficult time for all, especially for men like Walter, who had young families. Along with thousands of other local men he enlisted in the Cheshire Regiment. Leaving a wife to bring up small children alone, knowing that he might never return, must have been heart-breaking.

After a short spell of training, Walter was sent to France, disembarking there on 19 July 1915. He survived the military operations of that summer and sniper attacks during the winter. The spring of 1916 brought the Somme offensive.

Walter's particular theatre of war was Ancre in Thiepval, Picardy, taking part in the Battle of Ancre Heights, conducted from its start on 1 October, intermittently, until 11 November 1916. It was one of the last and bloodiest battles of the Somme and it was there that Walter was awarded his Military Medal. He was a private and military protocol dictated that had he been an officer, then his Military Medal would have been a Military Cross. His medal was awarded for rescuing comrades whilst under heavy German fire and in the face of one of the heaviest bombardments of mustard gas in the Somme battles. This was recorded in the London Gazette dated 19 February 1917 and confirmed in a formal letter signed by King George V. He also received the 1914–1915 Star, the British Empire Medal and the Allied Victory Medal.

Walter Joseph Keating

Walter returned from the war, a troubled soul. Mentally scarred by what he had witnessed and endured, he found it difficult to come to terms with everyday life. The effects of the mustard gas and trench foot had taken their toll and he was left with a racking cough. Despite this he managed to find work with Chester Corporation as a yardman and held down steady employment on the site which is now St. Werburgh's and St. Columba's Primary School, in Lightfoot Street, Hoole. He was unable to tackle physically demanding work, because of the effects of the mustard gas, encountered during his time spent in the trenches.

Home life was now close to the breadline. His wife and eight children made great demands on him, with which he was poorly equipped to deal and the death of a much loved daughter Margaret, at the age of 15, was a devastating loss to all the family. Our mother, Emily Cunniff, late of St. Werburgh's Parish, recalls him being constantly cold. He would sit in front of the fire on his return from a day's work and shiver. My grandmother would cover his shoulders with a blanket and sometimes he would weep for his lost comrades. I suppose today that we would say that he was suffering from Post Traumatic Shock in the aftermath of war.

Walter Keating's Military Medal

'Preamble'

To the London Gazette Supplement dated Monday 19th February 1917

His Majesty the King has been graciously pleased to award the Military Medal for bravery in the Field to the undermentioned soldier

18570 PTE W KEATING
9TH Bn Cheshire Regt.

George R I

Grave of Walter Keating in Overleigh Cemetery

Walter Keating died in 1942, in the middle of another war, age 61. He had been a lifelong parishioner of St. Werburgh's, where he had been baptised and married and where his children also had been baptised and had attended school. He was buried in Overleigh Cemetery.

All photographs are reproduced by kind permission of Angela Clark.

Angela Clark 2014

Sergeant Major Patrick Currivan

A True Irish Hero, but not in the Great War

The original Great War Memorial Board in St. Werburgh's Church was lost during alterations within the church. The present Great War Memorial Board lists Sergeant Major Patrick Currivan as a parishioner who died in the Great War. The sixty eight names shown on this current Memorial Board were collected in the late 1980's, by a group led by Fr. Andrew Lloyd. This team only had access to St. Werburgh's Parish Magazine records from this period and local newspaper reports, held by Chester Archives. That they identified sixty eight names was a remarkable feat. However, there are some names listed, which have been included erroneously, but understandably. The name of Patrick Currivan is one of them.

The research undertaken later, between 2012 –2016, had access to Government Great War records that were made available in anticipation that there would public interest on the 100th anniversary of the War. Edmund Kirby files in Liverpool Central Reference Library were also accessed, as they contained letters between Canon Chambers and the church architects, relating to the design of the War Memorial Chapel. These letters identified that there were a total of 96 names on the original War Memorial Board, purchased from Hardman's of Birmingham. Hardman's records in Birmingham were then accessed and these proved a major breakthrough in the research, as their records included the original 96 names placed on the board, plus one late addition, from a mother who had been ill and had been unable to see Canon Chambers and have her son's name included, when the board was originally commissioned. Comparison of the current war Memorial Board names with the original Hardman Board names, clearly showed that Sergeant Major Patrick Currivan had been wrongly included.

So who was this person, now described as a "True Irish Hero"? The bare facts of his life are that Patrick Currivan was born 12 October 1827 in Dundalk, Louth, Ireland and died 27 November 1916 in Lightfoot Street, Hoole. This would indicate that he was 86 years of age at the start of the Great War. His mistaken inclusion on the Great War Memorial Board is readily understandable. The Parish Magazine, January 1917, recorded the following as having recently died; Pte. A. K. B. Brandreth, Pte. Thomas Waldron, Pte. Hugh Beatty, Sgt. Major Patrick Currivan and Matthew Clayson, Australian Munitions Worker. So what was the history of this "hero"? Who was he? Just like the hunt for Lieutenant A. F. Hughes, described in another essay, the research into Sergeant Patrick Currivan revealed the fascinating history of a different type of hero, living in Chester during the Great War.

Patrick Currivan's father, also named Patrick, joined 86th (Royal County Down) Regiment of Foot at Roscrea, Tipperary, on the 12 February 1827. He had joined the Army of King George the Fourth, for the bounty of Three Pounds. His attestation papers showed he was aged twenty and unable to write his name. He served 21 years and 57 days in the army. His discharge papers showed that at the time of discharge, he was in receipt of four Good Conduct Badges and had remained a private throughout his army service, all of which was served at home. Patrick had three sons, John born 22 January 1823 in Thurles, James born 10 June 1825 and Patrick born 18 October 1827 in Dundalk. All three sons followed their father into the 86th Regiment of Foot, joining the regiment near the start of Queen Victoria's reign, signing to serve for a minimum of 21 years. They all rose to the rank of Sergeant and all served in India, during the period of the Indian Mutiny. A Private in the army at that time, could not marry except with their officer's permission.

James was the first of the Currivan boys to marry. He married an army widow, Mary Leeson, nee Mitchell, in 1856 at Upper Colaba Fort, which is 35 km. south of Mumbai. Patrick was best man at the wedding. Family believe Mary's correct maiden name to have been Mitchelson.

The other sons did not marry until the 86th Foot returned to Ireland, following the Indian Mutiny, in August 1859.[1] John, the eldest brother married Ann Moore, on 14 October 1862 at Killeshin, Laois, Ireland. A few months later, in April 1863, Patrick

Colaba or Kolaba Fort, 1855

Currivan married Mary Ann Maloney, at Ballybricken, Waterford City, Ireland. The regiment was posted to Gibraltar in 1864 and two children, Patrick James, and Kate Agnes were born there. An earlier daughter, Mary Ann Currivan had died soon after her birth in 1864. Patrick Currivan remained a Sergeant with the 86th Regiment of Foot, completing his 21 years of service in Gibraltar. He was discharged from the army on 9 April 1867, aged 39, indicating on his discharge papers that his intended place of residence would be Birkenhead.

It is likely that Patrick chose to reside in Birkenhead as his older brother James had retired there from the 86th Regiment of Foot, on the 15 August 1864, having also completed 21 years of service, over 17 years of which had been spent in the East Indies. James also would have only been aged 39 when he retired from the army. The Chelsea pension for retired serving men must have been insufficient for a married person raising a young family and James would have needed to find alternative employment. The 1865 Post Office Directory for Cheshire, shows James Currivan, Band Master to the 1st Cheshire Engineers Volunteers, living at 24 Mornington Street, Birkenhead. His work with the band was greatly praised in the Chester Chronicle 14 January 1865.

But why should Patrick Currivan be recognised as a 'hero' in Chester? To understand this, it is best to return to the records of his army career. Patrick Currivan attested as a boy in the army on the date of his 14th birthday, 12 October 1841. He served in that role until 26 September 1845 when he was promoted to be a drummer. 2 weeks later on his 18th birthday, being no longer under age, he attested again and signed up for 21 year service. He received his first good conduct pay award on 12 October 1850 and his second good conduct award on 12 October 1855. He was promoted Corporal 28 December 1857 and then Sergeant on 29 November 1858. Currivan served with the Central Indian Field Force and was involved in eight different engagements between

Jhansi Fort which the 86th Regiment of Foot besieged in April 1858

*The Light Company 86th (Royal County Down)
storm the walls of Jhansi*

17 March and 20 June 1858[2]. For these actions he was to receive the Indian Mutiny Silver Medal with Central India Clasps. The 86th Regiment of Foot formed part of the force led by Major-General Sir Hugh Rose, which besieged and captured Jhansi Fort. On the morning of the 3 April 1858, Major Stuart and the Light Company of the 86th, scaled the city wall under fire, while the remainder of the Royal County Down assaulted the breach in the walls. The 86th suffered one officer and twelve men killed and six officers and sixty men wounded. Although The Royal County Down Regiment did not gain a Battle Honour for their part in the siege, four Victoria Crosses were awarded to members of that regiment for this operation[3].

On his Military records, it stated that in 1858, Patrick Currivan was in the actions at Chanderee, Betwa, the capture of Jhansi, Koonch, Gowlowee, followed by the capture of Calpee, Morar and Gwalior. In one engagement the regiment went into action in full strength and came out only forty strong. Amazingly all three Currivan brothers were in this engagement and survived.

Patrick's records show that upon his return to England, he found employment as Sergeant on the Permanent Staff of the 3rd Btn. the Cheshire Regiment. He served in this role until 1883. The Cheshire Observer 7 August 1869, records the results of the Cheshire Rifle Association meeting at Shotwick, a three day event promoted by the Earl of Grosvenor, who normally attended all three days. The paper records event No. 19, Register Keeper's Prize, -To be Shot for by the register keepers. Five shots at five hundred yards, Hythe position. Any rifle of government pattern, except sergeants 5-grooved rifles. First prize, £3; second, £2; third, £1. It is recorded that Sergeant Currivan was second with 12 points. The following year he was third in the competition.

During this period Patrick's family grew, with the addition of four more boys and a girl. All these children were baptised at St. Francis' Church, as Patrick was residing in the Militia Barracks. Sadly, Patrick's wife Mary Ann died 7 October 1880, just over a month after the birth of their son Ernest Claude. The 1881 census shows Patrick's brother James and his twenty year old daughter Agnes staying with Patrick at the Militia Barracks in Chester, presumably helping Patrick with his young children.

In 1888, Patrick aged 60 married Margaret Richmond aged 31, in St. Francis' Church. They had two children, Percival Joseph Currivan born in 1889 and then Teresa Mary Josephine Currivan in 1890. Unfortunately Teresa died before her second birthday, in 1892. The 1891 census shows Patrick and his family having now moved from the Militia Barracks and to be living at 16 Queen Street. His occupation is shown as Day Waiter at an Inn. This job would have been in addition to his continued work with the Cheshire Regiment. His record shows he was working as D.D. (Detached for Duty)

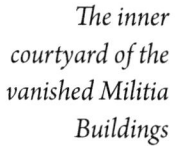

The inner courtyard of the vanished Militia Buildings

to the Officer in Charge of the Cheshire Depot until 21 April 1907 and then D.D. to the War Office. It was during this period, when no longer directly employed at The Cheshire Depot that Patrick served as Sergeant Major of the Javelin Men who escorted the Judge's coach to and from Chester Assizes.

Patrick became a well-known figure in the City of Chester. He attended all military funerals and other ceremonials and was interviewed on several occasions by local newspaper reporters.

In 1905, when H.R.H. the Duke of Connaught visited Chester Castle, he noticed the Sergeant –Major wearing the Central India Force Silver Medal, the Long Service and Good Conduct Medals. He went up and spoke to him. Replying to a question by his Royal Highness, Patrick said that he had seen two years' service in the Mutiny under

The Javelin Men preceding the Judge's Coach

Order of Merit Instituted by the Cheshire Regiment

Sir Hugh Rose and altogether he had forty one years' service. The Duke remarked that he carried his years well and shook hands with him[4.]

In January 1909, just prior to his retirement on 13 January 1909 at the age of 82 years, Sergeant Patrick Currivan was presented with the Meritorious Medal at Chester Castle. In presenting the medal Major Gosset said, "It is for your good service in the Indian Mutiny and for your long service in peace time in the Royal Irish Rifles *(86th Regiment of Foot had merged with other regiments to form this new unit)* that you have received this distinction."

Patrick Currivan was not only recognised as a hero in Chester. A cutting is shown below, taken from the Liverpool Weekly Echo, Saturday, 29 February 1908, entitled "More Crimean and Mutiny Veterans," Patrick Currivan is pictured in the centre of the photograph opposite.

When war broke out in 1914, though 87 years of age, Patrick apparently asked for army employment. He was possibly assigned to civilian duties at the Chester Castle Barracks. He died on 27 November 1916. At the time of his death, two of his sons were in the Forces. Ernest Claude, born 1880, was in the A.S.C. and served in France from 28 August 1915. Ernest entered the war as a Staff Sergeant Major and eventually rose to the rank of 2nd Lieutenant. His brother John Joseph joined the Cheshire Yeomanry in 1916.[5] This unit joined with the Shropshire Yeomanry to form 10th Shropshire Light Infantry Battalion at Cairo on 2 March 1917. They came under command of 231st Brigade in 74th (Yeomanry) Division. On the 7 May 1918 they landed at Marseilles for service in France and later Belgium. Another son James Herbert, Pte. 6802 Shropshire Light Infantry, had enlisted 22 August 1914 and served in France from 18 February 1915. He was discharged from the army and awarded the Silver War Badge, 21 March

1916, before his father's death. One of Patrick's younger sons, Percival Joseph, was a Civil Servant, carrying out a wartime posting in Madagascar. Four grandsons were also with the armed services, one in the Army canteens, one in the R.F.A., a third in the Cheshire Yeomanry, and the fourth in the Cheshire Regiment[4].

Patrick Currivan was given a funeral with full military honours. The band, firing party, and buglers were from the Castle, Chester. Bandmaster A. H. Graves was in charge of the band, which played appropriate music on the way to the old Overleigh cemetery, where the service at the graveside was conducted by Rev. Father Hayes[4.] The January 1917 edition of the Parish Magazine, recorded "Sergeant Major Patrick Currivan was a well-known figure, proud of the services he had rendered the Empire and intensely interested in the present war, was cheery and confident of the final success of the Allies, which alas, he was not permitted to see. He reaches the remarkable age of 91."

Patrick died whilst still supporting the Cheshire Regiment. He is surely the oldest member of the Cheshire Regiment to die whilst still being of service.

John W. Curtis   **July 2014**

References

1. https://en.wikipedia.org/wiki/86th_(Royal_County_Down)_Regiment_of_Foot
2. Patrick Currivan's Discharge Document issued Gibraltar 9 April 1867 – Detailed Statement of Services
3. https://www.royal-irish.com/events/storming-of-jhansi-the-indian-mutiny
4. Cheshire Observer 2 December 1916
5. The Cheshire (Earl of Chester's Yeomanry). B Squadron No.2 Troop, Pte. J Currivan No. 1564

Canon Hugh Welch

Parish Priest of St. Werburgh's and Prisoner of War

Any Parish Priest is interested in his predecessors: who sat in this chair, said Mass at this Altar, visited these hospitals and homes and looked after these schools and colleges? Parish Priests are birds of passage. We come, we go. But the people we serve stay for ever, the people who live in the streets and roads that go to make up the geographical parish. Here at St. Werburgh's, we can never quote too often the words of Canon Murphy (PP 1959–80) that our magnificent church was built with the pennies and tuppences of the Irish Catholics of Boughton.

Frank Murphy took over from Hugh Welch (PP 1944–59), Canon Maurice Hayes (PP 1927–1944), Canon Eugene Rooney (PP 1925–27), Canon Joseph Chambers (PP 1903–24) – these were just names when I arrived here in September 2006. But you cannot be long in any new parish before the names of your predecessors become familiar and your appetite becomes whetted to find out more. For Hugh Welch, the inspiration was clearing out a top floor junk room in the Presbytery. My immediate predecessor, Fr. Peter Sharrocks (PP 1992–2006) had shown me the outside of this room, and ruefully admitted it had been a lumber room since the days of his predecessor, Canon Vincent Turnbull (PP 1980–92). "It's the stuff of ages" he said, "And if I were you, I'd leave it that way." Not renowned for my tidiness, I had an uncharacteristic burst of energy and invited parishioners to come along and fill a couple of skips with all this lumber. But any junk room hides a few treasures, and for me, it was finding Frank Murphy's student books and notes from his time as a Seminarian in Maynooth in the 1930's, sent there by the Diocese of Cloyne. And then two little red volumes of Dickens, the *New Century Library* Edition of 1900, pocket-sized but, thanks to the marvel of India paper, able to contain all nine hundred pages in a book half an inch thick. "Martin Chuzzlewit" and "Pickwick Papers", both elegantly inscribed "Hugh A. Welch, 1920." Ninety years ago. What was he doing? Where was he when he read these books? Who was he?

This was the beginning of finding out as much about Hugh Welch as I could. His Diocesan Record was clear enough: born in 1897, in Whitchurch. Student at Ushaw, 1910–24. Ordained by Bishop Singleton in St. Vincent's Altrincham 3 August 1924. Four curacies – dear dead days beyond recall – at St. Peter's Stalybridge (1924–25), St. Vincent's Altrincham (1925–26), St. John's New Ferry (1926–27) and St. Alban's

84   A War-Torn Chester Parish

Canon Hugh Welch ca. 1957

Macclesfield (1927–32). Then Parish Priest at St. Mary's Congleton (1932–38) and Our Lady's Latchford, Warrington (1938–44), arriving here in Chester at the end of WW2. So far, so straightforward. But one statistic stands out there: fourteen years at Ushaw. He was thirteen when he arrived there and twenty-seven when he was ordained. But the normal age for Ordination today is 25, and it could be even lower a century ago, the most able students becoming priests at 22 or 23. Why the two extra years for Hugh Welch?

I could never have guessed at the answer before my researches began: that he had enlisted in the army in 1916, and had spent ten months in a German Prisoner of War Camp, returning to Ushaw early in 1919 to resume his studies for the priesthood and presumably, one winter's evening in 1920, settling down in his room with a nice little red volume of Dickens.

The Military Records were very sparse, with no surviving Service Record for him. But there was an entry for a Hugh Welch in the Medals Records, giving him as a member of the 18th Battalion, the Welsh Regiment. It may be our Canon, it may not. Known only to God, as our anonymous war cemetery grave stones so beautifully phrase it.

In any historical research, as the amazing work of our Parish Great War Group has shown, in this volume and the earlier *We Shall Remember Them*, every dead end is followed by buried gold. For Hugh Welch, it was contacting Ushaw College and asking if they had any information on him. Very little, the answer came back, just the bare bones of his official seminary record. But, of course, I did know, didn't I, that he'd written an account of his time as a Prisoner of War for the Ushaw College magazine…

So here we have Hugh Welch, speaking in his own words from a century ago. The language is a little stilted, the jingoism a little dated, but it's a marvellous piece and connects not just me, but all of us, with one of our greatest Parish Priests.

A Prisoner in Germany

[The writer of the following pages is one of our own students who returned to Ushaw on 17 February. Ed]

It was on 9 April, 1918, that I had the misfortune to fall into the hands of the enemy. The details of the fighting which preceded our capture need not now be related, so I begin my story with the white flag.

When the officer in charge had hoisted the sign of surrender, the Germans rushed from their cover, exceedingly excited and shouting, "Goot Tommy Goot!" We were greatly encouraged by this unexpectedly cordial greeting but it was not very long before we were abruptly and unceremoniously undeceived as to our new masters. As we went back under escort we were obliged to do the work of the German stretcher-bearers. For miles and miles, we walked, and it seemed as if the dressing station would never be reached. At last, however, we arrived, and we very thankfully left the wounded with their doctors. They then led us to a field, wet and badly drained, round which were extended a few strands of barbed wire. Sentinels kept watch night and day, within and without. There we were left with no cover, most of us without overcoats, many without hats, and we remained for three days and three nights under a persistent shower of snow and sleet. We saw no food the first or second day. From time to time the Germans would take a number of us and, still without food, we would be marched to the line again to carry shells and to push the guns into position. The third day we received our rations – 18 small biscuits each about ¾ inch square!

After those three awful days of indescribably hunger and fatigue, we were marched to Lille, a distance of perhaps ten miles. Never have I made such a journey! With craving stomach, tired and weary, with an awful thirst, we marched along the long road. The weather had changed, and now in the afternoon, the transport continually passing, the dust aggravated our thirst. Men were drinking the water of pools and ditches and endeavouring to eat the greens by the roadside. When all were almost exhausted, we turned along the banks of a canal into Lille. Here the French were running out to see us. "Ça ne marche pas, eh?" they asked, and one could read agony on their faces. We were led into a barracks, which for some reason or other was called the 'Arsenal'. Here we received our first soup. Oh, what a sight! I had never seen starving men after food before – though I saw it often later. There was a mad rush and the soup was collected in anything handy – amongst other things I saw used were soft service caps, steel helmets and mess-tins. Here we lay in some sort of cover, with a drink of coffee and a ladle of barley or barley water per day for six days. We were then marched out and paraded in a most filthy condition, and always starving, and after passing through a little place called Fivres, we arrived at Fort MacDonald. This was a real dungeon, and life in it was certainly the most terrible experience I went through.

We were split up into groups of 275 and marched into the fort at intervals. The place felt ghostly and damp. We entered a passage with iron gates barring the way every fifteen feet. On to the passage some six or seven cells opened. The cells were of uniform length, about 15 yards, with barred windows and iron doors. Inside the cells poles were fixed from floor to roof, and across these shelves were fitted to provide more accommodation. Here for seven days 1,600 men were herded together, a cell being allotted to each group of 275. We were allowed to leave the cell for about six minutes a day to draw our one ladle of watery soup and a piece of bread. That was a twenty-four hour ration. Again, no water or drink of any sort was allowed except in very exceptional cases. The six minutes per day was our only relief, and all that time was needed to take the soup and drink it. For no other reason, sanitary or otherwise, were we permitted to leave this Black Hole of the Germans. One can well imagine the state of the men and the billet after seven days of confinement such as this. We could hardly move and were covered with dirt and vermin. It was, indeed, a glad day for us when we were warned of our departure to Germany. We imagined our troubles were over, but again we were mistaken.

We were led fainting and falling through the streets of Lille to the station, and were packed into cattle trucks, forty to a truck. The doors were not opened during three days, save once to receive a plate of some fantastical mixture not worthy of the name of soup. We arrived at Dulmen in a deplorable state, and received a bath and later a few potatoes and a sort of shell fish. One could say of our stay at Dulmen that we just existed – only just: never did I feel otherwise than starving. At last the Red Cross parcels and the mail came from England. Oh, what a day, when for the first time lads heard from mothers and husbands from wives and children! Many were the scenes of weeping that day. We went to bed at midnight, and in our beds, sang 'Home, Sweet Home', and such like till morning. The parcels came regularly, and after that mail our worst sufferings ceased. We were moved to Cottbus, an NCO's camp, and there, with the theatre, the church and the football, we lived comfortably. Every hut was soon changed into a clean, comfortable apartment after the advent of the parcels. The Russians, who had no parcels, and suffered perhaps more than any, were very skilful workmen, and made us tables, chairs, cupboards, beds, and everything for the comfort of the hut, receiving food in return for their labour.

We had not had our parcels very long when the old hands came to warn us that the Germans would shortly be on our track to buy surplus stocks. Sure enough, they came: civilians were frequently at the wire and soldiers in the huts to try their luck. They never received anything from us at first, but when they offered six marks for a ¼ lb of tea and 12 marks for the same of cocoa, it became very tempting. The lads thought they could not possibly sell tea sent from England for our use to such a thing as a German, even at that price. At last, however, the difficulty was solved, for a budding young business man suggested the following scheme. The used tea leaves of the whole hut were collected in the evening, scrupulously dried in a sort of frying pan arrangement, and then carefully put back in the packets. It looked and smelt just like tea. Hundreds of packets were sold to civilians at 5 marks a packet. One man is said to have made 250 marks private profit out of tea alone, and another 150 marks.

The scheme was progressing very satisfactorily, but the above-mentioned business patriot became scrupulous. How could the Germans buy the second-hand tea if it were not good, he argued; and so he suggested a second brewing of the tea before we dried it for sale. The proposition was carried unanimously, but never proved a success, as the second brew, although good enough for a Hun, did not come up to an Englishman's fancy.

As another instance of the straits to which the Germans were reduced during the last year of the war, I may mention that a farmer once gave me over 50-lbs of potatoes for a piece of soap weighing less than ½ lb in weight.

At last the end of our troubles approached. The camp became very unsettled, and one could feel that something unusual was in the air. We were ignorant of what was going on, but the Germans assured us that the war would soon be over. One day at noon an aeroplane had flown over dropping revolutionary pamphlets, but all remained quiet until 9 pm, when a shot rang out, followed by shouting and the sound of struggling. Next morning, we heard that the Red Guards had caused the commotion and

Grave of Canon Hugh Welch, Overleigh Cemetery, Chester

had taken charge of the camp. They informed us that we could do whatever we liked as long as we confined our activities to the interior of the camp. Accordingly, men were told off to go to the German stores to obtain a few sheets, and before eleven the next morning, the sheets were transformed into four magnificent flags, British, French, Italian and Belgian. The band and orchestra (British and French, of course: the instruments were bought by us) were called out, and we all followed, headed by the four flags, each flag carried by a soldier of the nation to which it belonged. 'The Marseillaise' and 'God Save the King' were sung with great spirit, followed by the hymns of Belgium and Italy, and thus we celebrated as well as we could the victory of the cause for which we had fought and suffered.

Perhaps we should give the last word to Canon Welch's predecessor as PP. Saying the 11.00 am Mass on Sunday 3 September 1939, Canon Hayes was handed a piece of paper by one of his curates. At the end of Mass, he had to make the solemn announcement to the congregation that the ultimatum to Germany now having run out, England was once again at war; and as people left church, they saw sandbags being off-loaded on the corner of Grosvenor Park Road.

Fr. Paul Shaw **July 2017**

A War-Torn Chester Parish

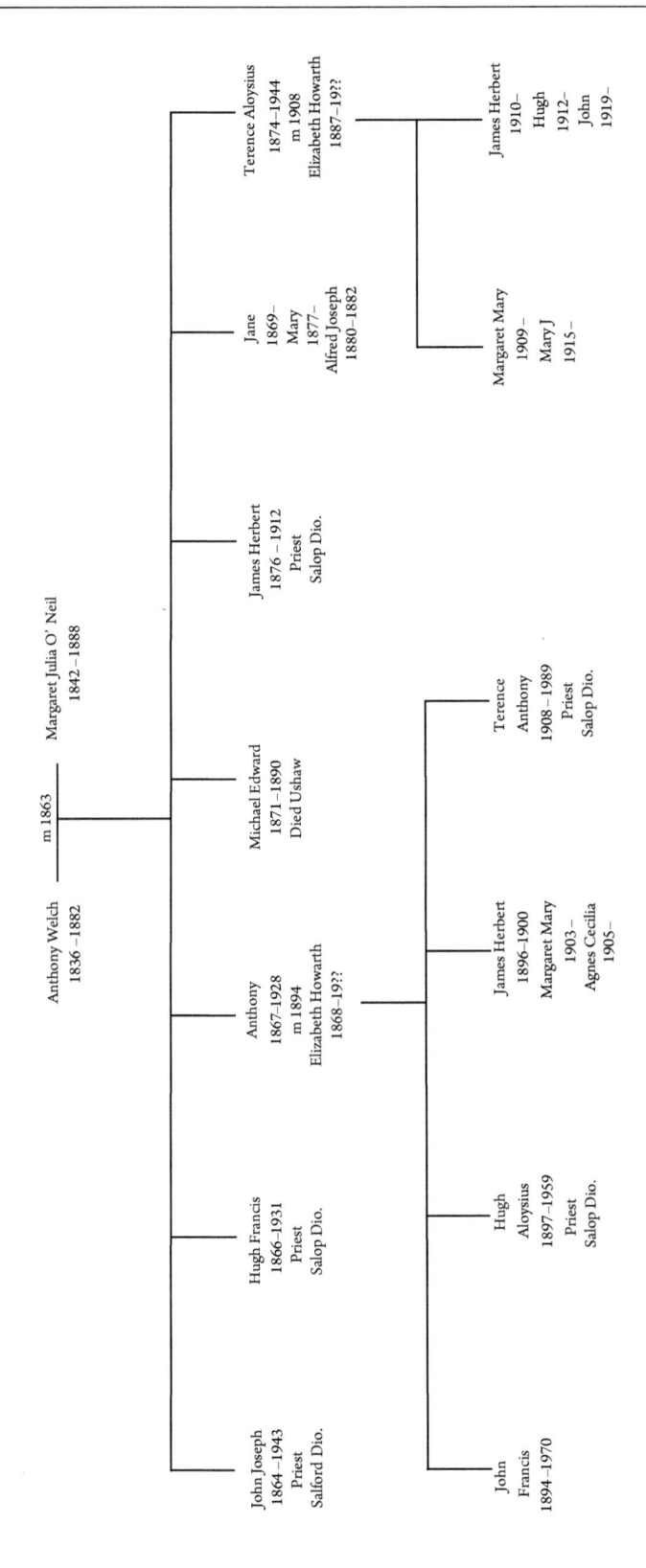

WELCH FAMILY TREE

Anthony Welch (1836–1882) m 1863 Margaret Julia O' Neil (1842–1888)

Children:

- **John Joseph** 1864–1943, Priest Salford Dio.
- **Hugh Francis** 1866–1931, Priest Salop Dio.
- **Anthony** 1867–1928, m 1894 Elizabeth Howarth 1868–19??
- **Michael Edward** 1871–1890, Died Ushaw
- **James Herbert** 1876–1912, Priest Salop Dio.
- **Jane** 1869–, Mary 1877–, Alfred Joseph 1880–1882
- **Terence Aloysius** 1874–1944, m 1908 Elizabeth Howarth 1887–19?:

Children of Anthony and Elizabeth:
- **Hugh Aloysius** 1897–1959, Priest Salop Dio.
- **James Herbert** 1896–1900
- **Margaret Mary** 1903–
- **Agnes Cecilia** 1905–
- **Terence Anthony** 1908–1989, Priest Salop Dio.

Children of Terence Aloysius and Elizabeth:
- **Margaret Mary** 1909–, Mary J 1915–
- **James Herbert** 1910–, Hugh 1912–, John 1919–

Child: **John Francis** 1894–1970

A Family of Priests – The Welch Family

After reading about the Great War experiences of Canon Hugh Welch of St. Werburgh's, as described in Fr. Paul's essay, we became curious about his family and origins. Researching them, we came to realise that it was no chance or random personal commitment which had led Hugh Welch to become a priest – it was inherited in his DNA! The Welch family seemed to exist for the primary purpose of providing priests for the Catholic Church in general and the Diocese of Shrewsbury in particular. The few family members who escaped this calling were mostly female. Possibly due to mutation, a couple of Welch men in each generation remained resolutely secular, in order to provide the next generation of priests and to keep a watching brief on their brothers in religion.

St. George's Catholic Church, Whitchurch, 19 Aug 2017

The Welch family were residents of Whitchurch, Shropshire. The first Anthony Welch had settled there, in Green End, possibly in the 1830's and had founded both a store and a family. There were very few Catholics in Whitchurch in those times and in 1853 the Welch family were granted permission to have mass said in their house, (which they shared with a Mr. O'Neil), whenever a Catholic priest was available in the area[2]. Over the years the numbers attending this mass centre grew and led in stages to the founding of St. George's Catholic Church, Whitchurch, in 1878. In 1863 though[1], when one of the Welch sons, another Anthony, wished to marry Margaret O'Neil, they had to travel to St. Mary's Catholic Church, Crewe for the ceremony[3]. The couple then settled in Castle Hill, Whitchurch and began to bring up a family of nine children, seven of them boys. The boys were mainly sent Whitchurch Grammar School, followed by either Ushaw or Cotton Colleges, for their education and four of them started training for the priesthood at Ushaw.

The eldest brother, John Joseph, was ordained for the Salford Diocese, because he particularly wished to serve the poor[4]. Apparently there were more poor people in Salford, than in rural Shropshire or Cheshire! The second brother, Hugh Francis was ordained at St. Werburgh's, Chester in 1892, after which he served in a variety of town and country parishes. He was particularly interested in the welfare of children, often personally providing them with suitable footwear[5].

St. Cuthbert's College, Ushaw. 2014

Sacred Heart Catholic Church, Whaley Bridge, 19 Aug 2017

The third brother, James Herbert Welch, served 5 years as a curate at Seacombe, after which, 1906–7 he had to take sick leave for one year. He lived during this year, with his brother Terence Aloysius Welch at Terence's house of Riverslie, in Whaley Bridge. Terence had qualified as a physician and surgeon in 1902 and had practiced in Whaley Bridge since 1905. He was later appointed Medical Officer of Health for Yeardsley-cum-Whaley[6]. In 1907 James Herbert returned to clerical duties and the Bishop appointed him as rector at Whaley Bridge[7]. This enabled him to continue living with his brother Terence who would be able to keep an eagle eye on his health. Thus, James Herbert Welch became the first resident priest at Whaley Bridge. Since 1900 there had been a Catholic Church of the Sacred Heart, designed by Edmund Kirby, in Whaley Bridge but there was no presbytery.

Terence Welch married Elizabeth Howarth in 1908. Although large, their house must have been very busy and noisy from then onwards. Patients would always be calling and three children were born in quick succession, one sadly dying in infancy. The third child was named James Herbert, after his uncle[8]. Fr. James Herbert Welch served for 5 years at Whaley Bridge. Then, despite the ministrations of his brother, James' health deteriorated once more and he died in 1912 at the comparatively young age of 36. He was buried at Whitchurch. After his death no successor priest was appointed and the church was served until 1920 by Dominicans from Errwood Hall. The presbytery, again designed by Edmund Kirby and Sons, was not finally built until 1924.

Riverslie, Whaley Bridge, house and name stone

After Fr. James Herbert Welch had died in 1912, his brother Terence and his family, moved to Salford. Terence had a practice in Regent Road[9] and was now in a prime position to keep an eye on the health and well being of his elder brother, Fr. John Joseph Welch. Fr. John Welch carried out his duties as a priest with dedication and was certainly in a prime position to serve the many poor people of this sprawling, fog-bound, slum-covered city, (vividly described in The Spinners' song "Dirty Old Town"). It was here that during WW2 Dr. Terence Welch, though of retiring age, was medical practitioner in charge of a First Aid Post[10]. His wife Elizabeth acted as an Auxiliary Nurse. Fr. John Welch died in Salford in 1943 and Dr. Terence Welch died in Salford a year later, aged 70. He died knowing that this country was still in the middle of yet another dreadful war and that his son John had won the DFC in 1942. Dr.

Terence Welch had worked right up until his last illness, supported two of his priest brothers and was described in the Manchester Evening News of 15 August 1944 as the "Dockers' Friend." Evidently, he also had been called to serve the poor of Salford.

The fourth brother to start training at Ushaw senior seminary, was Michael Welch. He entered his second year as a candidate for the priesthood, in the autumn of 1890. Michael was an athletic lad and one of the natural leaders of the seminary year group. The students always looked forward to winter, when the low temperatures on Ushaw Moor led to the freezing of ponds and the start of the skating season. On the morning of 18 December 1890 Michael set out with two fellow students, George Lamstead and Harold Burton, to test the ice on Broadgate pond near Ushaw Moor colliery. The ice, when tested, appeared to be suitable for at least one person to skate on and still erring on the safe side, the students decided to skate one at a time, in case it was not thick enough to support all their weights at once. Michael skated first. The ice cracked and Welch fell through a hole into the water. Fortunately he was able to hold himself aloft, by pressing his elbows along the ice at each side of him. He then managed to raise his knees to the surface but when he put any weight upon them, the ice again cracked and Welch was once more immersed. Welch had been calm and purposeful until this point but now he began to cry for help. Lamstead came across the ice to try to rescue him, but seeing the ice cracking around Lamstead, Welch forbade him to come any closer and told him to return. This was only just in time for Burton to be able to seize Lamstead's arms and drag him to the bank, before the section of ice around him, totally disintegrated. When the two students looked back, all they could see was Welch's cap and some surface bubbles. Later in the day, Welch's body was retrieved from the pond and two days afterwards a coroner's inquest was held at the College[11]. The verdict of the jury was "accidental drowning." An obituary, which stressed the fine character of the dead scholar, was placed in the College Magazine. Reading it, over a hundred years later, still evokes vividly the dire tragedy of a young life, so quickly snuffed out.

There were three Welch boys in this generation who had evaded training for the priesthood. Alfred Welch had died in childhood. Terence, mentioned earlier, had trained at the Universities of Manchester, Glasgow and Edinburgh, to become a doctor and surgeon, whilst, after the

Grave of Michael Welch, St. Cuthbert's College Ushaw

rather premature death of his father in 1882, Anthony had acted as both head of the family and head of the Marine Store Dealership in Whitchurch[12]. Living and working at 60 High Street, Whitchurch, he supported his unmarried brothers and sisters. Confusingly, Anthony and Terence later married two different Lancashire ladies, both called Elizabeth Howarth. The two ladies were almost certainly related, possibly cousins – it was common at that time to name children after older family members and so names were continually recycled within families. Anthony brought up his own family initially at 60 High Street, moving to 15 Dodington in 1896. He became a well respected citizen and businessman in the Whitchurch community, not to mention a fine amateur cricketer.

We come now to the next generation of Welch brothers and examine their responses to training for the priesthood. Anthony had a family of 4 sons and 2 daughters. One son, James Herbert, died in childhood. All three remaining sons, John, Hugh and Terence were partly educated at Ushaw College, going there at about the age of 13. John left Ushaw just as the Great War broke out. He enlisted with the Royal Fusiliers, 20th Public School Battalion, PS/5910. Once his training was completed, he found himself leaving for France, disembarking there on 14 November 1915. After taking part in much devastating action, he was transferred to the Shropshire Light Infantry. On 13 August 1918 he was Gazetted 2nd Lt. and transferred to the 1st Bn. Deoli Regiment (Indian Army), receiving his first commission on 30 October 1918[13]. After the end of the Great War, John saw service in India, where, in 1920 he married Norah Alice Lang at St. Patrick's Church, Karachi. John Welch enjoyed a successful career in the British/Indian Army, steadily gaining promotion.

Both younger Welch brothers trained for the priesthood, though Hugh's training was interrupted by his service in the Great War, as described in Fr. Paul Shaw's essay. Terence was too young for his training to be so interrupted and he was ordained for the Diocese of Shrewsbury in 1935. After a curacy of 5 years, Terence became Bishop's Secretary for 11 years and was then appointed administrator of the Cathedral, Shrewsbury 1951–83. He was famous for his organisational skills, as well as for his skills as a host and a raconteur. This generation of the Welch family were very proud, both of their Shropshire heritage and of the fact that their mothers came from English recusant Catholic stock[14].

In 1944, during the middle of WW2, Fr. Hugh Aloysius Welch arrived as parish priest of St. Werburgh's Chester. In 1946 he was appointed a Canon of the Diocese of Shrewsbury. Canon Welch quickly became immersed in the Chester scene. He was elected onto the boards of governors of the Hospital Management Committee and the City Education Committee, both of which he felt were of huge importance to the lives and well being of the people of Chester. However, it was in his daily contacts with parishioners and other Cestrians that Hugh Welch's good will to all men shone through. Though he suffered ill health, as a result of his experiences during the Great War, he never allowed this to prevent his serving his parishioners in a dedicated way. At his funeral in 1959 the church was filled with Diocesan and Civic dignitaries, parishioners and friends. There were so many people, that many had to stand outside whilst the Requiem Mass was said. They also lined the route to Overleigh Cemetery, where he was laid to rest. Present at his funeral were the remaining members of the Welch family: his brothers John the soldier and Terence the priest, his sister Margaret, sister-in-law, niece Clare and cousins[15]. Major John Welch died in Holywell in 1970 and Canon Terence Welch died in Shrewsbury in 1989. It is not often that we see today this scale of dedication to the Church within one family. What a huge debt is owed by the Dioceses of Shrewsbury and Salford, to the whole of the Welch family, both clerical and secular!

Ann Marie and John Curtis   **July 2017**

References

1. Census for 1841 accessed via Ancestry
2. Abbott, E.M. *To Preserve Their Memory* entry for James Herbert Welch
3. Marriage Registers of St. Mary's Catholic Church, Crewe Cheshire Archives and Local Studies (CALS)
4. Abbott, E.M. *To Preserve Their Memory* entry for James Herbert Welch
5. Abbott, E.M. *To Preserve Their Memory* entry for Hugh Francis Welch
6. *U.K. Medical Directory 1910*, entry for Dr. Terence Aloysius Welch, accessed via Ancestry
7. Abbott, E.M. *To Preserve Their Memory* entry for James Herbert Welch
8. Census for 1911, accessed via Ancestry
9. *U.K. Medical Directory for 1915* entry for Dr. Terence Aloysius Welch
10. TNA R39 4633 4633H
11. Durham County Advertiser, 26 December 1890, accessed via
12. Census for 1901, accessed via Ancestry
13. British Army WW1 Medal Roll Index Card for John Francis Welch, accessed via Ancestry
14. Abbott, E.M. *To Preserve Their Memory* entry for Terence Anthony Welch
15. Chester Chronicle Saturday 15 August 1959 CALS

Australian Influences in Chester

Matthew Clayson 1887–1916

Why should we remember Matthew Clayson, a man from Sydney who died in his "own" bed without hearing a shot fired in anger? He may have never attended mass at St. Werburgh's, as he only lived in Chester for just over a week. He was not included on the 1922 plaque nor the 1990 scroll.

The centennials of 1914–1918 are a fitting time to think back and reconsider some things that were taken for granted in days gone by. Who is a parishioner of St. Werburgh's (or Werbie as we are now called)? What was the ultimate sacrifice? Whom should we remember?

I believe that Matthew Clayson was truly a Werbie, who made the ultimate sacrifice and deserves to be remembered today. His is a sad story that spans the globe and includes both love and tragedy.

Matthew Clayson was born in 1887 to Matthew and Mary Ann Clayson. They had been married in 1884 in St. Bridget's Church, Bradford, Lancashire – not Yorkshire! His father was a "soap mixer" and his mother the daughter of a career soldier who had served in Canada, where Mary Ann Ward was born, the UK and India. After leaving the Army William Ward worked as a "tar distiller," a sideline of the coal industry.

Young Matthew Clayson grew up in Bradford, where the family lived next door to Mary Ann's parents. By 1901 the family had moved to Gorton Lane, Gorton, in South East Manchester, close to Matthew's paternal grandparents. As they lived only a few hundred yards from the Church and Friary of St. Francis, known locally as Gorton Monastery, they were probably parishioners and attended mass in the Pugin masterpiece of High Victorian Gothic architecture. Matthew attended the Technical School, but by age 14 he was already working as a mechanic. On leaving school he started an apprenticeship with Sir W.G. Armstrong Whitworth & Co Ltd, the famous armaments manufacturer.

By 1911 Matthew had moved with his mother and two sisters to another house in Gorton, and his father, Matthew Senior, was living close by. The 1911 Census

Gorton Monastery

describes the senior Clayson as a "soap maker (pensioned) – totally blind". He had a family boarding with him, so it is likely that he had some support from them. He died in 1911, soon after the census was taken.

In May 1912 Matthew set out on a great adventure by emigrating to Australia with William Linney, a friend of the family. Both men are described in the RMS Ophir's passenger list as "fitters." On arriving in Sydney, Matthew went to work on the NSW Government Railway in Cowra, a country town in rural New South Wales.

Cowra Railway Station

Just over a year later, Mary Ann Clayson, together with her daughters Edith and Annie, also migrated to Australia on RMS Suevic. They were joined on the ship by Jennie McCormick. The atmosphere on the voyage to Sydney must have been full of hope and anticipation for their new lives in Australia.

The Suevic docked in Sydney on Monday 15 December 1913. After a brief pause to catch up and finalise arrangements, on Wednesday 17 December 1913 the Claysons, William Linney and Jennie McCormick returned to the dock area of Sydney heading to St. Augustine's Church, Balmain North for a double wedding. The marriage register contains consecutive entries for the marriages of Matthew and Jennie followed by William and Annie. Jennie was also the daughter of a soldier, and had been born in Malta.

In 1916 Matthew left the NSW Railways and started a new job at the Naval Dockyard, Cockatoo Island, Sydney as a tool and gauge maker. In response to a shortage of workers with such skills in UK factories, the Australian and Imperial Governments agreed a programme to recruit chemists and other skilled men to bolster munitions production in the UK. The Australian Munitions Workers scheme started to seek volunteers in the middle of August 1916. The men had to be volunteers as Australia did not institute conscription during World War 1.

NSW Munitions Workers on SS Osterley October 1916. M Clayson Standing 2nd from Left. A Chambers Seated 2nd from Left. Photo courtesy of Roslyn Spiteri

Matthew Clayson stepped forward and volunteered for the scheme on 30 August 1916. This must have been a hard decision for Matthew as he was, by this time, the father of two girls. He was accepted as volunteer number 22 and in just over three weeks he sailed from Sydney on SS Osterley with 77 other volunteers. The voyage via Cape Town to Tilbury lasted six weeks but was not uneventful. There were numerous complaints about the food, service and standards in 3rd Class accommodation. The threat posed by German submarines also added to the unease on the ship.

The Osterley arrived at Tilbury on 10 November 1916. After a few days in London, Matthew and fellow volunteer Alfred Chambers travelled up to Chester on the evening of 20 November. They arrived in Chester the next morning. Later that day they reported at H.M. Explosives Factory, Queensferry. They signed on and were examined by the Factory doctor.

On returning to Chester, Clayson and Chambers found lodgings together with Mrs. Atkinson at 23 Cherry Road at £1.00 per week. It was reported that the lodgings were clean, very comfortable, and in a good neighbourhood.

Unfortunately during the stopover in Cape Town Matthew contracted a cold. After just three days work at Queensferry, the cold developed into lobar pneumonia. His condition deteriorated rapidly, and by Sunday evening he was too ill to be transferred to hospital. The help of Father Hayes was sought. He immediately sent for nursing sisters who remained with him day and night until he died at 1.00 a.m. on Friday 1 December 1916. The sisters were assisted by Jennie's sister who came over from Manchester.

On Monday 4 December 1916 Matthew Clayson was buried in Chester Overleigh Cemetery in a shared grave with Madam Bertha Krebbs and Emily Jane Whitehouse. They had died in 1906 and 1914 respectively. Matthew's grave is now marked with a Commonwealth War Graves Commission headstone. For whatever reason, a personal inscription was not added by his family. The original grave marker can still be seen in the cemetery.

The funeral arrangements were undertaken by Father Hayes, who was commended for being "in constant attention and took more than an ordinary interest in Clayson." Father Hayes also wrote to Jennie twice and to her local parish priest in Sydney.

Although Matthew Clayson did not die on the battlefield or of wounds, he gave his life as a volunteer in the service of Australia and the Empire. He certainly connected with St. Werburgh's in his short time in Chester. Therefore, we must remember and commemorate him and the young family that he left behind in Australia. After the

Original Grave Marker   Commonwealth War Graves Commission Headstone

Armistice, Jennie and the two girls were offered the opportunity to return to her family in Manchester. However it is not clear if they did return, or if they remained in Australia with his family.

Harper Wright 2016

Sources

Griffiths, T. (2010). *An industrial invasion.* 1st ed. Terrey Hills, N. S. W.: Toptech Engineering
The National Archives of Australia (NAA): MT1139/1, CLAYSON MATTHEW
The National Archives of the UK (TNA): RG, Census for England and Wales 1881
The National Archives of the UK (TNA): RG, Census for England and Wales 1891
The National Archives of the UK (TNA): RG, Census for England and Wales 1901
The National Archives of the UK (TNA): RG, Census for England and Wales 1911
General Register Office: Marriage Certificate, M Clayson & M A Ward 1884
The National Archives of the UK (TNA): BT, Passenger List: RMS Ophir May 1912
The National Archives of the UK (TNA): BT, Passenger List: RMS Suevic October 1913
NSW Registry of Births, Deaths & Marriages, Marriage Certificate M Clayson & J McCormick 1913
NSW Registry of Births, Deaths & Marriages, Death Certificate M A Clayson 1924

A Tale of Two Architects

John Douglas (1830–1911) and Edmund Kirby (1838–1920)

The area surrounding Grosvenor Park Road has traditionally been referred to as the Victorian Quarter of Chester. There are indeed several fine Victorian buildings in this sector, which give it a unique ambiance and which add to the general attractiveness of the city. This is largely due to the work of the two architects involved, John Douglas and Edmund Kirby and their co-operation with each other.

Superficially the two architects involved could not be more dissimilar. John Douglas was born in 1830, the son of a prosperous joiner and builder, in Sandiway, Cheshire. He attended the local Anglican village church and school. In 1841 he was a boarder at a school in the Main Street of Frodsham, probably the school which became Manor House School in 1852[1]. After leaving school, Douglas was articled, to architect E. G. Paley in Lancaster and for a few years acted as his chief assistant. Paley was an enthusiastic exponent of the High Victorian neo-Gothic style of architecture, introduced into this country by A.W. N. Pugin (1812–1852). In 1860 Douglas left Paley and came to Chester, in order to start his own business, setting up his workplace and home at 6 Abbey Square[2].

John Douglas

Edmund Kirby was born in Liverpool in 1838[3]. His father, also called Edmund, was the proprietor of a brass foundry in Cheapside, Liverpool and was listed on the electoral register for Liverpool in 1840. Family finances were sufficient to allow Edmund and his two younger brothers to receive a good education. Edmund was sent to a Catholic boarding school, Sedgley Park, near Wolverhampton[4]. After leaving school, Kirby was articled to architect E.W. Pugin (1834–1875), son of the famous A.W.N. Pugin and by 1860 was lodging in Birmingham, where he was working for John Hardman Powell, arguably the foremost maker of stained glass and metal artefacts in this country.

Edmund Kirby Portrait Reproduced by kind permission of Matthews-Goodman (incorporating Edmund Kirby & Sons)

The Pugin and Hardman Powell families had inter-married and their households subsequently intermingled and it was no surprise to any of them, when in 1861, Edmund made a proposal of marriage to Agnes, the beautiful and accomplished sister of E.W. Pugin. Despite the fact that she had several other eligible suitors, Agnes accepted. Wedding preparations were made but by the end of the year, Agnes had changed her mind[5]. Perhaps this was why Edmund began studies at the Royal Academy Schools 1862–1865, having been sponsored to do so by E.W. Pugin. Whilst a student in London, Edmund designed scenery for a Charles Keane production of Shakespeare's Henry IV. Kirby then came to Chester and joined Douglas at his practice in Abbey Square. It was whilst working here, that they developed the exaggerated chimney style which was to become a feature of both architects' domestic designs in the future. By 1866 Kirby had left Douglas' practice and moved to his own business premises in Liverpool, though he made his home in Birkenhead[6].

Douglas became the architect of choice for both the Duke of Westminster and Chester City Council. He was eclectic, both in the range of buildings and the style of buildings, which he designed. Churches and Ecclesiastical buildings formed a significant part of his work but these were far outweighed by the number of secular buildings which he designed. His work was often on a grand scale, such as the redesigning the whole of St. Werburgh Street, Chester in neo-Tudor style. He also designed the whole village of Eccleston. On stately homes throughout the county of Chester, we again see John Douglas' work, often in red Ruabon brick, with its signature grey brick interwoven pattern (diapering) and barley sugar twist chimneys. As far as I know, John Douglas is also the only architect of his calibre, who designed a public toilet facility – that on Frodsham Street in Chester.

One possible reason for Kirby leaving Chester is that Chester was too small a town to contain both himself and Douglas. In order to make his mark Kirby needed to work in a larger town and possibly to specialise. Kirby's range of work became much narrower than that of Douglas. Edmund Kirby had one main sponsor, the Catholic Diocese of Shrewsbury. He designed mainly churches and schools for this diocese, though he also designed individual churches for other Catholic and Church of England Dioceses. Liverpool warehouses and offices were also designed by him and the memorial to Queen Victoria in Hamilton Square, Birkenhead is regarded as one of Kirby's more unusual commissions.

Shotwick Park built by John Douglas 1872

Kirby too used red Ruabon brick but did not interweave it with a grey brick pattern. Instead he used the brick to great advantage when designing individual bespoke houses for rich Liverpool merchants, in the area around Birkenhead Park and Noctorum ridge. His first such design in 1876, was of "Redcourt" for the Liverpool banker, George Rae. Today it is home to "Redcourt St. Anselm" prep. school. On these merchant palaces Kirby placed the exaggerated chimney stacks which he had developed with Douglas in Chester. Kirby himself lived in the Birkenhead Park area and these merchants became his second most significant group of clients[7].

Occasionally Douglas and Kirby co-operated, as in 1867 when Douglas built the Lodge at Grosvenor Park and Kirby built the extension to the nearby Dee House Convent School[8]. The two buildings are different but co-exist in an harmonious way. A later co-operation was in the building of Port Sunlight Village during the 1890's. Lord Leverhulme employed several architects, each to design one or more terraces or streets of cottages. This was so that the cottages would not all be identical, though they had to blend with and complement each other. Douglas built several terraces and they are easy to identify due to their red Ruabon brick facades with "Dutch" gables and Douglas diapering. Kirby also built three rows of cottages, though arguably his best terrace, designed in 1893 and inspired by Shakespeare's birthplace in Stratford-upon-Avon, was pulled down in 1938, as part of a plan to make way for a new road through the village – the road was never built![9]

Throughout what became increasingly unsettled times in the lives of both their families, work still went on. Edmund Kirby built St. Werburgh's, Chester 1873–75, his first stone church, in what later came to be known as the "Kirby" style[10]. His design was in the neo-Gothic tradition but plainer and more elegant than the very individual style of Douglas' churches. The vaults of Kirby's stone churches are very high and the walls are pierced by two tiers of lancet windows. Only very light buttressing is needed for

Mere Hall built by Edmund Kirby for Sir John Gray 1882

John Douglas Terrace, 3-9 Bridge Street, Port Sunlight, 2015

Shakespeare's Cottages, Port Sunlight ca 1920, designed by Edmund Kirby
Reproduced by kind permission of Port Sunlight Village Trust

support and the interior is extremely light and airy. The stone for St. Werburgh's exterior was quarried in Yorkshire and the roof is of toning Welsh slate. The internal pillars are of Cheshire red sandstone. Here, the major influence on Kirby's work, appears to have been that of his former master, E.W. Pugin, who died the same year in which St. Werburgh's first stage was completed. (Due to lack of funds, St. Werburgh's Church was only partly built in 1875. It was later extended in two stages, in 1903 and 1913 and so was not finally completed until June 1914[11].)

In turn, John Douglas was a very committed Anglican and after he had moved his home to 33 Dee Banks in 1869, he redesigned and rebuilt his local parish church of St. Paul's in Boughton, a church which had at that time fallen into disrepair. The church was rebuilt in 1875–76 and is a unique example of the high Gothic revival style. The entrance of the church from Boughton is fairly unremarkable but the interior is a delight to the eye. It is furnished in a way which seems to be a fusion of A.W.N. Pugin (the elder) with Arts and Crafts. Sadly this church is closed at the present time, again due to problems of maintenance and staffing. Hopefully it will soon be restored and re-opened, in part as a fitting tribute to one of Chester's greatest architects.

The turn of the century marked the time of Douglas and Kirby's last great collaboration. Douglas had already built 6–11 Grosvenor Park Road in 1880 and his grand home of "Walmer Hill", Dee Banks, in 1896. The City Baths followed in 1901. In 1903 the City Council decided to make a new cutting from Foregate to allow better access to the City Baths. It potentially involved St. Werburgh's sacrificing some land around the west side of the church. Kirby was at the time designing the two sacristies at the western end of St. Werburgh's Church and overseeing their building. Douglas negotiated with Kirby and Chester City Council about this matter[12]. The church was left with barely sufficient land upon which to build its sacristies and if you walk around the western side of the church, you will see that in fact the ambulacrum connecting the two sacristies, protrudes slightly onto the pavement of Baths Street. However, agreement was finally reached and the famously ugly wall around the church boundary was erected by Chester City Council as a form of recompense.[13]

At the same time Douglas constructed the Prudential Assurance Building on the corner of Baths Street and Foregate, together with 1–11 and 13 Baths Street, on land which he himself had bought. This was probably a lucrative project for Douglas but at the same time it produced architecture which beautifully complemented the west end of St. Werburgh's Church. It has been described as a neo-mediaeval extravaganza and has been painted expertly by the artist Alister J. Winter Roberts.

From 1893–1904 John Douglas, was also involved in the rebuilding of Christ Church in Newtown, Chester. This was a tricky undertaking as the church was to be used

Baths Street, Chester

throughout the rebuild. In his design, Douglas did not use his more normal cruciform plan, nor did he use the same style as at St. Paul's, Boughton. Instead, he drew up a plan which superficially resembled that of St. Werburgh's. There is a difference in the heights of the vaults, that at St. Werburgh's being much larger and Christ Church also has a flat ended apse, rather than a rounded one. However, the effect on the interior is very similar to that of St. Werburgh's. During the years, 1900–1904 Douglas was almost permanently in Baths Street and even occupied a cottage adjacent to St. Werburgh's. Perhaps he was influenced more than he realised, by Kirby's design there. Incidentally, there was originally a plan for a tower on the north-west corner of both churches. In both cases this tower was not built, but a porch was added instead.

At about this time, John Douglas also wrote to Edmund Kirby, asking Kirby to verify his full name. This was because he wished to leave the sum of £20 to Kirby in his will, for the purpose of placing a statue of the patron saint, within St. Werburgh's Church, once it was finished! He thought that Kirby might prefer this to any other form of bequest.[14] I am not sure whether Edmund Kirby was pleased or not by this proposed legacy but I think that he would definitely have been pleased by the Baths Street façade, which allows St. Werburgh's to dominate the cityscape of the area, whilst Douglas' adjacent buildings link it to the City of Chester proper. It could only have been achieved by two architects who were in complete sympathy with each others' aspirations.

The domestic lives of the two architects were similar in some ways but developed very differently. They each had noteworthy wives and reared five children. Douglas had married Elizabeth Edmunds, a yeoman farmer's daughter from Bangor-on-Dee, in 1860[15]. Later, one girl and four boys were borne to them. However, Mary Elizabeth died 17 July 1968 at Chester, age 3. Jerome died only 3 days old, on 12 May 1869 at Chester. John Percy also died in Chester, 7 December 1873, age 12. Then Elizabeth, John Douglas' wife, died in 1878.

Walmer Hill, Dee Banks, Chester

After this, Douglas, never a gregarious person, became a complete workaholic. He never became a member of R.I.B.A. or of any other architectural organisation, even though he became the acknowledged local architectural master. Douglas rarely refused a commission, had no hobbies and took no interest in civic affairs. Architecture became his whole world. As he became wealthier John Douglas started to build his home, "Walmer Hill", in Dee Hills Park, overlooking the River Dee. "Walmer Hill" was designed on a palatial scale and even though it was not completely finished, Douglas moved into it, in 1896.

John Douglas still had two remaining sons, Colin and Sholto, who would be likely to continue the family business. The elder son, Colin did indeed become articled to his father but sadly died in 1887 at the age of twenty three. Allegedly, the only surviving son, Sholto, had severe problems. Life weighed heavily upon him and he resorted to alcohol to support himself. He was never able to follow a profession and Sholto's welfare must have been a constant worry to Douglas, particularly as, since the death of his wife Elizabeth, he had no-one with whom to share his concerns. Later, Douglas set up in partnership with two other architects in succession but

Douglas Family Grave
Overleigh Cemetary

the last partnership was dissolved around 1900. Douglas died in 1911 and was buried in the family grave in Overleigh Cemetery, Chester. Interestingly, Douglas' will, drawn up just before he died, made no mention of a bequest to anyone other than his only surviving son Sholto, for whom he had set up a trust.[16]

Perhaps a little wary after his first broken engagement in 1861, it was not until 1873 that Edmund Kirby married Rose Ann Dodsworth, of York[17]. However, the couple appears to have subsequently enjoyed a very close and happy marriage. Rose came from a staunch Yorkshire recusant family and the couple had three sons, Edmund Francis Joseph (Frank), Edward Dodsworth and Edmund Bertram (Bertie). Kirby had a more relaxed and rounded personality than John Douglas. Kirby had become an A.R.I.B.A. by 1881 and was president of the Liverpool Architects Association in 1887–89. He later became a fellow of R.I.B.A. and was elected to its council in 1888. He was a member of the committees of Catholic and other charities, in the Liverpool area. He never lost his love of the theatre and was often seen in the audience at the Opera House in Liverpool.[18] Like all the male members of his family, Kirby had a great interest in cricket and in the Kirby household this sport was raised almost to the status of a minor religion. In spite of designing some exceedingly opulent residences, Edmund Kirby's own home in Birkenhead, though large and comfortable by most people's standards, was certainly not palatial.

EDMUND KIRBY FAMILY TREE

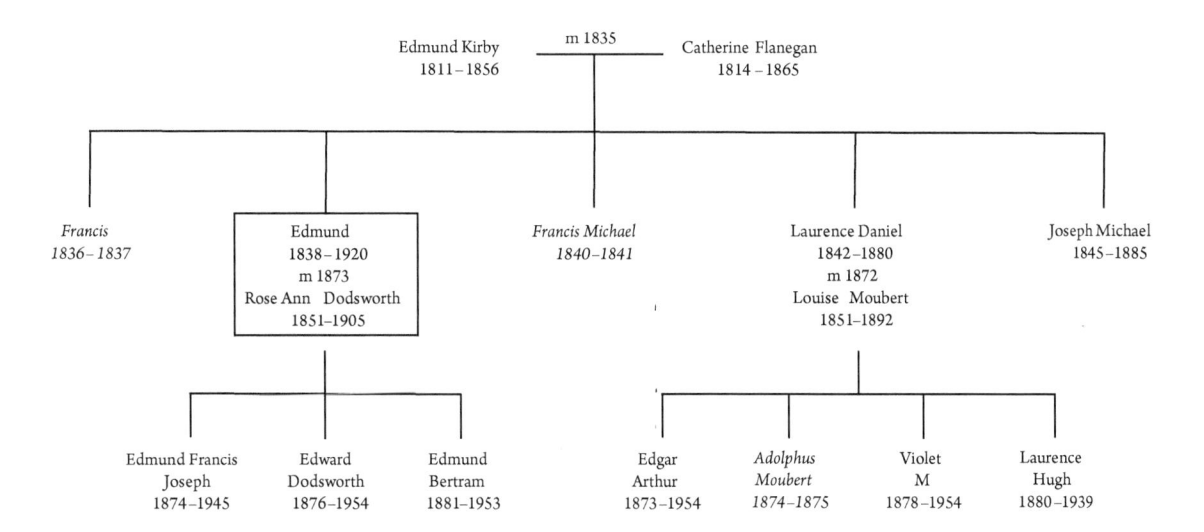

Edmund Kirby 1811–1856 — m 1835 — Catherine Flanegan 1814–1865

- *Francis* 1836–1837
- Edmund 1838–1920, m 1873, Rose Ann Dodsworth 1851–1905
- *Francis Michael* 1840–1841
- Laurence Daniel 1842–1880, m 1872, Louise Moubert 1851–1892
- Joseph Michael 1845–1885

Children of Edmund and Rose Ann:
- Edmund Francis Joseph 1874–1945
- Edward Dodsworth 1876–1954
- Edmund Bertram 1881–1953

Children of Laurence and Louise:
- Edgar Arthur 1873–1954
- *Adolphus Moubert* 1874–1875
- Violet M 1878–1954
- Laurence Hugh 1880–1939

Edmund Kirby's brother, Laurence Daniel Kirby, died in 1880, leaving a widow and three children. Four years later, Daniel's widow remarried and lived abroad with her daughter and new husband. Edmund Kirby was appointed guardian of his two nephews, Edgar and Hugh Laurence, Kirby. These nephews were then brought up by Edmund and Rose, with their own three sons and received a very good education, first at prep. schools and then at Stonyhurst College[19]. However the younger nephew, Laurence found it difficult to settle and he did not make the same type of academic progress as his elder brother and cousins had. In 1892 his mother also died. In that year Laurence was removed from Hodder (Stonyhurst prep. School) and sent for a year to the Ryleys school in Alderley Edge. Afterwards he spent a year at S.S. Conway School, moored on the Mersey[20]. This school educated prospective merchant marine officers. Eventually Laurence returned to Stonyhurst, where his progress, except at sport, was indifferent. After leaving Stonyhurst in 1896, he joined a Liverpool shipping company and trained to be a merchant marine officer, eventually gaining his masters certificate[21]. His elder brother Edgar had a distinguished academic career, obtaining a law degree at Cambridge and later trained for the priesthood. He was ordained in Rome in 1908.[22]

Rose Kirby died in 1905 and was buried in Flaybrick Cemetery, Birkenhead. In that same year Frank and Bertie Kirby became partners in their father's architectural practice, Frank being an expert in land surveying and Bertie having trained as an architect. Frank was also a good amateur cricketer and played for the County of Cheshire during his younger days. Latterly he played for and was President of, Parkgate Cricket Club, moving house so that he could live overlooking the pitch![23] Edward Dodsworth Kirby, Edmund's middle son, was ordained a priest in 1901 in Birkenhead and served as a curate at St. Werburgh's, Chester 1906–09[24].

In 1914 the Great War disturbed their lives in an unprecedented manner. Bertie joined the army, on 4 August 1914, leaving Edmund and his eldest son Frank to keep the firm together. However, Edmund had to retire in 1915. Frank was now in

Grave of Rose and Edmund Kirby, Flaybrick Cemetery, Birkenhead

St. Werburgh's Shrine

complete charge of the firm but was co-opted for war related business, concerning land acquisitions and uses. Bertie served with distinction as a Major in the 12th Lancashire Battery of the Royal Field Artillery. He was attached to the 2nd Canadian Division and was severely wounded in January 1916. After recuperation he then became involved in Intelligence work in London[25]. He was awarded an O.B.E. at the end of the war. His cousin Laurence Kirby was commissioned into the Royal Naval Reserve and also served with distinction.

After the war Laurence visited Portugal and on 19 February 1919 was made a Chevalier of the Portuguese Order of Avis. He was demobilized on 26 September 1919[26].

Though Rose Ann Kirby had died in 1905, Edmund had lived to witness his sons' and his nephews' service and success. Edmund Kirby died in 1920 and was buried in the same grave as his late wife, in Flaybrick Cemetery, Birkenhead. Frank and Bertie Kirby continued the work of the firm and remained involved with St. Werburgh's, Chester until their deaths in 1945 and 1953 respectively.

Bertie designed the War Memorial Chapel at St. Werburgh's in 1921[27] and then in 1923 he was asked to design St. Werburgh's Shrine inside the church. At this time he wrote to Canon Chambers (Rector of St. Werburgh's), telling the Canon not to concern himself with the cost of St. Werburgh's statue itself, as he had already obtained the wherewithal for it.[28] Perhaps the John Douglas bequest had been obtained after all and was now being put to the use for which Douglas had intended it!

John Douglas left a great legacy of work in Chester and is arguably mainly responsible for Chester's success as a tourist town. Edmund Kirby has little work still standing in Chester. However, in Grosvenor Park Road, where Douglas' work on the terrace and on Grosvenor Park Lodge, faces the front façade of St. Werburgh's, we are confronted by the achievements of both architects. This view is quite spectacular, though taken for granted by most Cestrians. However, in my opinion, it is even better to approach St. Werburgh's via the back way, from Foregate, down Baths Street. Here, the view as you approach St. Werburgh's is unrivalled. Douglas has given free reign to his neo-Gothic terrace design, which complements and paves the way for Kirby's more restrained but nevertheless impressive neo-Gothic architecture at St. Werburgh's. Perhaps the spirits of A.W.N. Pugin and E.W. Pugin are also rejoicing at what has been accomplished here.

Ann Marie Curtis   **July 2015**

References

1. Census of 1841 accessed via Ancestry
2. Census of 1861 accessed via Ancestry
3. Census of 1841 accessed via Ancestry
4. Census of 1851 accessed via Ancestry
5. Fisher, M., *Guarding the Pugin Flame* pp111, 119, 152–154
6. Report at beginning of the catalogue of deposits of Edmund Kirby and Sons, in the archives of Liverpool Library, 720/KIR
7. Redcourt, front & rear perspective views, including plan, published in *The Building News, August 28th 1885*.
8. Dee House Convent School plans, deposits of Edmund Kirby and Sons in Liverpool Library 720/KIR 891
9. deposits of Edmund Kirby and Sons in the archives of Liverpool Library, 720/KIR 1103
10. deposits of Edmund Kirby and Sons in the archives of Liverpool Library, 720 KIR 872

11. *St. Werburgh's Parish Magazine July 1914*, retained at St. Werburgh's Chester
12. deposits of Edmund Kirby and Sons in the archives of Liverpool Library, 720KIR 872
13. deposits of Edmund Kirby and Sons in the archives of Liverpool Library, 720/KIR 872
14. deposits of Edmund Kirby and Sons in the archives of Liverpool Library, 720/KIR 872
15. Marriage of John Douglas and Elizabeth Edmunds at St. Mary's Parish Church Bangor-on- Dee 25 Jan. 1860 accessed via Ancestry
16. Will of John Douglas, MF91/60, WR52 P263 Cheshire Archives and Local Studies, Chester
17. Marriage records of St. Wilfred's Catholic Church, York, 24 April 1873, retained at the church
18. Obituary in *Liverpool Mercury 26 April 1920* held at Liverpool Central Library Newspaper Archives
19. Records of the five Kirby students, retained at Stonyhurst College
20. Records of SS Conway, Register of Cadets, Liverpool Maritime Museum, Ref. number D/CON/13/11 Cadet No. 144
21. Masters Cert for Laurence Kirby, Board of Trade Cert of Competency 31936/1831109333/0091-00095 TNA
22. *To Preserve Their Memory* by Maurice Abbott, pp. 61 and 66, Shrewsbury Diocesan Archives
23. Report at beginning of the catalogue of deposits of Edmund Kirby and Sons in the archives of Liverpool Library, 720/KIR
24. Records of Frank Kirby at Stonyhurst College
25. Army records of Edmund Bertram Kirby accessed via Ancestry
26. Naval records of Laurence Kirby ADM340/80/19 No. 1816 TNA
27. deposits of Edmund Kirby and Sons in the archives of Liverpool Library, 720KIR 872
28. deposits of Edmund Kirby and Sons in the archives of Liverpool Library, 720KIR 872

An Irish Childhood in Chester

My first recollection of anything Irish was from listening to my Grandad talking to me and my Granny in his West of Ireland brogue. I first went to school in St. Werburgh's Primary in Queen Street, Chester. That first day was the most stressful, in my case because of the death of my twin sister Winifred, who died in the isolation hospital on Sealand Road of diphtheria, just before her fifth birthday. I was in there as well but thankfully recovered. First day at school was an ordeal not only for the new starters but mainly for the mothers who had tears in their eyes on seeing their 'little darlings' go through the big front door in Union Walk, past Mother Bernadette who was the head teacher in the Junior School. On whisking us into our first classroom, which was positioned under a steel fire escape which led to the senior boys section on the second floor, we walked past the statue of a Saint. I remember Mother Bernadette saying that it was Saint Patrick and on his feast day it was adorned with branches of shamrock and bunches of daffodils. The school stood where what is today the Tesco Supermarket in Queen Street. Mr. Cunningham was the head of the Senior Boys and Mother Helen was Head of the Senior Girls.

During the school year there were numerous feast days but Saint Patrick's Day stood out, for we would be taken to mass in St. Werburgh's Church in Grosvenor Park Road and boys and girls of Irish families would have sprigs of shamrock in their hair and

Mr. Cunningham, Headmaster 1924-50, another member of staff and a class of St. Werburgh's Boys

The Cross Foxes, Boughton 2017

their lapels. The girls would also wear green ribbon in their hair. Along the streets from City Road to Hoole Lane which had a large Irish community, many houses would have something suitably green displayed in their windows with the occasional Irish flag in a prominent position, after all this was the Irish Quarter.

As spring was approaching each year many Irish workers would return to the lodgings they or some member of their family had used in previous years. They worked mainly in heavy industrial labour, in the building trade, gas, electric and on water pipelines which at the time I remember as being laid or replaced throughout the length of Boughton. Also they worked at the Leadworks and in agricultural jobs in and around Chester. With regard to the pipe laying jobs, I remember seeing the Irish labourers getting paid in the Cross Foxes Public House yard in Boughton on a Friday afternoon. I suppose that this money would not last long by the time they had paid rent, put some aside to send home to their families in Ireland and what was left would be spent on beer.

There was always something going on in the street where I lived and many a fight would happen after closing time outside the many public houses in the area. Arguments that had occurred during the evening would be settled then forgotten and then it was back to work next day. Mainly they would return to their lodgings singing some well known

Irish ditty, happy nostalgic ballads about the 'old country' and the odd Irish rebel song thrown in for good measure.

Death was also a thing that brought out the customs of the Irish, with the inevitable wake and I have been to several, including my Grandfather and Granny. I would be sent home at about 9.00 pm leaving the adults to carry on with the drinking and reminiscing about the deceased and talking about the good things and the bad things that had happened during the deceased's lifetime. It is something I will always remember.

At the funeral the coffin lid would always be one quarter open, on which drinks large and small would be placed, with numerous toasts going on until the early hours. In the street at that time there were six to eight men of approximately similar height, mainly from the West of Ireland who were called upon to be regular coffin bearers to the Church and then onwards to the Grave. This went on for quite some time 'til one by one the grim reaper called and there were no more bearers left.

An old Irishman named Mick Burke, was a well known character. He used to play the Jew's Harp under the gaslight in the middle of the street during the summer and winter nights! He also played requests and locals would dance to his tunes. It was sad when one day he didn't turn up any more and it was the end of an era.

St. Werburgh's Church, in the years I am referring to, had a parish priest called Canon Hayes, who was in my opinion a great man, liked by everyone and often welcomed into their homes after Sunday Mass. On one particular Sunday, I had been sent by my Gran to The Waterloo, a local public house, for a half a pint of mild for my grandfather, which he liked to drink with his Sunday meal. As I came out of the Waterloo, which was only about 100 yards from my house, I met Canon Hayes on the corner of the street, and

Waterloo Public House
(now Backpackers Hostel)

he beckoned me to him with a crooked index finger. What have you got there my boy? I told him what it was and he put his hand into his pocket and gave me a sixpence! He told me I shouldn't do so again and with that he poured it (*the beer*) down the grid! Needless to say my Gran didn't ask me to do it again, because she was mortified!

On another occasion, the Bishop of Shrewsbury came to visit Steven Street in his bishop's robes. With a view to seeing some of his parishioners, he went into quite a few houses and called on my Gran who welcomed him into her home. She said afterwards how friendly he was and had she known he was coming she would have taken her apron off and looked a little more respectable for such an important visitor.

Some weekends when the weather was good, I would go walking on the meadows alongside the River Dee with my Grandad. On one particular balmy afternoon, we walked quite a long way along the meadows. It was a beautiful day, butterflies everywhere and the sound of birds in the air. Grandad stopped, got his pipe out and started to fill it with shavings of tobacco that looked like a liquorice stick! After filling his pipe, he leisurely took a ball of wire from his pocket and attached a rudimentary fish hook to a length of wire to make a fishing line. We had waited for quite some time when he suddenly noticed the line was going taut! "Think I've caught something" he said and there hooked on this line was the biggest salmon I had ever seen in my life. Grandad looked around furtively, because it was an offence at that time to have caught a Dee Salmon without a license. He made sure that the coast was clear and having wiped the salmon thoroughly on the grass, proceeded to stuff it into his duffel coat pocket! My Gran was not impressed and she was so alarmed the law would catch up with him that she made him sell it to a local publican who had a refrigerator. No doubt it became pride of place at the next wedding or wake that came along. These days of innocence however would soon come to end, with war (*WW2*) taking its toll on the nation, I would never go fishing with my grandfather again....

Walter Cunniff 2015

The Belgian Connection

After the invasion by Germany of neutral Belgium, on 4 August 1914 the first wave of refugees began to arrive in Britain. By the end of November 45,000 mostly destitute refugees had landed in England and a further 12,000 arrived in December. A National War Refugees Committee was formed, with offices at Aldwych in London and two large reception centres were set up at Earl's Court Exhibition Buildings and the Alexandra Palace. There were also public appeals for funds and accommodation. Local refugee committees were organised in most towns in the country and Chester was no exception.

The Cheshire Observer of 7 October 1914 reported the welcome given to the first of the Belgian refugees to arrive in Chester. Eleven refugees from Malines, which had fallen to the German army on 27 September, arrived in Chester from Euston after being temporarily housed in Alexandra Palace in London. They were met by members of the Chester Refugees Committee and their Honorary Secretary Mrs. D. M. Bibby. They were taken to their accommodation at 12 Eaton Road, which had been provided by Mr. Longueville Barker.

*12 Eaton Road
(left hand house)*

Oakfield House

A further report, in the Cheshire Observer of 31 October 1914, described the arrival of twelve more refugees who were to live in Dee Side Cottage, a property loaned by the Duke of Westminster. Oakfield House, which was later to become the family home of Chester Zoo founder George Mottershead, was also used as a home for a great number of Belgian refugees. In addition, many refugees were also accommodated in individual houses in Chester, including Father Joseph Loos, a Belgian priest, based at St. Werburgh's. (See essay on Fr. Loos).

In order to raise funds for other types of help for the refugees, a concert took place in Chester Town Hall on 14 December 1914. A notice advertising the event mentions that "the Talented Children of St. Werburgh's Schools" will be taking part. Five days after the entertainment a review of the event featured in the Cheshire Observer. The reporter writes "Almost in its entirety the entertainment was provided by the boys and girls, comprising the children of St. Werburgh's Schools, trained by the nuns and teachers ….."

Despite the fact that there were about 170 Belgians living in the Chester, Hoole, Upton and Eccleston areas, who might have made St. Werburgh's their parish, few Belgian names are noted in the parish registers. Perhaps this is because the refugees were mainly middle aged women with children over the age of 5 years and older men. Belgian males 18–25 were enlisted in the Belgian army. Nevertheless, there is one baptism, that of Marie Josephine Lemmans, daughter of Charles and Augusta Lemmans, on 28 November 1915. The Lemmans family lived at 52 Boughton. In the confirmation lists of February 1917 Rogerius de Vos, Augustus van Wouwe and Gottfried Croenan are named. Two marriages also took place, Joseph Valkenburg and Ellen Purcell in October 1916 and John Naylor of Beeston Towers with Louise Reine Aimee Delriviere of Brussels in March 1917. Sadly there were also three burials, which will be mentioned later. In addition to civilian refugees, injured Belgian soldiers were also brought to Britain for treatment.

The Little Sisters of the Assumption

In September 1914 the Little Sisters of the Assumption had offered their Convent as a hospital with beds for up to ten wounded soldiers; the ladies of St. Werburgh's parish promised to supply all the necessary bedding. Parishioners continued to support the Sisters in their mission throughout the war, contributing money for food and other supplies.

The first of the wounded soldiers began to arrive in December 1914 although the hospital had been ready to receive them for some time before this. Mrs. Barker of Heron Bridge, who had been working hard to help set up the hospital, collected donations from the parishioners on behalf of the Sisters.

By February 1915 the hospital was busy and the Sisters expressed their gratitude through the St. Werburgh's magazine to all who had helped and sent presents for the wounded soldiers. In April 1915 four of the soldiers were well enough to return to the Front and by the end of September 1915 the last of the soldiers had left the hospital. The Belgian soldiers' gratitude to the Sisters was demonstrated by the fact that every one of them was glad to return to visit the Convent, whenever he could, to see the Sisters. In August 1916 the parish magazine reported that it had been some time since the Sisters had received any wounded soldiers into their care and that it was unlikely that their offer to take more would be accepted, probably because of the limited number of beds available. They had therefore decided to cease to maintain their hospital. The remaining balance of £20 would be given to the Red Cross. After the end of the war, the Sisters were presented with the Queen Elisabeth Medal, by the King of Belgium. This was in gratitude for their outstanding service to wounded Belgian soldiers.

Union Street Convent ca 1950 – now Knightsbridge Court

Constant Wauters

One Belgian soldier who was nursed in Chester, was Constant Wauters, originally from Ghent, a married man with two young children. He was wounded during the early days of the war and brought to Chester for treatment at Richmond House Hospital, a private house which had been turned into an auxiliary hospital for the duration of the war. It was the main centre for injured Belgian soldiers in the North West and it also housed some British soldiers. Constant was recovering well from his injuries and probably went on the outing to Holywell, described in the newspaper article below.

Richmond House 123 Boughton
Reproduced by kind permission of Chester History and Heritage
Flintshire Observer
11 February, 1915

"WOUNDED BELGIANS" OUTING

On Friday last, two Chester gentlemen, Mr. Warden and Mr. T. Cotgreave[1] (cousin of Mrs. Llew Jones, The Bungalow) brought to Holywell a party of seven wounded Belgians, who have been invalided to Chester some three months ago, and are now convalescent. They were accompanied by Father Loose, also a Belgian.

On arriving at Holywell Junction Station a conveyance met them and proceeded to Englefield Colliery, where, through the kindness of the manager, Mr. Jones, they were allowed to descend and enjoyed the experience very much. Before leaving they thanked all the officials for the kindness shown to them.

After leaving the colliery they visited the Shrine of St. Winefride, Holywell, and the Catholic Church. Afterwards they were taken to Peckham House, where a capital dinner was served by Mr. and Mrs. Culling. The next visit was to Pantasaph, and upon arriving there they were met by Father Guardian and other Fathers and Brothers, who conducted them through the Church, Monastery and Mount Calvary. They were afterwards invited to visit the Convent, where they were received with great kindness and shown the institution through the kindness of the Rev. Mother and Sisters.

Returning to Holywell at 5 o'clock, they were entertained to tea at The Bungalow, Penyball, and left for Chester by the 6.20 train, having thoroughly enjoyed the day's outing. Nothing was wanting to make their visit a perfectly enjoyable one. The conveyance was supplied by Mr. Brown, King's Head Yard, Holywell."

However, when almost fit for release, Constant contracted meningitis. He was seriously ill for about six weeks and unconscious for about fourteen days. During this time, nuns from the Little Sisters of the Assumption Convent in Chester sat with him night and day, in order to take care of his needs and to release other nurses for duty on the rest of the ward. He died aged 26 on the morning of Thursday, 11 March 1915. His coffin, covered by the Belgian flag and the Union Jack was received into St. Werburgh's Church the following day and lay there before the high altar until his funeral, the first and only Chester funeral of a Belgian combatant, which was conducted with full military honours, on Saturday 13 March. A Requiem Mass, celebrated by Canon Chambers, Father Hayes, Father O'Hara and Father Joseph Loos, was sung at 10.00 am and, according to the Liverpool Daily Post of 15 March 1915, "was attended by all the Belgian refugees who are resident in the city on Saturday morning".

The coffin, covered in the flags of both nations and with many floral tributes, including a wreath of violets from Constant's wife, was conveyed to Overleigh Cemetery on a hearse drawn by artillery horses, followed by many of the Belgian refugees, with Chester residents lining the streets to witness the sad procession. The military procession included detachments of men of the Cheshire Brigade, the Royal Field Artillery, the Cheshire Yeomanry, the 5th Cheshire Regiment, the Royal Army Medical Corps and the Voluntary Aid Detachment of the Red Cross Society. Fr. Loos officiated at the interment in Grave 11864. A firing party and buglers from the Cheshire Regiment Depot were at the graveside and the ceremony concluded with the firing of three volleys and the sounding of the 'Last Post'.[2] Reports of the funeral were carried in newspapers throughout the region. Constant's name is also listed on the Great War Memorial Board in St. Werburgh's Church, Chester.

The British people continued to willingly support the Belgian refugees but inevitably problems arose from time to time. The odd fracas involving Belgian males visiting British pubs and getting involved in arguments, or an example of petty theft attributed to a Belgian, was reported in local newspapers. Another newspaper story involved a Belgian family in Chester who had visited Llandudno for a weekend, before their son went to join the Belgian Army. The family was arrested for being more than 5 miles distant from their registered domicile, without permission. The mother and two sisters had to appear in court, although they were later released, because of their inability to understand English legal jargon[3]. In another case, a fight broke out between two farm workers on their way home from the local pub. The Englishman accused the Belgian of being German, which the Belgian claimed was sufficient provocation[4]! The story has a sad ending, as the Belgian man took his own life a little later, whilst on remand in Shrewsbury Gaol – heaven knows what mental turmoil he was going through[5].

Negative incidents reported in newspapers and the horrific toll of British lives being taken in 1916 on the Somme may have weakened public support for the Belgian refugees a little. It was about this time that a national committee was set up to support the return of the refugees to their homeland after the war was over[6]. Controversially the people being asked to support this project, were the same people who were already supporting the refugees in this country!

When the Armistice had been signed, the Belgian and British governments began to prepare for refugees to return home. By the end of March 1919 over 95% of Belgian refugees had returned. Free transport was provided for those who registered before the end of December 1918. So, despite the great impact they made on British society at the time, there are few reminders of their presence in this country and their stories are virtually forgotten.

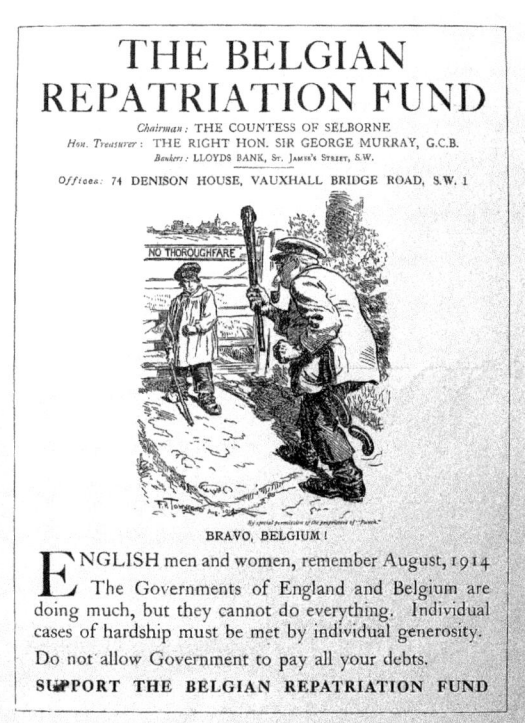

Advertising poster for the Belgian Repatriation Fund Reproduced by kind permission of CALS

Overleigh Cemetery

The grave of Constant Wauters can still be seen in Overleigh Cemetery. Close by, there is also the final resting place of Madame Marie Verbinnen, a Belgian lady who was very involved in organising fundraising activities for the Belgian refugees and combatants. She had lived on Lower Bridge Street and died on 1 December 1918 aged 68. She had lived long enough to hear the good news of the armistice but not long enough to return to her native land.

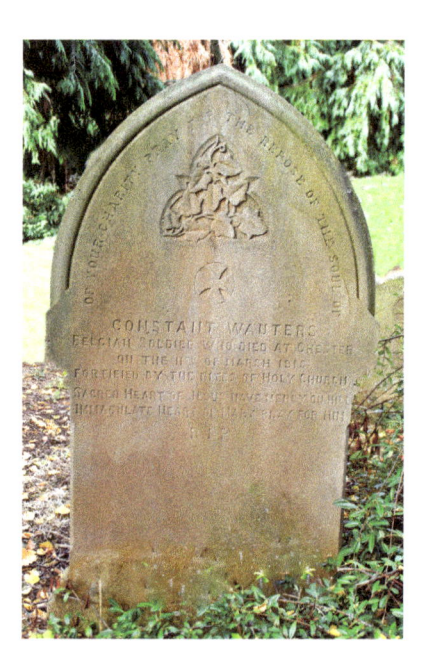

A headstone in the same area of the cemetery marks the grave of Henri Piessens, a two year old Belgian boy, who lived at 13 Westminster Road, Hoole. The communal grave where Henri was buried was originally unmarked but the new headstone, commissioned by the parish of St. Werburgh's, has been erected to commemorate him and the other persons buried there. These three headstones and the name of Constant Wauters on St. Werburgh's Great War Memorial are the only tangible reminders of the estimated 170 Belgians who lived in the Chester area during the Great War.

Stella Pleass 2017

References

1. The Cotgreave family were prominent parishioners of St. Werburgh's, Chester
2. Liverpool Daily Post, 15 March 1915, Liverpool Archives
3. Chester Chronicle 11 November 1916, CALS
4. Chester Chronicle 25 March 1916, CALS
5. Chester Chronicle 13 May 1916, CALS
6. Letter from Belgian Repatriation Committee, 7 March 1916 ZRP 14/37, CALS

Father Joseph Loos

A Belgian Priest at St. Werburgh's

On Saturday 31 October 1914 the following letter to the editor, appeared in the Cheshire Observer, marking the beginning of the ministry of Fr. Joseph Loos to the hundreds of Belgian refugees arriving in Chester and the surrounding area.

"Belgian Priest in Chester

Sir, Will you please make known through your paper that I have a Belgian priest residing with me? He will be only too pleased to be of any service to those who are giving hospitality to his people or to the refugees themselves. So far, in visiting the Belgian refugees and wounded soldiers, he finds them all more than happy and contented, and expressing gratitude for the kindness they are receiving and especially for the facilities offered them of practising their religion. It is well-known, and I'm glad to say, understood by the committees in Chester, who have the care of the soldiers and refugees, that they are all Catholic.

Yours faithfully,
J. Chambers.

PS Should anyone wish to write directly to the Belgian Father, the Rev. Father Loos, St. Werburgh's, Chester will find him.
St. Werburgh's, Chester. October 30 1914"

Institut Sainte Marie in Kuregem-Anderlecht (near Brussels)

Father Joseph Loos had been born in Minderhout, a town in Flanders about 25 miles from Antwerp, on 2 February 1890. He was ordained priest on 30 May 1914 and after ordination he started teaching in a diocesan college in Brussels (Institut Sainte Marie/St. Mary's Institute in Kuregem-Anderlecht). Within months however he found himself, at only 24 years old, at St. Werburgh's in Chester taking responsibility for the welfare of hundreds of his compatriots.

On 14 October Canon Chambers had taken the newly-arrived Fr. Loos to visit St. Werburgh's Girls' School[1] and later in the month the Canon wrote the above letter to the Cheshire Observer.

In the St. Werburgh's Parish Magazine of November 1914 Fr. Loos published the first of his monthly sermons in French and Flemish, addressed to his fellow Belgian refugees in the City and district.

Sermon recorded in St. Werburgh's Parish Magazine November 1914:

"To my dear compatriots

When I think of the fate of my homeland and that of these poor children, it feels like I am dreaming, for I am frightened by the image of a country burned and devastated. But nevertheless the fact remains, our brave Belgium, victim of her own heroism, is in flames and our fields are ravaged. How despicable, how shameful it is that these barbaric people have coldly and remorselessly dared to seize a neutral country, a peaceful people.

The innocent blood of our valiant soldiers has poured out in waves and reddened the soil of our homeland; the cloisters and churches have succumbed to flames and neither the ransacked and pillaged homes nor the devastated fields could satisfy the enemy's thirst for vengeance. Nevertheless, dear compatriots lift your hearts, have confidence! Reparation will come soon, victory is assured. The civilised world already admires our little Belgium, her valiant and heroic king and her brave soldiers who are fighting to the last drop of their blood for freedom and national independence.

We honour and thank England for her ready generosity in sheltering and feeding us poor refugees.

My dear compatriots listen to the voice of the homeland and never betray your Christian beliefs which are the honour of our dear Belgium.

J. L., Priest of Flanders
Chester, 26 Oct, 1914"

As you can see, the "sermons" are more like calls to the patriotism of Belgian refugees and soldiers, to honour their homeland in these difficult times and to put its welfare and that of its Catholic ethos, before all else. Nowhere was this more apparent than in the sermon of July 1915, published to celebrate the 85th anniversary of Belgian independence. A small extract will give the flavour of the whole:

"Let us imitate the wonderful example of our King, our royal family, our soldiers our fellow countrymen who are prisoners of war or living under the enemy's yoke. Above all, let us be like our illustrious Primate of Belgium who was not afraid of the enemy's threat when he faced them with their treachery, injustice and cowardice.

Let us hope. Already Noble Belgium has won the admiration of the entire civilised world because of her people's bravery and the heroism of her King who never hesitated for an instant in refusing the deceitful offer from an emperor who, violating the neutrality of a nation, has trampled underfoot his most sacred promises of 1839.

Finally, let us pray for the health of our homeland. Faithful to God and to our Religion, the Belgian nation will emerge from these ordeals greater and nobler."

During the early years of the war Fr. Joseph Loos ministered to the Belgian refugees living in and around Chester but as the war progressed other parts of the country were losing their Belgian priests as they were being called up to join the war effort and Fr. Loos was required to extend his ministry beyond the Diocese. At the request of the Bishop of Menevia he visited wounded soldiers and refugees in the Diocese of Wrexham and Chirk. He was also amongst those who took a party of convalescent soldiers on an excursion from Chester to Holywell, in February 1915, as described in "The Belgian Connection" essay.

A number of letters from Fr. Joseph Loos written during his stay in Chester in 1914–1915 have survived in the archives of the Archdiocese of Mechelen-Brussels[1]. They are written in French and addressed to Mgr. Antony de Wachter, auxiliary bishop of the archdiocese of Mechelen, who was given responsibility for the Belgian refugees in the UK by the Archbishop of Mechelen, Cardinal Mercier. Belgian priests working in the UK during the war had to report to Mgr. de Wachter, who spent most of his time in London but made many journeys throughout England to visit the refugees. In his first letter Father Loos seeks Mgr. de Wachter's help to allow him to remain in Chester to continue his work.

> "Loos
> St. Werburgh's Cath. Church
> Chester (Cheshire)

Monsignor,

The Very Reverend Canon Debroux, the military chaplain in London, has suggested that I ask a small favour of you. I am a Belgian priest, a teacher at the Sainte Marie Institute in Cureghem (Brussels). At the request of the Bishops of Shrewsbury and Menevia I came to live in Chester in October, where I enjoy the hospitality of the Very Reverend Canon Chambers.

I make regular visits to the Belgian refugees and wounded Belgian soldiers in the two provinces. I have approximately five hundred refugees and one hundred soldiers. I preach regularly every Sunday, sometimes in Cheshire sometimes in Wales. I can tell you Monsignor that in general the Belgians conduct themselves very well and attend Mass on Sundays if they are within travelling distance. The good conduct of the soldiers has been particularly noted.

This morning I received a letter from the Commander of the Military Bureau in London, 1 Finsbury Square E. C. After my address, etc. he asked if I would be interested in becoming a chaplain to a military hospital but don't you think, Monsignor, that the service I provide here every day is just as important? It would be a great honour for me, and for Canon Chambers, if we could welcome you to Chester. We could go and see some of the refugees in the area; in Northwich there are about 150 Belgian refugees.

I would also ask some pecuniary assistance from you, Monsignor, which would be very welcome. Canon Debroux has promised to put my case to you.

I would be very obliged to you, Monsignor, if you could inform the Commander of the Military Bureau in London that you wish me to remain in Chester where I am the only one able to address my compatriots in both Flemish and French and therefore best placed to attend to their spiritual needs.

I pray you bless me, Monsignor, and accept my respectful and grateful good wishes.

Your humble servant
Joseph Loos"

In the second and third of his letters Father Loos provides comprehensive details of the numbers and locations of Catholic Belgian refugees in the area. The area he covered was extensive – from Rhyl in the west to Knutsford in the east. An excerpt from his third letter gives an idea of the size of his task:

"I have around 600 Belgian refugees to visit regularly of which:

100	live in	Chester
160	"	Northwich
60	"	Crewe
80	"	Wrexham, Chirk, Llangollen
40	"	Upton
30	"	Eccleston
40	"	Nantwich, Acton
60	"	Rhyl
50	"	Knutsford, Mobberley

There are also other families dispersed in other places such as Winsford, Delamere, Manley, Frodsham, Tarporley, Calveley, etc."

As well as ministering to his people Father Loos helped to raise funds for those in need who were still in Belgium. In February 1915 he made an appeal to the members of St. Werburgh's Young Men's Society on behalf of the professors and students of his seminary in Brussels and received contributions totalling £7-10s. He also helped members of the various Belgian Refugee committees, when they needed to explain rather complex matters to Belgians who did not have a strong grasp of English. His facility in both French and Flemish was put to good use (see essay "Belgians at Deeside Cottage") Father Loos was successful in his efforts to remain in Chester for the time being and continued his ministry at St. Werburgh's until the end of August 1915.

On Tuesday, 31 August 1915 a Belgian Recruiting Commission, consisting of 3 officers, 6 NCO's and several Gendarmes (members of the Belgian Military Police), arrived in Chester. The Commission sat all day on Wednesday, 1 September at the Drill Hall, where 85 Belgian men from Cheshire had been summoned to appear before them. These men would have been between the ages of 18 and 25, unmarried and not working in munitions. Those who had travelled by train were first given dinner at the Castle. Then they were given medical examinations and 30 were found to be fit for military service. One of those 30 was Fr. Joseph Loos. The 30 men, accompanied by an NCO and several Gendarmes, then caught the 6.20 pm train for London. The rest of the Commission later travelled to Derby and York, where they were to sit during the following two weeks.[2]

Fr. Loos was quoted in the St. Werburgh's magazine of October 1915 as saying that he was sorry to have had to leave without bidding a proper farewell to his fellow countrymen etc. but had been obliged to leave hurriedly! However he was "only too willing to serve his country's interests on the field or here in England looking after his people". He was posted to the Auvours Camp at Sarthe in France, to receive training for Ambulance and Hospital work. Father Loos kept in contact with Canon Chambers and at Whitsun 1916 he returned to Chester, on leave from the trenches, where he was working as a member of the Belgian Ambulance Corps looking after the sick and wounded.

News of Father Loos continued to reach St. Werburgh's after his return to France and in September 1916 the parish magazine reported that he had been awarded the Croix de Guerre (War Cross).

In October 1917 Father Loos lost one of his sisters who was nursing at a hospital in Malines. She had nursed throughout the war, first at Malines through the terrible bombardment of the city, then in Ghent before returning to Malines, where she was taken ill and died.

Croix de Guerre

Fr. Loos remained in military service until 17 April 1919 and then returned to his college until 1925, when he became chaplain in the parish of Saint-Fredegandus in Deurne (near Antwerp). In 1926 he became chaplain of the chapel of Our Lady of Perpetual Help, again in Deurne, of which he was the first pastor (after the chapel had become a parish) from 1927 until 1936. His last post was in the parish of Saint-Gummarus in Emblem (a village near Lier in the province of Antwerp), where he was pastor from 1936 until his death on 28 September 1955.

Stella Pleass   **March 2017**

Translation of documents in French was undertaken by Cecilia Murphy and Stella Pleass. Translation of documents in Flemish was undertaken by Andrew Pleass.

References

1. Log Books of St. Werburgh's Girls' School, held at Cheshire Archives and Local Studies (CALS), Ref. DES/47
2. Three letters held in the archives of the Archdiocese of Mechelen were supplied by Gerrit Vanden Bosch, Archivist of the Archdiocese of Mechelen-Brussels
3. Chester Chronicle Saturday, 4 September 1915 held at CALS

Belgians at Deeside Cottage

On the afternoon of Monday, 2 November 1914 a train arrived at Chester Railway Station. It carried thirteen Belgian refugees, who were to live at Deeside Cottage in Eccleston. The Belgians had been accompanied by Mrs. Wilson of Eccleston Rectory, who had met them at Deptford and conveyed the party to Euston Railway Station, London. She then accompanied them to Chester, thoughtfully providing sandwiches for their sustenance during the train journey. They were met at Chester by several local dignitaries, amongst whom were Canon Chambers and Fr. Loos from St. Werburgh's[1].

Deeside Cottage had been prepared for them during the past several weeks. A Refugees Committee had been set up in late August 1914, which included members from the surrounding villages of Eaton, Pulford, Claverton, Marlston-cum-Lache Dodleston and Lower Kinnerton. Each household in this area had been contacted and had agreed to contribute one penny per week to support the refugees, in addition to personal donations of furniture, linen, crockery, etc[2]. Deeside Cottage was in fact quite a large house, with surrounding gardens and outhouses. Previously it had been rented for several years by Hon. Cecil Thomas Parker but for the past two years it had been unoccupied[3]. The Duke of Westminster offered it free of charge to the Belgian Refugees and it had been cleaned and made ready by local volunteers.

There had been some chaos on the platform of Chester Station, as one Belgian lady was heard to cry out "Le bagage, le bagage" and refused to leave the station until she was assured that it would follow. The same lady then caused another sensation when she realised that a well-meaning Mr. Rowe Morris had taken her two young children by the hand to lead them to a waiting motor car. The lady was not to be separated from her children at any cost. The same performance was re-enacted when the three reached the car. She would not enter it until her husband had joined the party! It was probably a good thing that Fr. Joseph Loos, a Belgian priest staying at St. Werburgh's, was at hand to interpret – he was fluent in English, Flemish and French. Eventually a motorcade transported all thirteen persons to Deeside Cottage, which was described as a large house, well fitted out and situated in one of the most pleasant villages in England[1].

We do not know how the persons sent to Deeside Cottage were chosen but we do know that they formed three family groups: Mr. and Mrs. Harvent and their four children, Mr. and Mrs. Meyermans with their daughter, mother and an elderly aunt (Marie Hermans), Mrs. Joanna Palmans and her adopted son Jacques. Although the refugees were probably glad to reach Eccleston, this was only the beginning of their lives in Britain and like most ventures, it was to present difficulties, as well as to bring rewards.

It could be assumed that the children enrolled at Eccleston School and on Sunday mornings, Fr. Loos makes it clear in his letters, the Belgians at Eccleston walked into Chester to attend mass at St. Werburgh's. Possibly they would meet up with fellow countrymen from 12 Eaton Road, or Handbridge and exchange gossip. Christmas was fast approaching and the names and ages of any Belgian children were asked to be sent to Chester Rural District Council, in order to obtain Christmas presents from various charities. The names of the five children we know were at Deeside Cottage, were listed: Marie Virginie Meyermans, age 14, Rosalie Harvent, age 13 and her siblings Adolf, age 11, Petrus, age 7 and Maria, age 5. Hopefully they were able to celebrate Christmas with some degree of comfort and hope.

On 11 February, the party increased in size when the sister-in-law of Mr. Meyermans arrived, along with her two children. It is difficult to give exact names at times, because Belgian names could be spelled in either the French or Flemish way, which can differ considerably. Often English clerks gave up, as seems to have been the case with the names of the last three arrivals. The chief problem for the refugees was to obtain employment and so not be a drain on the British economy. In February 1915 the Government Commission for Providing Occupation for Belgian Refugees asked each refugee committee for a list of unemployed Belgian men and women and made it clear that every aid should be given to get the refugees into the workplace.

At around this time, peace in Deeside Cottage appears to have broken down. The frictions consequent upon having three very different family groups sharing a house had not possibly been fully appreciated. There was a breakdown of relations between the Meyermans family and its adherents and the Harvent/Palmans family. Mr. Harvent was an umbrella maker who had owned his own shop in Malines but was not able to practise his trade in Eccleston or Chester. This must have made things very difficult for him. He eventually took a job at the motor garage in City Road, Chester. Four other Belgian refugees, living in Hoole, were also employed by this firm.

Mr. Meyermans was a former postman and shoe repairer. He was always willing to repair shoes for villagers in Eccleston as needed but was unsuccessful in obtaining a job in Chester. As late as December 1915 there is a letter from the manager of the Labour Exchange in George Street, Chester, explaining that there is no vacancy for a Belgian boot repairer at the moment. If Mr. Meyermans had not had a small allowance from the Postal Workers Association in London, it would have been very difficult for him to maintain his family. However, this allowance paid to Mr. Meyermans appears to have been the cause of envy in other members of the Deeside Cottage household. Mr. Meyermans was eventually taken on as a gardener on the Eaton estate in 1916 and earned twenty-four shillings for two weeks' work. The Estate had employed around sixty gardeners pre-war but the workforce was reduced by half during the war. Mr. Meyermans remained so employed until the end of February 1919[4].

Jacques Clement Palmans was a young man aged about 25/30 who had a delicate constitution and was not contacted by the Belgian army. He seemed unable to find an occupation in the Chester area but eventually found employment as a draughtsman in London and left Eccleston for the big city around March 1915. This left his mother, known as Joanna or Jeanne or Jeanette, to her own devices and she was probably somewhat lonely. She talked a great deal with the two elderly ladies in the house, one of whom became dissatisfied with her own position at Eccleston. Marie Hermans, decided to go to Holland, where her former masters were interned. (Holland was a neutral country and the estimated 1 million Belgians who had sought refuge there, were held in internment camps, to prevent their escaping to Britain to join the war effort.) She had received letters from them and decided that life there was not too bad. Fr. Loos was called in to talk to her about the difficulties and the folly of such action in a lady aged over 70. However, she remained steadfast in her determination to go. Fr. Loos was of the opinion that if Joanna Palmans left Eccleston, the other problems would soon subside.

In the middle of this domestic chaos, the Eccleston Belgian Refugee Committee had notice that Count Goblet D'Alviella, Vice President of the Belgian Senate, would be visiting on Monday, 28 June 1915. The Count was making a tour of Belgian Refugee homes in Cheshire, to check on the domestic and work facilities available to the refugees. His schedule was crammed with visits over two days and he was due to visit Deeside Cottage at 5.15 pm on 28 June. He was then due to be at 12 Eaton Road by 5.35 pm and at "Oakfield" Upton at 6.00 pm. His visit obviously constituted an in-depth investigation and he afterwards wrote a letter of thanks, from his lodging in the Grosvenor Hotel, to the General Secretary of the County War Refugees Committee, stating that he was "very satisfied" with all provision for Belgian Refugees in Cheshire. Perhaps there was a strong sigh of relief upon receiving this letter.

Meantime the Eccleston Belgian Refugee Committee had contacted Jack Palmans, in London and explained that as he was now earning a good salary he should be supporting his mother, who, in any case, wished to be with him. After several letters had passed between the two, Joanna Palmans set off for London in July 1915. She went to her son's lodgings, instead of to the Aldwych centre, as she had been told and somehow her luggage was mislaid! After several more mishaps and problems, the two Palmans were re-united. Jacques Palmans lived at 4 different addresses in London, not needing to claim a living allowance, before returning to Belgium via the SS Guildford Castle on 3 February 1919[5].

Earls Court Exhibition Centre, ready for Belgian Refugees

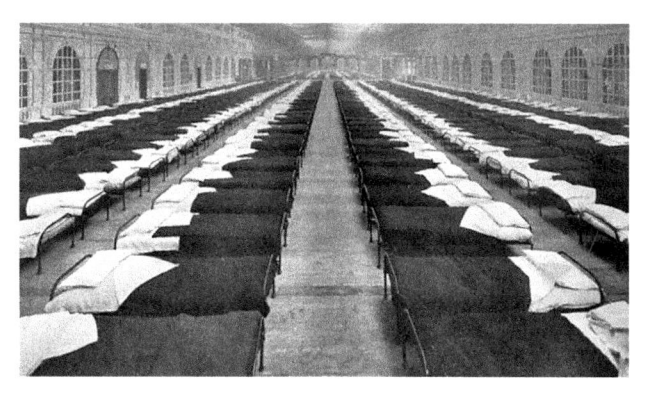

In the meantime the Harvent family decided that they too would go to London and meet up with the Palmans. Jacques Palmans would be able to find a job for Mr. Harvent and the two families would share a house. Again they were advised by the Refugee Committee to remain in Cheshire, where Harvent had a job and the family had support from the Committee. However, Harvent remained "stubborn" and the family went to London in July 1915. They lived at the Earls Court Centre for Belgian Refugees whilst they looked for accommodation in London. It was from there that Rosalie, the eldest child, sent a letter of thanks to the Eccleston Belgian Refugee Committee.

Later, the National War Refugee Committee in London wrote to Eccleston to enquire about the family and their reasons for leaving. It seems that Pierre Harvent was now working as an umbrella hawker but did not earn enough to support his family. The family needed a grant of sixteen shillings per week. Letters from the Eccleston Belgian Refugee Committee revealed that the family had received twenty-five shillings per week whilst in Eccleston, as well as receiving free rooms, fire and lighting. The mother was reported as having been a good manager and kept their rooms very clean. The girls were charming, though the boys could be somewhat mischievous. The Harvent parents had not really taken to such a quiet village as Eccleston and preferred town life. The Harvent family lived at three different addresses in London and received sixteen shillings per week, until they all left for Belgium on 15 December 1918. Their Belgian address was stated as 103 Rue de Malines, Louvain[5].

Back in Eccleston, Marie Hermans was still determined to go to Holland but had no passport or other necessary papers. Her passport was with her former employer in Holland. After being contacted by Hermans, via Joanna Palmans, whilst she was still resident in Eccleston, Mr. L. Van Gobbelschroy had written to the Belgian Consulate in London, enclosing Hermans' passport and saying that she would be welcomed in Holland and looked after. Hermans and Meyermans then obtained papers giving permission to travel to London, from the Police in Chester. In August 1915 George

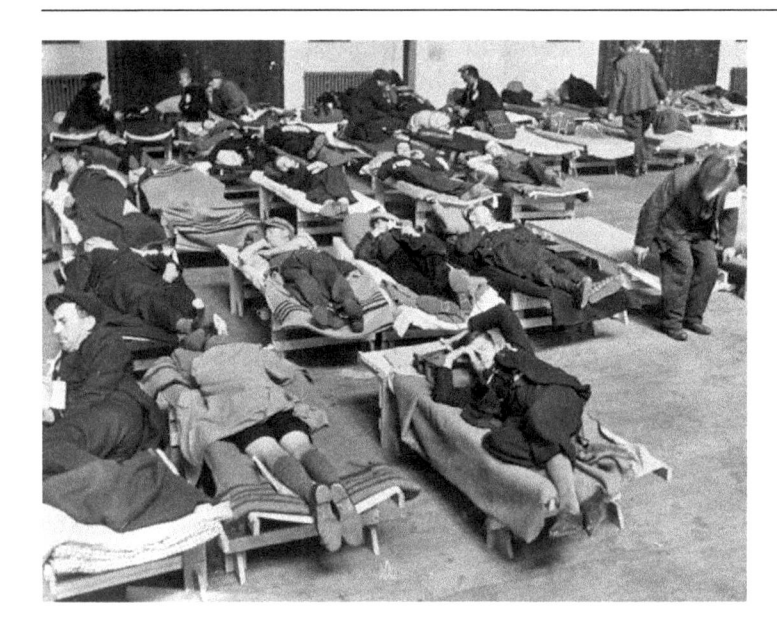

Alexandra Palace Belgian Refugee Centre with new male arrivals

Meyermans accompanied his aunt to the Belgian Consulate London, to obtain the passport, then to the British Permit Office in Downing Street for a permit to leave the country and finally to the port of Tilbury where she boarded a ferry to sail for the Dutch port of Flushing.

It is truly amazing how much time and effort the Refugee Committees and other organisations put into arranging these transfers of personnel to the places which they had requested. The letters and telegrams exchanged were numerous. The complex system whereby the National War Refugee Committee was at Aldwych, the Belgian Consulate at 37 Bedford Square, London WC and the main personnel processing centres at Earl's Court or Alexandra Palace was not helpful. Belgians who spoke very little English would have been passed from pillar to post, not understanding why or wherefore. It was also very difficult to get a permit from the British authorities to leave the country, during time of war. That these transfers occurred at all seems like a minor miracle.

George/Maurice Meyermans then returned to Eccleston, where he remained working on the Eaton Estate and with his extended family, continued to live at Deeside Cottage. In 1919, when it was time for him to leave his employment and the family to return to Belgium, there were sad feelings on both sides. Meyerman requested leave to attend the last meeting of the Eccleston Belgian Refugee Committee, in order to express the thanks of himself and his family, for their reception and hospitality in Eccleston. The Committee accepted his thanks and returned his feelings of fellowship. In the words of Committee member Mr. Wilson, Rector of Eccleston, the family "came as homeless strangers and will leave as old friends".

In 1919 Mrs. Adele Wilson, Secretary of the Eccleston Belgian Refugee Committee, received an order from Queen Elisabeth of Belgium, in recognition for its work on behalf of Belgian refugees. In 1920 Deeside Cottage was demolished and Eccleston Village Hall was built on the site[3].

Ann Marie Curtis   **2017**

References

1. Chester Chronicle 7 November 1914 held at Cheshire Archives and Local Studies (CALS)
2. Eccleston Belgian Refugee Committee documents ZRP14/35-40 held at CALS – contain most of the information about the refugees at Deeside Cottage, which has been referred to in this article. Individual letters and documents are not given separate catalogue numbers.
3. Eaton Estate Rent Book, held at the Estate Office
4. Eaton Estate, Gardeners Account Book, held at the Estate Office
5. Belgian Health and History Cards MH8 /41, 42, 43, 44, 45, and 46 National Archives, Kew (TNA)

Eccleston Village Hall 2016

Memories of Steven Street, Boughton, Chester

Ireland's many social problems culminated in the "Potato Famine" which decimated the country and it's population between 1845 and 1852. The proliferation of small holdings rented from "absent" landlords and over reliance on the potato as the foundation of a staple diet, lead to mass starvation, illness and death. Many native Irish sought a better life beyond Ireland's shores. In the years immediately following the failed harvest, mass emigration saw large numbers depart for America, Australia and England. Amongst those who landed at Liverpool and made their way to Chester around 1884 were John Jennings born 1857 and his bride Bridget Collins born 1856. John and Bridget were married at Castlebar, County Mayo in Ireland in 1884 after "running away from home."

They were to find rented accommodation in Steven Street, Boughton, Chester, originally occupying No. 11. John's brother Martin also arrived in Chester about that time, living at No. 13. John secured employment as an agricultural labourer with Dickson's Nurseries who cultivated many acres of land in both Newton and Upton, near Chester. Most of the residents in Steven Street had Irish Catholic heritage and the children attended St. Werburgh's school. Russell St., Steam Mill St., Victor St., Fosbrook St. and especially Steven Street, saw their residents form a strong Irish/Catholic community. Almost all of the properties were owned by a small number of landlords and were rented to grateful families. Notwithstanding the lack of basic amenities that we take for granted today, all were considered a vast improvement on what they had left behind in Ireland.

Steven Street ca 1950
Reproduced by kind permission of CALS

Bridget was to bear six children; Margaret (Maggie) born1885, Martin born1887, Peter born1890, John born1893, Delia born1895 and Rose Ann (my grandmother) born1899. All were baptised at St. Werburgh's Church within a few weeks of their birth and all were to attend St. Werburgh's school. It would appear that all were born within the house and not in hospital. Each delivery was no doubt conducted or at least supervised by some highly respected "Senior Neighbour" as was the case in many close communities. In the 1911 Census, the family had moved from No. 11 to No. 14.

Maggie married Patrick McDonnell in 1904 and they had a son John in 1905. They initially lived at No. 16. Patrick was killed in WW1 (see "We Shall Remember Them") and following this Maggie suffered depression and neglected herself, dying "of a broken heart" (according to Rose, my grandmother) in 1921, aged just 36. Margaret's funeral account was paid for by brother John Jennings Jnr. Margaret's son, young John Mc Donnell, was left in the care of the family. Times were extremely hard and the house was severely overcrowded and so it was decided that John would have far better opportunities if he were to live in America with two aunts (his late father's sisters). It was agreed that his uncle Martin would accompany him and return later. They sailed from Liverpool aboard the SS Havaford (White Star Line) on 25 August 1923 and landed in Philadelphia. Apparently, the arrangement (of living with his aunts) did not go to plan and for many years young John lived with Martin. Neither were ever to return to England. John joined the US Army and was killed in 1942/3 during WW2. Martin remained living in Philadelphia and worked on the railroad. He never married and wrote many letters to family back home, some very moving. He died in 1969. In fact none of the Jennings boys married and remained bachelors for life.

John McDonnell, killed 1942
Reproduced by kind permission of
Margaret Murray

Delia was to marry Albert Edward Capper. They had three sons; Desmond, John and Albert. They lived first at 24 Steven St., and later moved to Clover Lane, Lache, Chester.

Rose Ann married Joseph Earlam (my grandparents) of Abbots Mead, Chester at St. Werburgh's in 1923. They lived at 14 Steven St. The house was always overcrowded (two up/two down) and at this point it's inhabitants were, John Jennings Snr, wife Bridget, sons Peter Jennings, John Jennings Jnr, daughter Rose Ann and husband Joseph. To this day, it remains a source of mystery as to where they all slept!

Rose Ann at this time was working as a silver service waitress at the high class Bollands restaurant on Eastgate (now incorporated into the Debenham's building). Joseph was working at The Remount in Crane St., training horses for the army. He later worked on the railway. John Jnr. worked on the railway as an engine cleaner, never enjoying good health. Peter, who saw army service in WW1 and at one time also worked for Dickson's Nurseries, sought work where he could and experienced many periods of unemployment. He was to seek regular solace with a pint or two! This need was adequately catered for by the profusion of pubs in Boughton at that time.

Around 1924 Rose Ann became pregnant and endured a traumatic time, with poor health in no small way exacerbated by the appalling living conditions. She lost the child and came near to death herself. Years of ill health and emotional turmoil followed.

In 1928 Bridget the matriarch of the family died, never to see her second grandchild Margaret, who arrived on 14 February 1929, born to Rose Ann. My mother Rose Marie was to follow on 12 December 1930. Both girls arrived without complication and were born at St. James, later to become the City Hospital.

Peter Jennings (standing, extreme right) and friends during the Great War
Reproduced by kind permission of Margaret Murray

The house in common with most, consisted of a front kitchen with range, a back kitchen with a shallow brown Belfast sink. The stairs were off here leading to two small bedrooms. The toilet was situated in the back yard and was simply a scrubbed top plank with a hole in it. Cooking and the boiling of water were done on the open fire and range. Lighting was by means of gas downstairs and either oil lamp or candle upstairs. Margaret can recall as a small girl, lying in bed and scratching and picking at the plaster until straw was revealed beneath.

In later life my Auntie Margaret often wondered if perhaps her Grandfather John and his sons Peter and John slept in the same bed, knowing the size of the room. As she, sister Rose Marie (my mum) and parents Rose Ann and Joseph occupied the equally small bedroom two! Margaret recalls playing games in the narrow street; hopscotch, skipping, marbles, conkers and ball on the wall. The latter often incurring the wrath of one resident or other!

Most of the tradespeople visiting the street would have hand carts or horses and carts, and strangely it was a source of amusement that many horses would almost flood the street when "spending a penny". It was common for people who maybe had allotments (probably at Boughton Heath) to clean up after the horses for the benefit of their crops!

The shops in Boughton, near to Steven Street, were Mullin's, the proprietor of which was an Irish woman with grey hair, always worn as plaited buns over each ear. She had a son who was a huge man. Pegram's was the grocers. Tom Butler kept a sweet shop. Rose Ann asked him not to serve Margaret with sweets as she thought she was being spoilt by Uncle Peter Jennings who was always giving her a copper or two!

Foden's sold sweets and ice cream, some of which was in a cardboard wrapper that needed squeezing in order to get the last bit! Power's was the greengrocers and Ike Barlow's was "open all hours." Other shops seemed to sell all sorts of stuff and most definitely paraffin! Rose Ann recalls a serious fire in one shop, in which a woman died. The cause was thought to be a paraffin spillage. The tram lines were still in place along Boughton but the trams no longer ran. Buses had taken over in 1930.

Mrs. Agnes Coriam of Victor Street, sister in law to Mr. and Mrs. Andrew Cunniff Snr. of 15 Steven St, was a dress maker and made all the dresses for Church Processions and events.

I remember mum telling me of "The Boughton Gold Rush". Following the draining of the canal, a gold sovereign was spotted shining in the mud. Before long, as word spread, almost all of Boughton had jumped in, in the misguided hope of becoming

The Boughton Gold Rush, June 1927

rich. Apparently an old mattress dumped in the canal following a house clearance, was the culprit!

It is known that whilst those living in the area were predominately of Irish/Catholic extraction, there was often scant regard for the police, who would always patrol in pairs. In fact, it is recorded, that in the late 1800's there was major civil unrest in the area, culminating in riots! However, the appearance of a priest was always sufficient to calm the waters! In the 1930's Canon Hayes was tasked with pulling his parishioners into line.

Another tale, this time told by a member of the Jones family, related to funerals in Steven Street. My great uncle, Joe Jones following WW1 service in France, became an accomplished horseman and would often claim to be one of the few men in Chester capable of driving a "Four in Hand". Whilst in the employ of Hallmark's Undertakers he would often help conduct funerals from Steven Street. On occasion it was necessary to reverse the hearse and horses in, from Boughton. Whilst he and the other men entered the house to fasten the lid on and lift the coffin (amidst masses of empty bottles and glasses following the traditional wake) the children would be busy pulling the horses tails and trying to remove the black head plumes. When the coffin was placed aboard the hearse the cortege proceeded at a sedate pace to St. Werburgh's Church, often followed by the same group of mischievous children, only for them to attempt the same tricks as earlier!

After the service it was off to Overleigh Cemetery at a slightly faster trot, the group of following children getting steadily smaller until none were left. All was well until when passing the Castle Square the band of the Cheshire Regiment struck up. From there to the cemetery the horses pranced all the way!

The Earlam family; Joseph, Rose Ann, Margaret and Rose Marie, were to leave the street in 1938 for better housing in Handbridge, resulting in a rent rise from 5/- a week to 11/- a week! John Jennings Jnr. moved with them but Peter Jennings remained at No 14 until his death in 1953. Steven Street was pulled down in 1956–57. The only present day reminder of its presence, is Steven Court, built near to the site of the original street.

The above accounts and stories are not supported by my first hand knowledge or experiences, owing to the fact I'm a mere youngster of sixty four years. They do, however provide a snapshot of life within what was a very poor, close, sometimes tragic and yet often a very happy community. I remain eternally grateful to my late mother Rose Marie, her sister Margaret, my late grandparents Joseph and Rose Ann (nee Jennings), late great uncle John Jennings jnr. and late great uncle Joseph Jones, all of whom took time to recall the above people and events during my formative years.

Recalled by Margaret Murray (nee Earlam) and compiled by her nephew, Tony Jones.

Michael Anthony Jones   **May 2016**

The Easter Rising and St. Werburgh's, Chester

"England's difficulty is Ireland's opportunity" was a well-known slogan, which reflected the uneasy relationship between these two parts of the United Kingdom, at the outbreak of the First World War. Home Rule for Ireland was a subject which had occupied much Parliamentary time at the end of the 18th century, Prime Minister Gladstone taking the lead towards "pacifying Ireland." His first two Home Rule Bills were soundly defeated and the ruling Tory party concentrated on introducing reforms that might "kill Home Rule by kindness," but this did not placate the Irish people. Under the leadership of John Redmond a Third Home Rule Bill was introduced in 1912 but was not destined to become law until 1914, thanks to the passing of the 1911 Parliament Act which allowed the House of Lords to delay the enactment of Home Rule for a maximum of two years (but no longer). Because of the outbreak of the First World War, Ireland, minus the Ulster counties, would have Home Rule delayed until the European hostilities were overcome. This was not expected to be for more than a few months.

Thousands of Irish people had emigrated during the 19th century, particularly at the time of the potato famines in the 1840's. This meant that in 1914 St. Werburgh's parishioners were mostly from Irish backgrounds, many of them descendants of the 19th century famine refugees. They lived in the Boughton area and, with their meagre earnings, contributed to building of the beautiful church which we now attend. When war broke out in 1914 the men from these families volunteered for military service in huge numbers. Nonetheless their loyalty was suspect in some quarters. On 18 April 1914 Robert Foulkes wrote in the Chester Observer, questioning the decision to grant Ireland Home Rule: "The thing is absurd.... It is not safe to commit a Protestant minority to such keeping..... If you give them a Parliament in Dublin, the priests will control them and run the country." Mr. Foulkes was answered by someone calling him/herself "Sursum Corda" (Lift up your heart). He wrote "Thanks be to God. There is a good time coming. The loyal and faithful Irish peoples, who are ever disloyal to hateful tyranny, will soon .... give a taste of their quality and worth." On 7 November 1914 another correspondent to the Observer quoted from a letter written by Corporal O'Mara of the Irish Guards: "We are British soldiers and proud of the name and proud to belong to the Great British Empire.... We have also in our mind to add, if we can, more lustre to the fair name of Erin." Corporal O'Mara fought with the Munsters, the Leinsters and the Connaught Rangers.

In March 1916, a month before the Easter Rising, a letter appeared in the Chester Observer from Mrs. Dora Frost, Lady Mayoress of Chester, explaining that a

Dublin Post Office, O'Connell Street ca 2010

committee to which she belonged had decided "to set apart Friday, 17 March as "Irish Soldiers Flag Day" to give the people an opportunity of expressing their appreciation of the soldiers of Irish Regiments who were prisoners of war in Germany. By refusing to change sides and join the German army these men had been condemned to suffer inferior conditions.

Just a month later the Easter Rising took place in Dublin when members of various Republican groups seized the General Post Office and proclaimed the Irish Republic. The Rising was put down within a week after the leaders, Padraig Pearce and James Connelly surrendered to British Forces sent from England.

Many Irish citizens had not supported the rebel action but their opinions quickly changed when Pearce, Connelly and thirteen other insurgents were executed between 3 and 12 May. Two thousand captured Republicans were sent to Britain to be interned; among them was Eamon de Valera. After the failed Rising, support for John Redmond and the Irish Party at Westminster decreased and many people turned instead towards Sinn Fein.

The results of the Easter Rising in Dublin sent ripples as far as St. Werburgh's Boys' School in Chester. Items reported in the School Log Book for 1916[1] include the following:

1 May Owing to travelling facilities having been interrupted by the Sinn Fein rebellion, Miss M. J. Hannigan has been prevented from returning from her holidays in Ireland.

5 May Miss M. J. Hannigan is still absent from duty.

12 May Miss M. J. Hannigan resumed duties this morning.

31 August Miss M. J. Hannigan finished her duties in this school this afternoon.

It would perhaps be interesting to ask Miss Hannigan why she decided to leave her position in the school.

For the remaining years of the war Chester's newspapers carried reports concerning events involving Ireland which led to some strong debate in the correspondence columns of all the local papers. In March 1916 the Military Service Act was passed which imposed military service – with some exceptions, on all single men aged between 18 and 41; married men were included in a second act passed two months later. Conscription was not applied to Ireland because of the Easter Rising, although many Irish men still volunteered to fight.

On 13 May the Chester Observer carried a report "Ireland Exempt". "As a result", it read referring to the exclusion of Ireland from the recent conscription legislation, "Ireland is the only part of the islands where men of military age will be allowed to shirk their military obligations." Sir Edward Carson declared that exemption was "a disgrace to Ireland." Another correspondent to the Cheshire Observer wrote in October, "Week by week we pay tribute without invidious distinctions to the gallantry of the Irish soldiers. It is the Irish Nationalists who stay at home and threaten to resist compulsory service whose loyalty is in question." When an Irish nationalist living in Chester wrote and protested against "the mixing up of Irish Nationalists, Sinn Feiners and Independents, all in one group," the paper's editor added a footnote "… will the thousands of able bodied young Irishmen who are evading military service now come forward and prove their loyalty and patriotism by helping to defend the Empire?" When the Irish patriot queried some figures given by a government official for the numbers of Irish men involved in the fighting and pointed out that Mr. John Redmond had quoted the figure of 150,000 soldiers in arms, the editor again added a note to point out that the government officer's numbers might be more reliable "because his return is official while the correspondent is just "interested." [2]

In the Cheshire Observer a correspondent calling him/herself "Cosmopolitan" added a postscript to his letter "I cannot allow the imputation of cowardice against the Irish to pass unchallenged. The Irish as a race, whether Catholic or Protestant are even, if possible, less deserving of such a charge as the British…." The editor again added his own comment "No imputation of cowardice in the Irish was published in our article. The Irish, on the contrary, are always spoiling for a fight…."

Another area of discord during the years of the war was centred in the countryside where it had been the custom of Irish people to come and work in the county during the summer months. A Mr. Sadler was quoted in the Daily Dispatch, which reported that little Irish labour was employed in the Crewe and Nantwich district. It was suggested that local labourers were saying "You have taken away our mates and we will not have these Irish slackers. They should fight the same as our men." Mr. Sadler had not met with this objection except in the Chester area.

Chester War Memorial – Unveiling and Dedication 1922

It is good to finish this brief look at Anglo-Irish relations in 1916 by mentioning that on 13 May two reports of the same Irish action on the Western Front, appeared in the Chester papers. One was headlined "Another attack on British. Enemy Successfully Repulsed" and the other had "The Gallant Irish Division – A clean and quick job at Hulluch." The troops involved included the Inniskillings, the Dublin Fusiliers and the 16th Irish Division.[3]

It is not difficult to imagine how vilified, parishioners of St. Werburgh's so many being of Irish descent, must have felt during this time. Their men were falling in extraordinarily high numbers (as shown in "We Shall Remember Them") and those who returned often struggled for a life-time, with mental and physical health problems. Perhaps wounded feelings were mollified when the Great War Memorial was placed in the grounds of Chester Cathedral. It was unveiled in June 1922 by two Chester ladies, who had each lost three sons. They represented all the bereft mothers of Chester. One lady was Mrs. Lydia Sheriff Roberts, wife of a former Mayor of Chester, whose three sons had been officers in the Royal Welsh Fusiliers. The other lady was Mrs. Mary Beatty, the wife of James Beatty, an Irish immigrant gardener. Their three sons were servicemen of other ranks. The two mothers were united in their grief.[4]

Celia Murphy   **January 2017**

References

1. St. Werburgh's Boys' School log book Z DES 46 CALS
2. Letters in Chester press re. Irish exemption from conscription
3. Reports in Chester press re Irish soldiers at Hulluch
4. Chester press re unveiling of WW1 Memorial June 1922

Bibliography

"The Seven: The Lives and Legends of the Founding fathers of the Irish Republic" Edwards, Ruth Dudley. The author states that fewer than 1,800 people were involved in the Easter Rising and that about 200,000 uniformed Irish men served in the army 1914–1918. This figure is not believed to include Irish men, or men of Irish ancestry, recruited to English regiments.
Coffey, T.M., Agony at Easter – 1916 Irish Uprising.

In recent years the BBC broadcast a programme about the aftermath of the Great War in Ireland. Descendants of some of the men who volunteered for service were interviewed and explained that their families left Ireland post 1918 because they were ostracised on account of their action.

The Enigma of Roger David Casement 1864–1916

Whilst many men of St. Werburgh's parish were fighting in various WW1 arenas, there was an environment of discontent fast developing in Ireland. Just over one hundred years ago, the 1916 Easter Uprising shook the whole of Ireland and a man who had links with Rhyl, was one of the prominent figures. Reporting on his trial, an article in the Chester Chronicle of May 1916 states that his main focus was to conquer Ireland with the assistance of Germany!

Born in Co. Dublin in 1864, Roger David Casement was the son of Roger Casement and Anne nee Jephson. Though Roger's mother was a Catholic, Roger's father was a Protestant and their male children were baptised and brought up in the faith of their father. Their daughter, Nina, was probably baptised in the Catholic faith of their mother, as was a fairly standard practice in a "mixed marriage" at this time. Casement also had family roots in the Isle of Man. His great Grandmother was Catherine Cosnahan, daughter of Rev. Joseph, vicar of the parish of Braddan, Isle of Man and it was here that Roger Casement was baptised on 29 October 1865 at Maughold.

Anne Casement did not enjoy good health and in 1868 was staying in Rhyl to recruit her strength. For reasons at which we can only guess, Anne Casement took the opportunity to have Roger and his two elder brothers baptised in St. Mary's Catholic Church, Rhyl. Anne Casement died five years later, her husband Roger became incapable of looking after the family and Roger David Casement was then brought up in Ballymena, by his father's brother. He attended local Protestant schools and grew up to be a pillar of Loyalist society.

Casement Baptisms 1868 St. Mary's Rhyl

After a spell working in Liverpool, Roger entered the colonial Service in 1892, where he had a distinguished career serving the British Government. He served as Travelling Commissioner of the Niger Coast Protectorate, then as HM Consul to Lourenco Marques in Portuguese East Africa (Mozambique), to St. Paul de Loanda in Angola, then to Kinshasa in the Congo Free State. In his 1903 report he condemned the exploitation of workers in the rubber industry and this lead to the extinction of rubber trade in the Congo. His later appointments were in South America, where he held consular positions in Santos and then Para in Brazil, before becoming Consul General in Rio de Janeiro. In 1911 he received a knighthood for his humanitarian work and retired from the diplomatic service to Dublin, due to ill-health.

The horrors that he had witnessed during the previous years had turned him against imperialism of all kinds, including the imperialism of the British Government and from this time onwards Casement took a great interest in the nationalist movement in Ireland. In 1913 he joined the Irish Volunteers and later sought to obtain German aid in support of Irish Independence. During negotiations with the German Government, whose support was gained, he attempted to raise an Irish Brigade from Irish soldiers in a Berlin prisoner of war camp, who had been captured on the Western Front. The result of this was very limited, as he was regarded as a traitor by most of the prisoner population. Ironically, he could have been trying to recruit some St. Werburgh's men who had been captured. The vast majority of prisoners, who had refused to follow Casement, were then subjected to very poor treatment and caused Mrs. Dora Frost (wife of the Mayor of Chester) to inaugurate the Irish Prisoners Flag Day, on 17 March 1916. The proceeds would be used to send food and other necessities to these Irish prisoners of war.

Later in 1916, Casement was arrested, sent for trial and executed. Many newspapers published accounts of the events leading up to these events. For example, The Dover

Grave of Roger Casement
Glasnevin Cemetery, Dublin 2016

Express and East Kent News of Friday 28 April 1916, reports that an attempt to land arms and ammunition in Ireland was made by a boat disguised as a merchant ship, but which was a German auxiliary, accompanied by a German submarine. The auxiliary was sunk and amongst prisoners taken was Sir Roger David Casement.

Casement was arrested near Tralee, as he disembarked from the German submarine which was transporting arms into Ireland. He was brought to the Tower of London, taken to the Old Bailey, tried and sentenced to death on 9 June 1916, for high treason. The Irish Post records that he had support from such prominent figures as Arthur Conan Doyle, W. B. Yeats and George Bernard Shaw but that their words fell on deaf ears.

Interestingly, it is widely reported that Casement was received into the Catholic Church on 3 August 1916. This is perhaps a misinterpretation of events. He would not need to be officially received, if he had already been baptised in Rhyl. Perhaps though, as he was only four years old at the time, he did not remember this event. Whatever the situation, he was hanged in Pentonville Prison that same day, aged 51 years. In 1965 his remains were returned to Dublin and re-interred in Glasnevin Cemetery.

Casement's books, "The Black Diaries", were originally suppressed by the Government but when scrutinised later, they revealed matters concerning homosexuality, which brought much opprobrium on him at that time. The contents were disputed and later thought to be a forgery. More recent work indicates that the diaries are probably genuine after all.

John R. Caley   **2016**

Author's Note

While Casement was planning to overturn the Irish Government with the help of German arms, many of the parishioners of St. Werburgh's gave their lives at Gallipoli and the Somme. An account of their service is published in "We Shall Remember Them."

Bibliography and further reading

Records of the Cosnahan Family, Canon E Stenning M.A. Manx I-Museum
Chambers Biographical Dictionary, B L Reid, "The lives of Roger Casement". (1976)
A genealogical survey of the peerage of Britain as well as the royal families of Europe
   – Compiler: Darryl Lundy
Casement's speech following his conviction.
Irish Post 2016 "Ten facts about the Irish Patriot Executed A Century Ago"
Sinn Fein Rebellion Handbook, Easter Rising 1916
Agony at Easter – 1916 Irish Uprising by Thomas M Coffey.
We Shall Remember Them – Biographies of men associated with St. Werburgh's who
   gave their lives during World War 1.
Archived National and Local Newspaper articles.

Missionaries in Chester

In 1767, following a government order, the Anglican vicars of all the Chester churches drew up a list of the Papists in their parishes and came up with a total of 129.[1] The 129 Catholics were living in "Mission Country". There was no Diocesan structure as we know it but the whole country was divided into 4 Vicariates. Chester fell within the Northern District Vicariate. There were no parishes, Churches or schools. In 1797 Fr. Thomas Penswick was appointed as Resident priest in Chester; in 1816, Fr. John Briggs followed him. Chester was about to benefit from the presence of two memorable churchmen.

Fr. Thomas Penswick

Thomas Penswick was born in 1772. His father was the steward to the Bryn family of the Manor House at Ashton-in-Makerfield where Thomas spent his early years. He was educated at Haighton House near Preston and Mr. Seatle's School at Prescot. When he was 15 years old and expected to start a career, he expressed a wish to study for the priesthood.[2] With very few options at that time, his wish was met by sending him to Douai in northern France where, for 200 years, a seminary had existed to provide priests for the English Mission during Penal times. Thomas arrived at the seminary aged 16 years to follow an education similar to that of a Public or Grammar school in England, with the addition of his religious studies. He was a good student and progressed steadily through the different "Schools" at Douai, proving his ability, and by the age of 20 he was one of the Colleges "high" philosophers.[3]

During Thomas' years of seminary training in Douai, France suffered the constant upheaval of Revolution, which saw the fall of the Bourbon monarchy, followed by the Reign of Terror. Leaders rose and were replaced, many died on the guillotine. French armies invaded the Netherlands and in 1793 England declared war on France. The French National Assembly called for the imprisonment of all British subjects in France and armed guards were stationed in the college at Douai. Thomas and his friends did Trojan work saving precious items such as church plate. They hid some property in the town, some in the collage grounds, some up chimneys or under floors.

When the French authorities decided to move the college, staff and students, to Doullens, Thomas, with six friends and the help of a local countryman, managed to escape the transfer. The seven young men reached the Channel coast safely but were refused passports by the English Consul because he thought they were French.

Parry's Entry, Chester

The travellers managed to cross the Channel without passports. In the Douai Register for 1793 there is an entry "Thomas Penswick. Went 12 October".[4]

After a short spell at home in Lancashire, Thomas travelled to "Old Hall" in Hertfordshire to resume his seminary training. It was now February 1794. Thomas was almost 22 years old. Unfortunately, good relations among the Douai students now settled in England, did not last. Northerners and Southerners were in conflict, to the point where the Northerners asked their Bishop for a new home. They were accommodated at Crook Hall near Durham, where Thomas completed his theology training and was ordained on 1 April 1797. In late summer he left for the Mission in Chester. He was 25 years old.[5]

The priests' accommodation in Chester was in a small rented building in Parry's Entry, a narrow street off Foregate Street near Claremont Walk. Fr. Thomas had limited space and the Chapel was in poor condition. Sadly, the Chester Mission had lacked development because of the illness or death of previous clergy. There was a need for someone with good health and plenty of energy to take up the task of establishing a Catholic presence in the City.[6] Thomas' mission field would stretch from Chester to Northwich and to the Welsh border. His travelling would be on foot because he could not afford a horse of his own; sometimes he hired or borrowed one. He walked 8 miles to Puddington Hall, Wirral for Confession, to the Massey family's Chaplain.[7]

Fr. Thomas was the right man for the Chester Mission. In April 1799, only 2 years after his arrival in the city, he had registered, as was required by law and opened a new Catholic Chapel in Queen Street. It was described in a Directory as a "small but handsome brick building." The church cost £445 to build with additional payments for painting and the final bill was paid in 1801.[8]

This larger Chapel was built in time to receive numbers of Irish people who fled to England after the failure of the 1798 Rebellion in Ireland. Unfortunately, although there was work for the immigrants there was also tension between the local people and the newcomers. On several occasions during the building of the Chapel, the construction work was demolished during the night, by those who objected to the building of a Papist Chapel. The problem was solved by the Connaught Rangers, then stationed in Chester, who volunteered to guard the building site at night.[9] It should be remembered that the first three decades of the nineteenth century was the period when the campaign for Catholic Emancipation was at its height. There was strong opposition from many quarters but the call to repeal the Penal Legislation against Catholics was persistent and in 1829 political freedom for Catholics was granted. When Daniel O'Connell, one of the leaders in the fight, died on his way to Rome in 1847, his body was returned for burial in Ireland. His coffin rested overnight in the new Chester Chapel before the last stage of his journey to Dublin.[10]

Fr. Thomas too, had encouraged his parishioners to support the cause of Catholic Emancipation. While frowning on "disturbing the settled order" he preached a

Penswick Family Gravestone

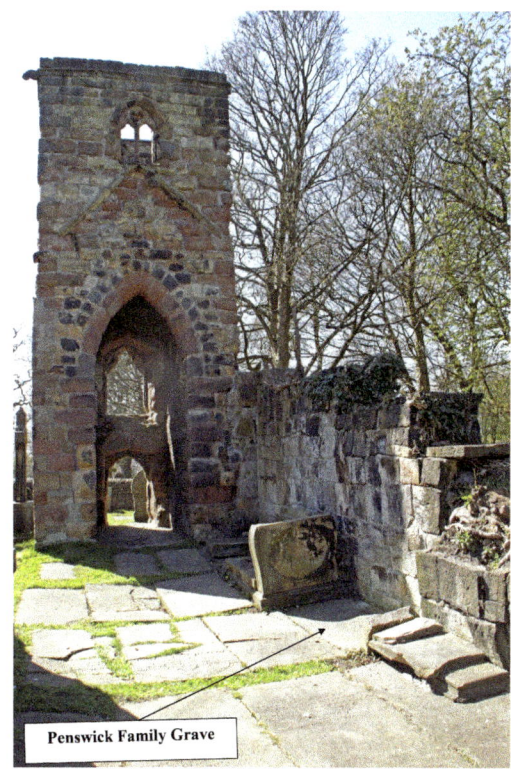

Grave in Ruins of Windleshaw Chantry

Ruins of Windleshaw Chantry, St. Helens Cemetery

sermon which included the words "far be it from me however, to insinuate that you are never to endeavour to ameliorate your condition….Princes who hearken to the petitions of private persons, will not refuse the demands of a considerable body of people." When the Bishop of Chester arranged a meeting for an anti-Catholic petition against Catholic Emancipation, several leading members of Chester society opposed it and invited Fr. Thomas to refute any anti-Catholic slanders. Fr. Thomas replied to his enemies in the Chester Courant with two lengthy letters which protested against the anti-Catholic calumnies.[11]

In 1814 Fr. Thomas was moved to the pro-Cathedral of St. Nicholas in Copperas Hill in Liverpool. He was consecrated as co-adjutor to Bishop Smith, whom he succeeded in 1831 as Vicar Apostolic of the Northern District. He did not forget his time in Chester and when there was occasion to write to the city he always sent "his compliments to all his friends in Chester". In Liverpool he worked as hard as ever, concerned about conflicts between Irish immigrants and local labour. Often there was a fine line between men banding together to improve their work and living conditions and the formation of groups with political or secret overtones. In a Pastoral Letter in January 1834, he asked the poor to accept their lot rather than involve themselves in illegal action.

Fr. Thomas died in 1836 in his old home in Ashton-in-Makerfield, where his brother Randall had brought Thomas as his health failed. Thomas is buried in the family grave in the ruins of Windleshaw Chantry, where many Northern English recusant Catholics are buried, in St. Helens cemetery.[12]

Fr. John Briggs

Two years after Fr. Thomas Penswick left Chester, Fr. John Briggs came to the city to begin his ministry as the resident Catholic priest. He was 28 years old and known to Fr. Thomas who was delighted that John Briggs had been appointed to look after Catholic Chester. Fr. John was an extrovert, a tall man of great energy. When he was later appointed Bishop of Beverley in 1850 he took as his motto "non recuso laborem".[13]

Right Rev. John Briggs, Bishop of Beverley Reproduced by kind permission of St. Cuthbert's College, Ushaw

John was born in 1789 at Barton-on-Irwell outside Manchester. His family were farmers owning land in Lancashire. John's young years were less troubled than Thomas Penswick's. At 15 he proceeded to Crook Hall and later to Ushaw to study for the priesthood. He was ordained priest in July 1814 and came to Chester two years later.

Like those who came before him, Fr. John had to travel considerable distances from Chester. He was responsible for the Southern section of Cheshire which required him to visit Crewe, Nantwich and even Wrexham in all weathers. The railway to Crewe was not built until 1837 so the journey would have to be made on horseback and in 1825 Fr. John spent £19 13 shillings 4 pence on a horse and gig.[14]

From available records it is easy to discover what a devoted pastor Fr. John Briggs was for his parishioners. The number of Catholics in Chester increased greatly between 1816 and 1833 when Fr. John left the city; many of the newcomers were Irish and they had great confidence in him. Numbers of them trusted their small savings to his care – witness a note which survives:

> Thomas Kelly left £4 in my hands, 2 June 1826. If not called in 12 months to Lord Dillon's office, Mr. McGuire, for John Kelly, Kiltobanks, Loughlin, Roscommon;
>
> OR
>
> Martin Mahoney left in my hands 39 sovereigns 29 August 1827. John Briggs signed it.[15]

His parish work among his flock was equally dutiful. For example, in 1829 he baptised 70 infants nearly half of them on the day of their birth or in their first week. Most of the remainder within a fortnight or three weeks.[16]

Fr. Briggs was also mindful of the future for young seminarians. One such was Thomas Grant the son of an Army sergeant who had fought at the Battle of Waterloo. Thomas was born in Ligny-les-Arles in France where his father was part of the army of occupation following the battle. During his early life, both John's mother and his brother died. When his father was posted to Chester, Thomas came too. He became an Altar Server in the Catholic Chapel and felt confident enough to tell Fr. John that he would like to study for the priesthood. For three years he studied with Fr. John and then went on to Ushaw in 1829. After his ordination he was appointed as Secretary to Cardinal Acton. Then, at the age of 28 he became the Rector of the English College in Rome. Following the Restoration of the Hierarchy in 1851 he was appointed the first Bishop of Southwark.[17]

Another kindness from Fr. Briggs – in June 1823 he had a message from Archibald McAllister who was held on a prison hulk called "Ganymede" moored in the Thames off Chatham, maybe waiting for transportation to Australia. McAllister asked Fr. John to tell his wife where her husband was and to tell his friends in Chester Castle that "this is a great deal better place than what was represented."[18]

From the time he arrived in Chester Fr. John involved himself in the debate about Catholic Emancipation. He was interested in local affairs and wrote regularly to the local papers. He wrote several letters attacking the Bishop of Chester's anti-Catholic speeches in the House of Lords.[19]

Fr. Briggs enjoyed the friendship and co-operation of Fr. John Hall, another great Missioner in Macclesfield. The two men, aware of the growing Catholic community in Cheshire, called for an annual meeting of all the County clergy, to discuss and organise this expansion. The two priests visited the Earl of Shrewsbury who was a generous benefactor of the church. A circular letter to the laity in the County, maybe written about 1830, could justly boast;

> The large chapel in Duckinfield…..has been completed; the Gallery in Stockport Chapel has been raised; an entire new Mission has been founded in Congleton, a handsome Chapel having been there erected; and with feelings of exultation we announce it to you that we have penetrated even into Wales…. We have still further promoted the religious education of the rising generation, by contributing to the erection of Day and Sunday Schools in the new Missions mentioned; namely Duckinfield, Congleton, Wrexham as also to the endowment to the Schools at Stockport and Chester.[20]

In 1836, Fr. Briggs succeeded Fr. Penswick as Vicar Apostolic of the Northern District. He became Bishop of Beverley at the Restoration of the Hierarchy in 1850 and he was held in very high esteem by the other Bishops. Sadly, in 1860 he resigned his See because of ill health and he died in the following year[21]. He was buried in St. Leonard's Chapel, Hazlewood Castle, nr. Tadcaster, then home of the recusant Vavasour family.

Celia Murphy 2016

References

1. Mary Winefride Sturman "Catholicism in Chester" (MWS) p.20 & Peter Phillips (PP) "Two Chester Missionaries p.4
2. PP p.2
3. MWS p. 28
4. MWS p.30 and PP p.3
5. PP p.3
6. Ibid p.4
7. Ibid pp. 3–4
8. PP p.5 and MWS p.30
9. PP pp.5–6 and MWS p.31
10. MWS p.31
11. PP pp.6–9
12. MWS p.31
13. Ibid pp.32 and 34
14. PP p.10 and MWS p.36
15. MWS p.35
16. Ibid p.35
17. pp 13–14
18. Ibid p.12
19. Ibid p.10–11
20. Ibid pp.12–13
21. Ibid p.37

The Wallis Family and St. Werburgh's

Recusant Family Connections joining Cheshire and Yorkshire

Following the reformation, the Catholic Church in Chester consisted of a small community of recusant English Catholics, later joined by Catholic Irish Linen traders who visited the city. Originally mass would have been held privately, in individual's houses, but by 1799 following the Catholic Relief Acts, a more permanent establishment, the Catholic Chapel, was built in Queen Street.

English recusancy was for the most part nurtured in the north of England on individual family estates where the Catholic owner was able to afford the penal taxes levied on Catholics. These estates, with attendant tenant farmers and workers owing loyalty to their Lord of the Manor, formed the focus for small centres of the Catholic faith to survive for the 250 years following the reformation in England. The local landowner often had a Catholic Chapel attached to his home and supported a local Catholic priest or teacher living on the estate. The agricultural and industrial revolution, starting in Georgian times, broke down this link with the Catholic landed estates, as people moved to the newly emerging towns and cities, looking for work. Priests and new centres for delivering the mass needed to be established in the fast growing towns and cities.

The impact of the Irish Famine in the late 1840's accelerated the movement of Irish Catholics to England and the New World in search of work and a better life. In Chester the population increased to such an extent that by the mid-19th century the Franciscans had been invited to form a mass centre serving the West of Chester and North Wales. Queen Street Chapel was proving too small for the increasing population in the East of Chester and new more permanent larger churches for both parishes were proposed. St. Werburgh's was envisaged as the large new diocesan church to replace the Queen Street Chapel in Chester.

For the previous 200 years, there had been no English Catholic Hierarchy and with tacit support from Rome, which had ambassadorial links with England, English recusant Catholics had developed unusual ways to circumvent the prescriptive penal laws. In Georgian times, to be considered legal, all marriages had to be conducted in an Anglican Parish Church. Catholics followed this practice, which was considered valid by the Catholic Church, even if they had a second catholic ceremony later, when a priest was available. Children born to Catholics had to be at least registered at the Anglican Parish Church. Catholics were not allowed to inherit land or property. One way sometimes used to circumvent this, was for the first born son to actually be baptised in the Anglican Parish Church. In a country where Catholicism was a minority religion, it was fairly common for there to be marriages where the partners were of differing religious faiths. On occasions such as this, it was not uncommon for a typically English compromise to occur, where any sons followed the religion of their father and daughters followed that of their mother. Such was the case of one York family, the Wallis-Dodsworth's, and this was to have a significant impact on the development of St. Werburgh's, Chester.

Clare Wallis was born 28 December 1818 and baptised at the Little Blake Street (Catholic) Chapel in Jan. 1819. Her parents Edward Wallis and Margaret Dale were recusant Catholics and sent her in 1829 to attend the Bar Convent School. This school for young Catholic girls was established in 1686 in York and is the oldest surviving Catholic convent in England and the oldest girls' school in the country. A short study of Clare's background and early life helps us to understand the future development of her marriage and the impact her family would have on Cheshire and in particular St. Werburgh's Chester.

Clare's father Edward, born 1773, married Margaret Dale in 1818. She was the widow of Thomas Smith and already had 4 children. Edward had been appointed a surgeon at the York Dispensary from 1801. In Baine's Directory, 1823 it was indicated that the objective of the Dispensary was to dispense gratuitously advice, medicine, and surgical assistance, to those who were unable to pay for them. This establishment was opened on the 28 of March 1788, more than 150 years before the formation of the National Health Service. Later, on 23 October 1834 Clare's father was recorded as holding the post of lecturer in Anatomy at the Hull and East Riding of Yorkshire School of Medicine and Anatomy. He resigned as surgeon to the York Dispensary on 18 March 1839 when he was thanked and in recognition of his 38 years' service, asked to become a consulting surgeon to the institution. He was by then 66-years-old. On 6 April 1839, the Yorkshire Gazette reported that Edward Wallis' Blake Street partner Benjamin Dodsworth had succeeded him as surgeon at the York Dispensary.

Upon retirement, Edward moved his extended family to London, living at 11 Montague Place, Bryanston Square. In London, Edward kept himself active in catholic social affairs. He supported "The Tablet", the catholic journal founded in 1840 by Fred. Lucas & Joseph Quin. Quin was the husband of Edward Wallis' step-daughter, Mary Ann.[1] Wallis and Quin ensured that the journal survived through its early tumultuous period. In 1842 Joseph Quin edited "The Tablet", during the disputes between Lucas and the publishers. Quin died in 1843 and Wallis a year later. Edward Wallis' son, John

Edward Wallis, continued the family link with "The Tablet" being both its Editor and Proprietor from 1855 to 1868, until its purchase by the Rev. Herbert Vaughan who also founded the Mill Hill Missionaries.[2]

In 1841, Benjamin Dodsworth, Edward's former medical partner in York, came to London and married Clare, Edward's eldest daughter, by licence, at St. John's Anglican Parish Church, Paddington, Westminster. The couple then returned to York, where Benjamin continued his medical and other business interests. Benjamin Dodsworth is listed as a Sheriff in 1848 in Baines Directory. He was also chairman of the York Union Bank. As a surgeon, he was one of the first people to successfully remove an appendix. Clare and Benjamin brought up their family of five boys and four girls, with the boys following the religion of their father, all being baptised at their local Anglican Parish Church, either Saint Michael-Le-Belfry, or Saint Olave, York.

The eldest son, George Edward Dodsworth was sent to The East India Company Military Seminary, at Addiscombe, Surrey, in what is now the London Borough of Croydon. It was opened in 1809 and closed in 1861. Its purpose was to train young officers to serve in the East India Company's private army in India. The second son, Francis Savage joined the Royal Navy and at the age of 18 was a Mid Shipman on the newly launched HMS Renown, a 91 gun, 2nd Rate, screw-powered ship of the line serving in the Mediterranean. The third son William Wallis Dodsworth, born in 1855, entered Pembroke College, Oxford 26 May 1874, aged 19 and gained a B.A. 1877. He was then appointed as Curate of Annunciation Church, Chislehurst.[3] This was a new church, consecrated in 1870. Its Rector, Canon Francis Murray, was part of the Anglo-Catholic revival in the Anglican Church. It is certain that the newly appointed Curate,

DODSWORTH – KIRBY – BARKER FAMILY TREE

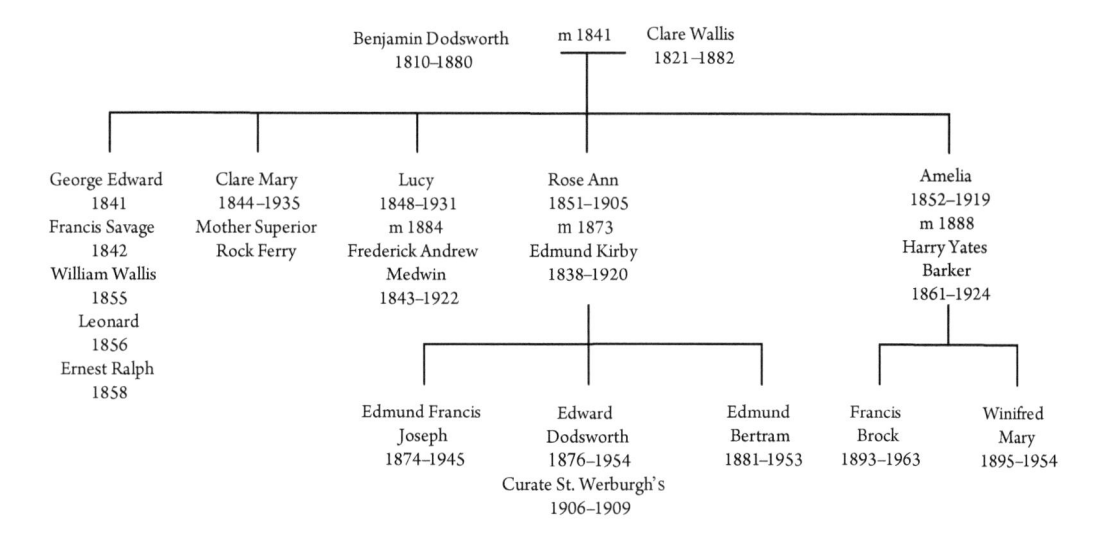

Benjamin Dodsworth 1810–1880 m 1841 Clare Wallis 1821–1882

- George Edward 1841
- Francis Savage 1842
- William Wallis 1855
- Leonard 1856
- Ernest Ralph 1858

Clare Mary 1844–1935 Mother Superior Rock Ferry

Lucy 1848–1931 m 1884 Frederick Andrew Medwin 1843–1922

Rose Ann 1851–1905 m 1873 Edmund Kirby 1838–1920

- Edmund Francis Joseph 1874–1945
- Edward Dodsworth 1876–1954 Curate St. Werburgh's 1906–1909
- Edmund Bertram 1881–1953
- Francis Brock 1893–1963
- Winifred Mary 1895–1954

Amelia 1852–1919 m 1888 Harry Yates Barker 1861–1924

William Wallis Dodsworth growing up in a family where the boys were members of the Anglican Church and his sisters followed their mother in the Catholic Church would feel immediately at home in this environment. He later returned to York to serve at Saint Michael-Le-Belfry, York, the church at which his elder brothers had been baptised. The remaining two brothers, Leonard and Ernest stayed in Yorkshire, the first becoming a farmer and the second a solicitor.

If George Dodsworth was ensuring the boys of the family had a full education to prepare them for life, Clare was ensuring the girls were equally well equipped. All four girls, Clare Mary, born 15 May 1844, Lucy born 4 July 1848, Rose Ann born 27 March 1851 and Amelia born 29 December 1852 were baptized at St. Wilfred's Catholic Church York, the new church which had succeeded the Blake Street Chapel where their mother Clare had been baptised. There is no evidence that the girls were sent to the Bar Convent in York, but the 1861 census shows Lucy Dodsworth as attending the Convent Ladies School, Clapham, a school run by the Sisters of Notre Dame. However school records are not available for this time.

Clare Mary, the eldest sister, became a nun and was eventually the Mother Superior of the Sisters of Charity at Rockferry, Cheshire. Canon Chambers attended her Golden Jubilee in 1922. Rose Ann married Edmund Kirby, the architect who had designed the beautiful church of St. Werburgh's Chester, and many other churches for the Diocese of Shrewsbury. Her sister Amelia married Harry Yates Barker, a Chester lawyer and she became deeply involved in both civic life and parish life at St. Werburgh's, the Chester church her brother–in-law had designed.

Heron Bridge, Eaton Road 2016

Baptismal Font with original cover, St. Werburgh's Church Font Donated by Mrs. Amelia Barker 1893. Cover donated in her memory, by her husband Harry Yates Barker and her children, Francis Brock Barker and Winifred Mary Barker, 1922.

Mrs. Barker became President of the Ladies of Charity at St. Werburgh's. She led confirmation groups at the church and each summer entertained the school children at her home, Heron Bridge, Eaton Road. Amelia Barker also provided the baptismal font which is still in use today. The font was first used at the baptism of her own son Francis Brock Barker in 1893. The date and initials are carved into the side of the font.

During the Great War, Amelia Barker worked tirelessly for civic and parish causes. She raised sufficient money and goods to equip ten beds at the Little Sisters Convent in Union Street. Here wounded Belgian soldiers were nursed[4]. Amelia's nephew, Edmund Francis Dodsworth, son of Amelia's eldest brother George Edward Dodsworth, died of wounds in July 1916. He is therefore, one of the few Anglicans commemorated on our Great War Memorial. (see "We Shall Remember Them")

Amelia Dodsworth Barker died in 1919. Her son, daughter and husband provided a carved wooden cover for the baptismal font, in her memory. This was designed by her nephew, Bertram Kirby, son of the original architect of St. Werburgh's Church [5]. Sadly, in recent years, the wooden lid developed a fault and has had to be replaced by a simpler modern lid. The original Amelia Barker lid is still stored at St. Werburgh's. So, through the Wallis family and particularly Amelia Barker and her sisters, recusant Yorkshire folk had a considerable influence on the development of Catholicism in Cheshire at this time.

John W. Curtis   **2017**

Acknowledgements

Use of Ancestry to obtain dates of births, marriages and residence locations through census data.

St. Wilfred's Catholic Church, York for baptismal data of Clare Dodsworth's (nee Wallis) daughters.

References

1. Wikipedia 2017
2. "The Tablet" Page 15, 16 December 1950
3. "Oxford University Alumni, 1500–1886" about Rev. William Wallis Dodsworth
4. St. Werburgh's Parish Magazines 1914–1917 for information on the work of Amelia Barker
5. Edmund Kirby and Sons, Architects, Records, Liverpool Central Library, 720/KIR 872 Letters from Freda Barker to Bertram Kirby 1923–25

The Tragedy of the Vickers Family

There are a lot of clichés about death in war such as "the supreme sacrifice" or "lives cut short" but how can anyone adequately describe the tragedy that befell the Vickers family of Chester and Salford? Joseph and Mary Vickers proudly sent their only surviving children off with the Lancashire Fusiliers to fight Kaiser Billy, but within the space of 6 months and 11 days all three were killed in action.

Joseph Vickers was born in Great Saughall, near Chester, around 1862, and Mary McLoughlin was born three years later in Chester. They were married in 1890, and lived at 64 Cornwall Street, Chester, just to the north of Hoole Way. Joseph is listed in the census as a bricklayer.

Joseph and Mary's first son, John Shepherd, was born the next year on 12 April 1891. The following year Harry was born on 28 June 1892 and Percy on the same day in 1893. Sadly John died on 15 July 1895. John Louis completed the family on 13 August 1896. All four children were baptised at St. Werburgh's Church, about a 15 minutes walk from home. There is no record of them being confirmed at St. Werburgh's.

By 1901 the family had moved two streets over to 31 Talbot Street, another terrace of small two up two down houses. The family moved again and in 1911 they were living at 74 Harmsworth Street Seedley, Salford. The area has been redeveloped in recent years but the house was probably a "back to back" with 5 rooms.

Joseph was still a bricklayer, but the boys had grown up and were working. Percy and Harry were chickers (porters) with the Great Central Railroad and Louis was a shop and errand boy. Within a couple of years Percy changed jobs, and went to work for Smith and Coventry, machine tool engineers in Ordsal Lane, Salford. The family then attended St. James' Catholic Church in Pendleton which has since then been replaced by a new church.

Percy was the first of the boys to enlist, after war was declared in August 1914. He stepped forward and signed up with the 7th (Salford) Battalion of the Lancashire Fusiliers, a Territorial Army battalion. On 20 August 1914, 7th & 8th Lancashire Fusiliers marched to their training camp north of Bolton at Turton. They weren't there long as they were on board the Saturnia and headed overseas by 10 September 1914. After passing Gibraltar and Malta, the battalion arrived in Egypt on 25 September 1914 and continued their training in the desert around Abbasia and Cairo.

The Allies opened a new front in April 1915 by attacking the Ottoman Empire at Gallipoli, also called the Dardanelles. The 7th Battalion travelled on the SS Nile as part of the East Lancashire Division. They landed on V and W beaches on the morning of 5 May 1915 and were immediately involved in the Second Battle of Krithia. Percy survived this battle and seven more months of gruelling combat. He was wounded during an attack by the Turks on Sunday 6 June 1915.

The Dardanelles proved not to be "the soft underbelly" of the Central Powers, and in early December 1915 orders were issued for the evacuation of the Allied troops. Percy was killed by heavy enemy artillery fire on 20 December 1915, just 8 days before the last troops of the 7th Battalion were withdrawn. In that time the 42nd Division had lost two thirds of its normal establishment. Private Percy Vickers has no known grave, but he is remembered on the Helles Memorial.

Percy's death was reported in the Salford Reporter on 11 March 1916:

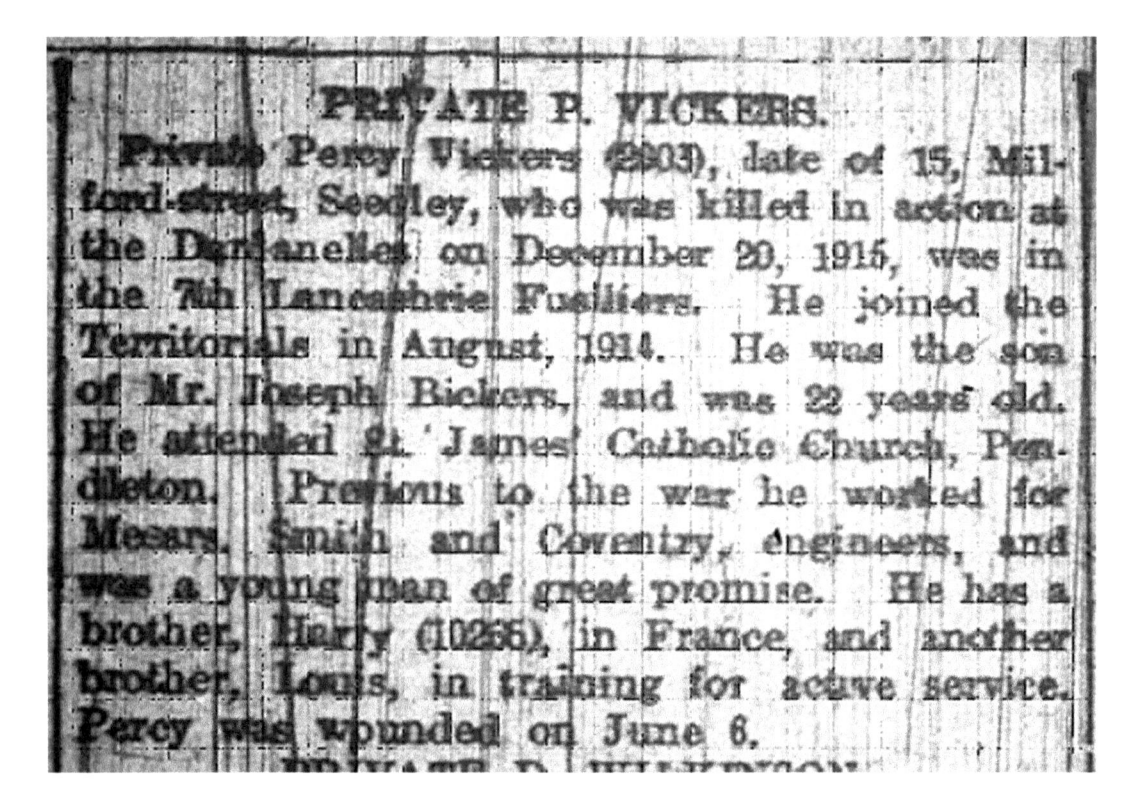

> **PRIVATE P. VICKERS.**
> Private Percy Vickers (2303), late of 15, Milford-street, Seedley, who was killed in action at the Dardanelles on December 20, 1915, was in the 7th Lancashire Fusiliers. He joined the Territorials in August, 1914. He was the son of Mr. Joseph Vickers, and was 22 years old. He attended St. James' Catholic Church, Pendleton. Previous to the war he worked for Messrs. Smith and Coventry, engineers, and was a young man of great promise. He has a brother, Harry (10255), in France, and another brother, Louis, in training for active service. Percy was wounded on June 6.

Percy's elder brother Harry enlisted in November 1914 and joined the 15th Battalion Lancashire Fusiliers, also known as 1st Salford Pals. In late December 1914 the Pals first went to a training camp at Morfa, Conwy, North Wales. Harry surely attended the drumhead mass on St. Patrick's Day and probably joined in the sports afterwards. In August 1915 the Pals moved to Codford St. Mary, Wiltshire to continue their training.

Harry was a member of B Company when a year after enlisting, the Pals arrived in France on 23 November 1915. The Battalion enjoyed good luck in the early days of their time on the Western Front, as a result of which they were nicknamed "God's Own" by the other Pals Battalions.

Their good luck did not hold on the morning of 1 July 1916, when the 1st Salford Pals went over the top to attack the German trenches at Thiepval on the opening day of the Battle of the Somme. Harry was in B Company and they were led that day by Captain Heald who shouted "Come on Salford; it at them" as they followed on after A Company. Heald, Harry and many other Pals fell that day. Most of them are remembered on the Thiepval Memorial, although Harry may lie in one of the many graves marked "A Soldier of the Great War – Known unto God". Harry is also remembered on the Thiepval Memorial in Sacred Trinity Church, Salford along with all the other Pals who fell that day.

Louis was the youngest of the Vickers boys. He enlisted, in the footsteps of his brothers in the Lancashire Fusiliers. However he was attached to the 2–5th Royal Warwicks. He was still in training in March 1916. His Battalion was posted to France in May 1916. On the evening of 1 July 1916 the 2nd–5th Warwicks. were in the trenches in the Moated Grange Sector, some 60 kilometres to the north of the Somme, where the offensive had started that morning at Zero Hour, 7:30 am.

At 9:00 pm the Germans opened an "intensive bombardment" of the front line. Over 50 yards of trenches were obliterated. Sometime in the night of 1 July to morning of 2 July, Private Louis Vickers was killed, about 18 hours after his brother Harry. Louis is buried at Number 1 Military Cemetery, Laventie. Mary Vickers had a personal inscription carved on his headstone. It reads "ALSO HIS BROTHERS HARRY (GRAVE UNKNOWN) AND PERCY (AT GALLIPOLI).

We don't know when Joseph and Mary Vickers were informed of the deaths of Harry and Louis but they would have read in the Eccles Journal that the Pals had been in "heroic charges" and the "Rolls of Honour" started to list the local men who had fallen. They must have learnt fairly quickly because their deaths were reported in the August edition of the St. Werburgh's magazine.

Sometime afterwards the three brothers were honoured in a local newspaper:

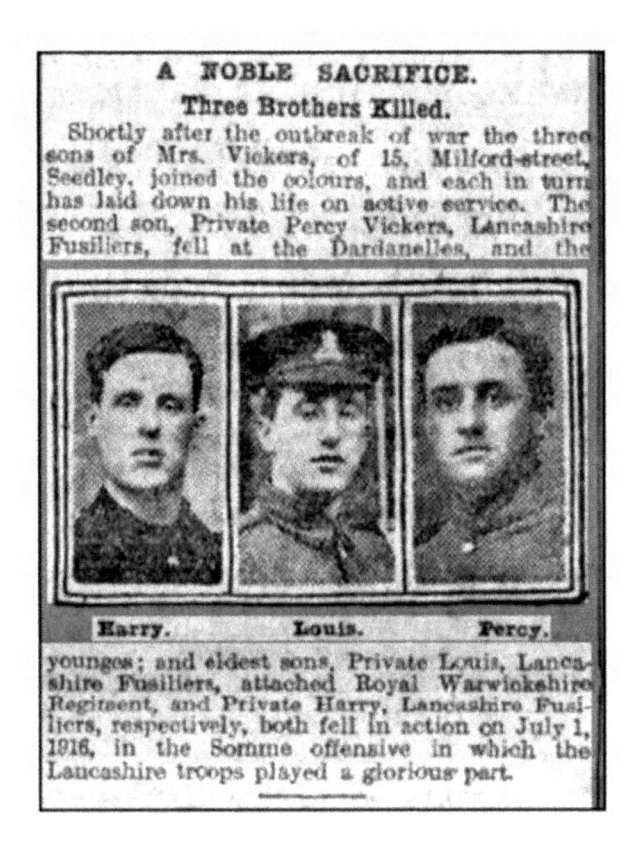

A NOBLE SACRIFICE.
Three Brothers Killed.

Shortly after the outbreak of war the three sons of Mrs. Vickers, of 15, Milford-street, Seedley, joined the colours, and each in turn has laid down his life on active service. The second son, Private Percy Vickers, Lancashire Fusiliers, fell at the Dardanelles, and the youngest; and eldest sons, Private Louis, Lancashire Fusiliers, attached Royal Warwickshire Regiment, and Private Harry, Lancashire Fusiliers, respectively, both fell in action on July 1, 1916, in the Somme offensive in which the Lancashire troops played a glorious part.

Harry.   Louis.   Percy.

Percy was remembered in December 1916:

Memoriam Notices

"VICKERS: In sad and loving memory of our dear PERCY who was killed in action December 20, 1915. He is in heaven with his dear brothers HARRY and LOUIS both killed in action July 1st. R.I.P.
Days of sadness still come o'er us,
Tears in silence often flow,
Thinking of the day we lost you
Just one year ago.
Still dear and daily mourned by your sad and lonely
MOTHER and FATHER
15, Milford Street, Seedley, Manchester."

On the first anniversary of the Somme the Manchester Evening News paid tribute to the fallen soldiers, including Harry and his two brothers.

> "**VICKERS** – In sad but ever loving memory of Private H. VICKERS Lancashire Fusiliers (1st Salford's), who was killed in action on the morning of July 1st, 1916, aged 24. R.I.P. Mother will always deeply mourn the loss of her dear friend and companion, Harry, a better son never lived, he was the soul of honour, truly one of God's Own.
>
> In fond memory also of his youngest brother, LOUIS, Lancashire Fusiliers (attached to the 2–5th Royal Warwicks) Who was killed in action on the night of July 1st, 1916, in his 20th year. R.I.P.
>
> He was always merry and bright, loving and willing, the sunshine of the home, and loved and liked by all who knew him. Both passed to the Great Beyond, to join their dear Brother PERCY 1/7th Lancashire Fusiliers, killed in action at the Dardanelles, December 20th 1915, aged 22 R.I.P.
>
> One of the nicest and dearest, only to be known to be loved, a great favourite.
>
> Three good sons and brothers, fondly attached to each Other in life, and in death not divided.

Mothers Group.

Gone are the faces to us so dear,

Silent are the voices we longed to hear,

Too far away from sight and speech,

But not too far for our thoughts to reach.

They have passed the shadowy portal,

They have borne the mortal strife,

They have left this world of sorrow

For a world of heavenly life.

And our hearts are grieving for them,

Aching with the deepest pain,

Knowing we shall never see them,

Our loved ones here again.

A heart breaking and terrible loss and a lifelong regret for
their deeply sorrowing
MOTHER and FATHER
15, Milford Street, Seedley."

Joseph died in Salford in 1925, 9 years after his sons. Life must then have been very lonely for Mary who lived for another 27 years without her beloved boys, and died in the Withington Workhouse on 10 February 1952, aged 86 years. Her death was reported by a niece, M.E. Davies who lived in Birmingham.

All that we can say today is that we hope and pray that the whole Vickers family rest in peace wherever they may lie.

Harper Wright 2015

Sources

1st Anniversary of the Somme 1 July 1917–3.pdf, n.d.
3bros_zps3c9e4456.jpg, n.d.
Census for England & Wales, 1881.
Census for England & Wales, 1891.
Census for England & Wales, 1901.
Census for England & Wales, 1911.
CWGC – Casualty Details Harry Vickers [WWW Document], n.d. URL http://www.cwgc.org/find-war-dead/casualty/817992/VICKERS,%20HARRY (accessed 10.6.14).
CWGC – Casualty Details – Louis Vickers [WWW Document], n.d. URL http://www.cwgc.org/find-war-dead/casualty/281933/VICKERS,%20LOUIS (accessed 10.6.14).
CWGC – Casualty Details – Percy Vickers [WWW Document], n.d. URL http://www.cwgc.org/find-war-dead/casualty/683772/VICKERS,%20PERCY (accessed 10.6.14).
Death Certificate – Mary Vickers, 1952.
Drum, N., Dowson, R., 2003. "God"s Own' 1st Salford Pals 1914–1916. Neil Richardson, Manchester.
Drum, N., Dowson, R., 2005. "Hell Let Loose" The 1/7th (Salford) Territorial Battalion Lancashire Fusiliers 1914–1915. Neil Richardson, Manchester.
Roll of Honour – Killed in Action, 1916. St. Werburgh's Parish Magazine.

Racehorses and Altars

Donations of the Topham-Hall Family

In 1936, Rector of St. Werburgh's, Canon Maurice Hayes, wrote "When the writer came to Chester 37 years ago, the shell of St. Werburgh's stood bare and gaunt and bleak against what was then Grosvenor Park Road. Union Street was a mud road, if road it might be called. Where the Chester Corporation Baths, now stand was the part of a disused tanning yard with an old house at the end. The present Bath Street was a series of Courts within Courts, a vile and horrible place where the poor existed during the week, and on Saturday nights knifed their fellows there and in Union Street, leaving the few clergy of St. Werburgh's to spend sleepless weekends, and compelling a Bishop of Shrewsbury to declare, on the occasion of a visit that "never had his ears drunk viler language."

Later in his article Canon Hayes recalls the names of out-standing benefactors, living and dead, who had supported the building of the church in 1873, its extension and completion in Edwardian times and the later decoration, lighting etc. that resulted in the outstanding edifice that is our church today. Who were these benefactors to whom the present generation owes so much, where had they come from and what was it like to live in Chester in those times?

At the start of the 18th century, Chester was still a very small compact city where the mayor and freeman of the City were shopkeepers, business men and lawyers. This changed as England and Ireland entered the industrial age. When the railway system was extended to Holyhead, Chester became a strategic location on the quickest route for travel between London and Ireland, with two different railway companies, the London and North Western Railway and the Great Western Railway running services between Chester and London. In the 18th century, there were very few Catholics in Chester and no Catholic Church but as the century progressed, numbers increased and the Queen Street Chapel, the first Catholic Church in Chester since the reformation was built in 1799. It was built by collaboration between the few recusant Catholics of Chester and Irish Linen merchants who traded at the Linen Halls. In 1875 this was followed by its replacement, St. Werburgh's and also the construction of a 2nd Catholic Church in Chester, St. Francis. So, who were these Catholic benefactors who supported the building of the two churches in Chester? A few were indigenous Cestrians who had lived in Chester through penal times, others came from elsewhere in England as opportunities for advancement arose, with the relaxation of laws which prohibited Catholics entering various professions, such as the law. Their numbers were then swelled by immigrants fleeing from the Irish famine in the middle of the 19th century.

One family which came to Chester around 1830 made outstanding contributions which resulted in its name being recognized country wide. Surprisingly this name is not usually associated with Chester and there are no Blue Plaques or any other public memorials that demonstrate links to Chester. It is only here in St. Werburgh's Church and in Overleigh Municipal Cemetery that these links to Chester can be found.

It was a recusant English family, the Tophams, from the Catholic heartland of Northern England. Edward William Topham married in Richmond, Yorkshire in October 1830, but immediately moved with his bride to Chester, living on Foregate Street. Their first child, Alice Dorothy Topham was baptized in St. Werburgh's Church on 11 September 1831. The 1851 census shows Edward Topham's profession as Clerk of Races. His family name is forever linked with one of England's premier horse racing events, the Grand National. The Grand National was originally founded by William Lynn, a syndicate head and proprietor of the Waterloo Hotel, on land he leased in Aintree from William Molyneux, 2nd Earl of Sefton. As a result of Lynn's ill health, Edward Topham, a respected handicapper and prominent member of Lynn's syndicate, began to exert greater influence over the National. The event had originally been a weight-for-age race but Topham turned it into a handicap in 1843. In 1848 he took over the land lease and in 1949 the Topham family bought the course outright, from Lord Sefton, from whom the land had previously been leased, since the racecourse's opening in 1829. Edward William Topham lived in Chester for more than 30 years before moving to Darland Hall, Allington, Denbighshire. Chester claims to have the oldest racecourse in England, yet there is no memorial in Chester for the man who introduced handicapping to horse racing and whose family name is still today associated with this great sport.

The Topham family were also great benefactors of both St. Werburgh's and St. Francis' Churches. In 1861 Edward Topham's daughter, Alice Dorothy Topham, married John H. A. Hall, an Anglican Chester banker. Later, their two daughters, Cecile and Josephine became prominent members of St. Werburgh's parish.

At the end of the 1890's, twenty five years after St. Werburgh's was constructed, the Church would have looked very different from today. The structural fabric of the Sanctuary, part of the main chancel and the new presbytery were completed but the internal fitments were very basic. Pews were brought from the old chapel and some are still in use to-day, but there was no electric lighting, nor any heating. The Altars were simple wooden tables covered in white cloth. Vestments, chalices etc. in daily use would be those brought from the original Queen Street Chapel. The church would have been very dark as the walls were of bare stone.

Much effort by the clergy and laity was spent during this time, raising funds to pay off the debt on the church. This left very little money to be spent on adorning the internal structure. Any more permanent improvement would have to come from the generosity of wealthy parishioners, benefactors of the church. Early examples of such generosity were the acquisition of the pulpit in 1894, a gift of Pat Collins. In the same year, Mrs. Barker of Heron Bridge made the gift of the Font.

The first permanent altar gifted to the church was the Sacred Heart Altar in 1900. The donor of the Sacred Heart Altar and the stained glass windows to St. Cecilia, St. John, and St. Dorothy, located in the Sacred Heart Chapel, was Miss Josephine Hall[2] in memory of her parents and sister who had recently died. The inscription across the three windows reads: "For Love of the Sacred Heart, Pray for the souls of John, Alice and Cecile Hall to whose memory this window and altar are erected. AD 1900." The choice of Saints for the windows reflects the names of the Hall family, Mr. John Hall, Mrs. Alice Dorothy Hall (nee Topham) and Miss Cecile Mary Topham Hall. These three members of the family died between October 1898 and April 1899. The altar was designed by Edmund Kirby and the windows were produced by Hardman. It was not until about twenty five years later that the permanent High and Lady Altars were placed in St. Werburgh's.

The Sacred Heart Altar

| St. Cecilia | St. John | St. Dorothy |

Sacred Heart Chapel Windows

The Hall family lived at Montrose House in Hough Green, at the time of the parents' deaths[3]. For a short time Cecile and Josephine Hall lived with one of their mother's family in North Wales. Later they returned to Chester and took up residence at Park House, Grosvenor Park Road, directly opposite St. Werburgh's Church. Sadly Cecile became ill and the sisters returned to their uncle's house in Bangor. Cecile died there in April 1899[4] and she is buried in Overleigh Cemetery in the same grave as her parents.

Josephine continued to live with her uncle's family but in 1905[5] returned to Chester and resumed her work in St. Werburgh's parish. Canon Chambers welcomed her in the Sept. issue of St. Werburgh's Magazine but there is no mention of where she is living. Her first project was to persuade Catholic nurses to come to the parish and establish children's clinics in Queen Street. However, according to St. Werbugh's Parish Magazine for November 1909, Josephine Hall had to leave Chester for the good of her health. Even so, in 1911, she was instrumental in enabling the Little Sisters to come and establish their wonderful work amongst the sick of Chester. Josephine Elizabeth Hall died in Holywell in 1974 at the age of 100 and is buried at Pantasaph. She had given a lifetime of service to the Catholic community of Chester, particularly within St. Werburgh's parish.

John W. Curtis   **April 2017**

References

1. 1936 Commemorative edition of St. Werburgh's Parish Magazine, to mark the Consecration and Diamond Jubilee of the church, held at St. Werburgh's
2. 1936 Commemorative edition of St. Werburgh's Parish Magazine, to mark the Consecration and Diamond Jubilee of the church, held at St. Werburgh's. Donor Miss Josephine Hall
3. Probate details of the wills of John and Alice Dorothy Hall accessed via Ancestry
4. Probate details of the will of Cecile Mary Topham Hall accessed via Ancestry
5. St. Werburgh's Parish Magazine, September 1905, held at St. Werburgh's. Miss Hall is returning to Chester

The Nelson Cup

One of those objects periodically handed in at St. Werburgh's, was a trophy cup, tarnished and non-descript. Fr. Paul Shaw suggested that we might be able to discover something about its history. We did.

When cleaned in a rudimentary fashion, the name of T. C. Nelson J.P. was seen to be etched on one side of the vessel. On the other side was a list of dates with the name of either St. Francis or St. Werburgh alongside. Reading through the parish magazines of the pre war years, we gradually pieced together the story of the Nelson Cup.

Thomas Cormac Nelson was a member of the Nelson family and firm of cattle importers. Thomas' brothers were either directors of the Nelson Shipping Line, which operated out of Liverpool, or cattle ranchers in Argentina. Cattle were reared, killed and the meat packed in Argentina. It was then transported to Britain in refrigerated ships of the Nelson Line.

Thomas Nelson, his wife Margaret nee L'Estrange and their family of two boys and two girls moved into the Mollington Banastre in 1906. They were parishioners of St. Francis' but their influence extended throughout Chester. Thomas Nelson visited the Young Men's Club of each parish, encouraging the men to make efforts in both their civic and religious lives. Margaret Nelson opened St. Werburgh's Christmas Bazaar at the Town Hall in 1908 and also visited the school. Thomas became a local magistrate and possibly because of his seeing at first hand how easily young people can commit crimes, if circumstances encourage this, he redoubled his efforts to support young men.

Mollington Banastre ca. 1912

Thomas Nelson (standing) with possibly his wife, youngest child and another passenger, in the car.

One result was the setting up of the Nelson Triathlon and Trophy. This cup was first presented by Thomas Cormac Nelson Esq. of the Mollington Banastre, in 1909. It was awarded to the winning team of a triathlon event between the young men of St. Francis' and St. Werburgh's Parishes. The three events were football, boxing and shooting. It was hotly contested, as only a local Derby can be and became the highlight of the sporting season.

The trophy was first awarded in 1909–1910 and in all pre-WW1 years it was won by St. Francis. It is surmised that much of the practice and competition took place on Thomas Nelson's land, adjoining the Mollington Banastre. The youngsters grew used to making their way there by whatever means possible, bicycle and "Shank's pony" were the favoured methods. The last year in which the trophy was awarded, was 1914–15. After that the competition was suspended, due to lack of participants, until the end of the war.

In August 1914, Mr.T.G. Frost of Mollington Hall, Mr. Ravenshaw of Mollington Grange and Mr. T.C. Nelson of Mollington Banastre set up the first Citizen Volunteers unit in the country[2]. Here, men who had not yet been called for army training, or were too young to enlist, learned marching, drill etc. and carried out target practice, on land owned by the three men. About fifty young men, mainly from Saughall and Mollington enrolled in the organisation. The movement spread and became countrywide.

One young St. Werburgh's parishioner who cycled out to Mollington every week to drill, was Thomas Goulding. Tom was wounded in action on the Somme on 7 October 1916. He died three days later.[3]

Thomas Nelson became increasingly ill as the war progressed and he died in December 1917. His requiem mass was said at St. Francis' and his body was taken to

*Grave of Thomas Cormac Nelson and his wife
Margaret L'Estrange Nelson, Glasnevin Cemetery, Dublin*

Glasnevin Cemetery in Dublin for interment in the family vault.[4] His family moved to London and the Mollington Banastre was leased by other persons. Eventually it was converted to the hotel which we see today on Parkgate Road, near the village of Mollington.

After the Great War, competition for the Nelson Trophy was resumed and the balance of victories was fairly evenly divided between the two parishes until it was suspended again, this time indefinitely, after the 1931–32 season.

One member of the group visited Lowe's of Chester, in an effort to discover details of the origin of the cup itself. Lowe's verified that the cup was made of Chester hallmarked solid silver and had been manufactured by Nathan and Hayes of Birmingham, in 1903.

This firm of manufacturing silversmiths was established in Birmingham in 1885, the partners being George Nathan and Ridley Hayes. Their first premises were at 285 Icknield Street, Birmingham. Their first London showrooms were at 95 Hatton Gardens but moved in 1906 to 13 Hatton Gardens. The Birmingham factory also subsequently moved to Institute Works, Howard Street, Birmingham.

It has been written that George Nathan commenced his commercial career in a jeweller's office at the age of fifteen and for ten years studied and mastered that particular section of the craft. Perceiving the great commercial possibilities in the manufacture of artistic looking silver articles at a moderate price, he launched out into the silverplate trade. Upon this basis the firm of Nathan and Hayes was founded.

In the endeavour to produce goods of a special character, Nathan used to the utmost his knowledge of styles and design gathered from the various art collections as far abroad as Italy and Greece, to produce copies of Mycenaean cups based on the finds now in the National Museum of Athens. The most popular were the Vaphio Cup, a small mug-shaped cup chased with bulls and similar cups chased with palm leaves and scrolls and

Nelson Cup

even with "arch and herringbone" decoration. Less popular were the Assyrian Bowl, a small one-handled bowl and the two handled Nestor Cup found at Mycenae.

The majority of Nathan and Hayes silverware bears the Chester hallmark. Because of this and also because most of their pieces were well made and designed, these makers are very popular with collectors today.

We are indebted to Lowe's of Bridge Street Row, Chester for this information and also for their expertise in the professional cleaning of the Trophy Cup.

Ann Marie Curtis and G. Tighe   **2014**

References

1. Details of the presentation of the cup and Thomas Nelson's life were obtained by reading St. Werburgh's Parish Magazines 1904–1917, held at St. Werburgh's
2. Cheshire Observer 8 August 1914 held at Cheshire Archives and Local Studies (CALS)
3. Details of the death of Pte. Thomas Goulding from an article in the Cheshire Observer of 28 October 1916 held at CALS
4. Details of Thomas Cormac Nelson's funeral were obtained from article in the Chester Courant of 19 December 1917 held at CALS

The Hunt for Lieutenant A. F. Hughes

How Fortune occasionally Favours Persistence

The death of Lieutenant A. F. Hughes is mentioned in the May 1917 edition of St. Werburgh's Parish Magazine. However, his name is not on the Town Hall Memorial nor was it on the original Hardman Memorial erected in St. Werburgh's. His is therefore one of the few names recorded in WW1 Study Group's first book, "We Shall Remember Them" where there is no information provided. This essay is an account of the search to identify him and the amazing insight into life in Victorian England, particularly in Chester, that was uncovered as a result.

Finding details of an officer is generally easier than finding details of a Private, however a review of Common Wealth War Graves Records and local Cheshire newspaper records for this period, brought no success. Further search ceased whilst the study of Fallen Men with more readily identified local connections continued. With a rapidly approaching publishing deadline, a final search was made, with efforts concentrated on reviewing Hughes families found in St. Werburgh's and St. Francis' baptism, confirmation, school and parish records. Again this met with no success. However, some possibilities did come to light.

The name Mr. Frank Hughes appeared a number of times in the St. Werburgh's parish magazines. Early mentions were Mr. Frank Hughes organising musical evenings at the Young Catholic Men's Club. An F. A. Hughes sang from the lectern with Arthur Brandreth at the High Mass on St. Werburgh's Feastday in February 1910. Later in 1916 a Mr. Hughes was Choirmaster at St. Werburgh's. A further possible clue was the F. A. Hughes bequest to Shrewsbury Roman Catholic Diocesan Education Fund[1]. Unfortunately Francis Augustine Hughes who left the bequest died 3 December 1942 in Hereford, hence could not be the Lieutenant A. F. Hughes referred to in the May 1917 St. Werburgh's Parish Magazine. However with these strong connections to St. Werburgh's, there was the possibility of the missing A. F Hughes being a cousin or other family member. To explore this possibility, a family tree for Francis Augustine Hughes and his parents Charles Henry and Laura Hughes nee Davies, was produced on Ancestry, a Family History Forum.

On 19 August 2015, the author received a message via Ancestry from USA stating "I am the granddaughter of John Timewell Hughes, one of Charles Henry and Laura

Hughes children – one of four that came to America. I'm wondering how you tie into the Hughes family". From this simple query, and many shared e-mails later, the remarkable story of the Hughes family emerged.

This story reflects the social changes and the hardships of life in Victorian England. It is also an account how people of different religious backgrounds adapted to their location and to changing circumstances. That we have this remarkable record is a tribute to the Hughes family who were great letter writers and to their American descendants who have so thoroughly researched their family history. The key Chester link in this story is Charles Henry Hughes, born 24 September 1836, baptised 25 September 1836 in the Queen Street Catholic Chapel, Chester who kept in contact with his sons, including those who had emigrated to America. Being so far from their family roots, these letters were treasured by the American branch of the family.

Establishment in Chester

Charles Henry Hughes was one of three children born in Chester to John Henry and Mary Stevenson. John Henry was a Catholic from Newry, County Down. Family stories maintain John Henry had joined an insurrection against the British because of the Corn Laws. Perhaps this was why he had left Ireland to live in England. Mary his wife was born in Ayr, Scotland, the daughter of a Wesleyan Minister, the Reverend Humphrey Stevenson. According to the Methodist Recorder of 1871, he was claimed to be the greatest Methodist minister of his time." John Henry and Mary were married at St. John's Anglican Parish Church in Preston, before moving to Chester. The 1841 census shows the Hughes family living in Northgate Street where they were next door neighbours to Greenwood Campbell, one of the Irish Linen Merchants who supported the building of the Queen Street Catholic Chapel. Unfortunately Charles Henry's father died in 1847, five months after the birth of his younger brother Henry. After this the family appears to scatter. The mother and youngest brother Henry are found living in Chester in the 1851 census. Daughter Eliza is found in London, being a boarding scholar at St. Aloysius Convent School, Clarendon Square, St. Pancras, an industrial school, where girls were given a simple education. It is very likely that Charles Henry had also been sent to school in London, although his location in 1851 was not found. On the 6 October 1861 he married Laura Davies, an Anglican, in the Parish Church of St. Anne, Stepney, Middlesex. On his marriage banns Charles Henry is described as a victualler. The couple eventually had a family of at least thirteen children, seven girls and six boys.

Early family life

Charles and Laura had six children born in London, who were baptised in the Anglican Parish Church. Because of the difficulties in bringing up a young family in a public house in London it appears that the young children were looked after by other family members such as grandparents etc., living elsewhere. Religious affiliation for the children was interesting and depended chiefly upon whom they were currently living with. For example, Alfred Davis Hughes, was baptised 24 February 1865 in the Anglican Parish Church at Abbots Langley, Hertfordshire but 5 years later, when he is staying with his Catholic grandmother Mary Williams, nee Stevenson, in Chester, he is taken to St. Francis and given a conditional baptism there. The 1871 census shows further dispersion of the family. Charles, Laura and their eldest daughter Laura are staying with Laura's mother Sarah and stepfather John Timewell at Staplegrove Lodge, Somerset. The eldest two boys, Charles Henry and Alfred Bishop, are living with their grandmother Mary Williams in Chester and there are 3 other children living with unknown adults, in this same census. Laura's step father died in January 1875, possibly prompting their moving from Staplegrove Lodge to Bawdrip, Somerset, where a son, Francis Augustine was born to Charles and Laura, 2 November 1875.

Return to Chester

The family were then re-united and returned to their father's roots in Chester to support his mother, Mary Williams who had her own millinery business, located in Northgate Street West. Charles established himself as a Linen Merchant, living at 25 New Crane Street, importing linen from Ireland and selling it at the Linen Hall. A further three of his children, Laura, Emily Sarah and Francis Augustine were conditionally baptised at St. Francis' Chester on 27 March 1876, a few months before their grandmother died. Mary Williams' address in Overleigh Cemetery records is given as Shoe Makers' Row. Six more Hughes children were born in Chester, all baptised at St. Francis.

Five years later in the 1881 census, Charles Henry then aged 44, is described as a Retired Draper. This is an unusually young age to be retired. It is believed that Laura had been left an annuity for life by her wealthy step-father John Timewell. In the census, five of their children are living at home and are described as scholars. Education must have been important to the Hughes family as Laura the eldest daughter is aged 15 and her brother William Manley and sister Emily are aged 13 and 12 respectively. This is at the time when the school leaving age for most children was 13 years and most parents were keen for their children to leave school and start working on that date, supporting the family income.

Hughes Diaspora from Chester

All of the Hughes boys appear to have been strong independent characters, possibly due to their having been brought up by grandparents etc. Charles Henry, the eldest son, was confirmed by the Bishop of Shrewsbury on the 22 September 1877 and made his First Holy Communion the same day (normal practice at that time). Two days later on 24 September 1877 at the age of 14, he was accepted into the Novitiate of the Franciscans at Pantasaph. He was solemnly professed into the Order on 4 October 1881, taking the name, Brother Albert. He would only have been 18 years of age – remarkably young by today's standards. During what turned out to be only a short life as a Franciscan, Bro. Albert later lived at monasteries in Dulwich and Pontypool.

During this time he composed and collected religious poems, then hand wrote them into a well-thumbed note book. This fragile book is retained at Franciscan headquarters in the Friary at Erith, Kent.

At St. Alban's Franciscan Monastery in Pontypool, Br. Albert Hughes began studying theology, with a view to being ordained as a priest. In the summer of 1884 he was part of a bathing party of about six students from the monastery, who went to the nearby River Usk. Br. Albert was an indifferent swimmer and sadly drowned after being caught in deep water whilst trying to cross the river[2]. Needless to say, the death of the eldest sibling greatly affected the whole Hughes family.

The other Hughes boys appeared equally determined to make their own way in life, away from Chester. The second son Alfred Bishop initially worked as an Ordnance Surveyor in Much Wenloch, Shropshire. He then joined the Royal Engineers at Chester in March 1886. He stayed in the army until June 1888 and then emigrated to Nebraska. Alfred Bishop Hughes died 14 February 1900 in Council Bluffs, Iowa, USA and was buried in Saint Mary's Catholic Cemetery, Wood River, Hall County, Nebraska, USA.

Alfred Bishop Hughes in Military Uniform ~1887

The third son William Manley Hughes joined the Royal Navy Marines on his 17th birthday and having graduated from training he was transferred to HMS Conquest where he served until 31 May 1889. During his service with HMS Conquest, William Manley fulfilled his wish to see the world. In 1885 HMS Conquest was sent to patrol the South American waters, then on to San Francisco, British Columbia and Hawaii before returning to England in 1888. He purchased his release from the Navy on 9 August 1889 and subsequently emigrated to America in 1890. He married an English immigrant, Catherine Connelly on 4 December 1894 in Pittsburgh, Allegheny, Pennsylvania, USA. Catherine had been born in 1869 in Sheffield, England, though her parents were both from Ireland.

William Manley Hughes – picture taken in San Francisco 1887

The fourth son, John Timewell Hughes, the last child born in London, surprisingly attended the Wesleyan School on St. John Street, Chester. In the 1881 census the family is recorded as living at 25 Middle Crane Street. This is just outside the city walls beyond Watergate and would be close by the entrance to Chester Race Course. John Timewell emigrated to America in 1887 and eventually settled as a farmer in Grand Island, Nebraska. He married Susan Melinda Guy, a local American girl, in 1891. Their granddaughter, Charlotte Hoak, made contact with the author and provided much family information.

John Timewell recounting his time in Chester to his daughter, shortly before he died in 1960, said "Despite the fact that I was a Catholic, I was sent to a Wesleyan Methodist school, and this was strange, since Dad was a staunch Catholic. Every day, while going to school and back home, I passed by God's Providence House. This house is said to be the only one in Chester that lost none of its members in the Black Death, a plague that hit Chester in the 1700's. (The Black Death actually occurred during the 1600's)

John Timewell Hughes taken in England before May 1887

A fifth son, Antony Hughes was sent by his father aged 13 to stay with his brother John Timewell in Nebraska, but returned to England 2 years later at the first opportunity, saying that he was a city boy, not one for the open prairie.

"Recollections of John Timewell Hughes" re his brother, Tony's 1892–1894 stay in Nebraska, JTH said:

"That fall of 1892 I really had a big surprise. Uncle Sam Guy, brother of my father-in-law, came driving in the yard, and he had with him my youngest brother Tony (Anthony Vincent Hughes)! All the way from England! His coming was a complete surprise. Without letting me know, my father just sent him out to me. A friend of the family, Ellen Jarvis O'Conner, married to Jack O'Conner who lived in Pittsburgh, had gone back to England to visit her folks in Chester, and when Dad heard that she was returning to America, he sent Tony out with her. He was just a child, thirteen years old. We tried to be very good to him, but being a city boy and from another country, he found everything strange and unfamiliar. Life on a farm was lonesome for him; really, we were pioneers. He attended school at District 16, a mile north of us, but he couldn't get used to it here, and was homesick for his homeland. In the spring of '94 we heard of a Mr. Hankey at Alda, Nebraska, who was going with a shipment of his cattle to England. Mr. Hankey said he would be glad to take Tony back to England with him."

The sixth son was Francis Augustine Hughes, the person we originally thought might be the Lieutenant A.F. Hughes mentioned in the 1917 Parish Magazine. He was the only son to stay in England. Francis worked as a Telegraphist for the General Post Office. He married Elisabeth Ann Simcock at St. Francis' Church on 23 September 1903.

No evidence was found that Francis was called up during the Great War. Francis would have been over 40 years of age when conscription was introduced in 1916 and it is also likely that as a telegraphist he would be classed as working in a reserved occupation and would therefore be exempt from conscription. Francis and Elizabeth had no children, this is might explain why after his death in 1942, Francis Augustine Hughes left money to the Shrewsbury Diocesan Education Fund.

A selection of Hughes Family Letters:-

Letters between William Manley Hughes and his father in Chester

William Manley to his father, 2 months after having joined the Royal Marine Light Infantry.

Royal Marine Depot Walmer 30 July 1884.

"I received the prayer book, picture and Observer quite safe. Thank you very much for sending them. …. They expect the Cholera here soon and are taking precautions against it. I hope it won't come for I don't want to die just yet. I want to see the world before the dead march is played over me. I expect we shall have to camp out in the fields if it comes."

William Manley to his father from Royal Marine Depot Walmer 20 August 1884

"I received your kind letter and newspapers quite safe and was glad to hear that Charlie was so much respected by the people of Pontypool. I received a picture (religious) from a gentleman of Walmer who had heard and got to know that Charlie was my brother; his name is Mr. Martin Edwards and lives at a beautiful house close by our church in Walmer. He sent it by a Marine whose name is Wm. McCarthy who goes to his house very often. I see you took one of my brothers to the funeral, which of them? They wanted to know whether I wanted to go home when I showed them the paper. I could have got 7 days pass if I wanted it."

William Manley Hughes Letter to his father whilst training at the Royal Marine Barracks Plymouth 10 April 1885

"You made my mouth water when you mentioned Welsh Mutton. I daresay it was a treat; we generally have a bit of bear or a nice piece of horse and for a treat sometimes get a leg of a large dog, fine stuff to live on especially the horse."

Charles Henry Hughes to his son William Manley in Pittsburgh, Pennsylvania, January 1898

"Tony could not keep out of trouble. He left Chester very suddenly November 26. His present address is 19 Vummer Hill, Dublin. … I expected all along he would get the gentlemen in blue on his track, but I was unable to pay his passage back to Nebraska. So he had to take his chance. What will become of him goodness only knows."

Charles Henry Hughes to his son William Manley in Pittsburgh, Pennsylvania, 28 January 1898

"Tony returned home a week ago in a state of destitution. He has parted with every mortal thing, "2 boxes full of belongings". Worked his passage from Dublin to Liverpool, and reached home at 1 am when we were all in bed, in a suit I had never seen before and never wish to see again. He said he was too late for the barracks and went off to bed. He told Frank it was the first time he had slept in 6 weeks, "poor devil". He went next morning to be sworn in and now he is at the castle and will I suppose get another 5 weeks learning his drill at the end of which time he will have to join some regiment for the next 7 years. I hope he will pull through all right but that it will do him good. It was a great pity he left Nebraska. I sent him there to keep him out of trouble but all to no purpose.

Brother Linus died on Saturday 16th just as the 11o'clock mass was finished, aged 76 he was buried at Pantasaph on Wednesday the 19th; it was exactly 45 years ago on that day he first arrived at Pantasaph from Holland along with the late father Seraphim who gave that bell that used to hang at the bottom of the church (St. Francis'). There has been an awful lot of deaths in Chester this winter, but we have kept healthy so far. I hope you got the pictures I sent you at Xmas and that you had a pleasant time. We manage to tumble through somehow, but we have long ceased to celebrate that glorious event and so leave it to those who are better able to apply their money to the jollifications, but state we are all alive so Xmas hasn't killed us. The weather has been what is called milk last dull, heavy and cold, damp, no sun.

Frank is working at the Telegraph, Tony is drilling, the band is playing the march fast; Laura is making a dress, Emily is mending up her old clothes. Gertie and Alice have just finished their lessons and are now practicing duets. Your mother is lying down for the afternoon and I am in the kitchen writing this letter.

All join in kind love hoping you are all quite well,
From your Affectionate dad,
Charles Hughes"

The Hughes Family taken during the visit of William Manley and his eldest son Charlie, September 1899

Author's Note re Antony Hughes. Having completed his training with the Cheshire Militia, Antony Hughes signed his attestation papers on 7 May 1898 in London with the Grenadier Guards, and on the 13 May he transferred to the Cheshire Regiment. He saw service in India from 5 October 1899 and served there until 11 November 1904. On the outbreak of the Great War Antony was sent to Egypt on 10 September 1914, returned to England 28 March 1915 and was finally discharged from the army 18 January 1920. On his discharge papers, the commanding officer wrote the following, "has been Exemplary, thoroughly reliable, honest, sober and hardworking, a very capable and efficient warrant officer. Good at police duties". The author wonders whether his father (who died in Chester on Good Friday 14 April 1911) would have recognised this commentary on a son who had given him so many worries in his youth.

Antony Hughes maintained contact with his relations in America. He lived in Northwich where he served as a postman. Following complaints about the of the brevity of his letters and a request to recount his experiences in the Great War, he wrote the following

Antony Hughes letter June 1, 1938 to his nephew George in America

"I will tell you some of my exploits in the Army, from asking for more food as a recruit & getting a black eye for doing so, to raising myself to the next step to commissioned rank. I have letters from generals, the King, etc. for good service rendered; I finished a First Class Warrant Officer (a real Regimental Sergeant Major with 6 medals). I was not quite 18 when I joined and stayed 22 years & 300 days and never had one black mark against me for that period. I mustn't brag too much, but there you have my record."

Antony Vincent Hughes in the uniform of the Cheshire Regiment ca 1900

Recollections of John Timewell Hughes in the USA shortly before his death:

"When I was almost seventeen, I migrated to America. Dad was always getting literature about America and its opportunities. I read all this avidly and it stirred my youthful imagination and desires. Perhaps being away from my parents and my home all my early years made it easier for me to leave home now. Dad placed a map of the United States on the table, and together we studied it. We'd had literature from steamship companies on the state of Nebraska. We decided upon Nebraska – but which place? Dad noticed a place name St. Paul; he thought having saint attached to the name would be an indication of the people's religion, and so that was the place that we decided upon. The next problem was money for transportation. Sister Laura loaned me money for steamship and railroad tickets. Dad took me to Liverpool the twentieth of April and we bid good-bye. There he stood on the deck in his Plug hat, waving his umbrella as the Steamship Peruvian of the Allan Line pulled away! I was both happy and excited in the adventure ahead of me!

We stopped at Ireland's Queenstown, now Cove of Cork, and took on an unruly bunch of Irish emigrants who fought and quarrelled among themselves all the way over. One of the emigrants was an old, old retired soldier and pensioner of the British Army. The others were constantly prodding him, trying to pick a quarrel with him. He would pound his hand on the table, defying them to fight, and saying, "Cowards! Spell it!" None dared take him up. His name was Mulcaey.

After the ocean crossing, we stopped at St. John's, Newfoundland, to discharge some cargo. We stayed on the ship the twenty-four hours it was there, then proceeded to Halifax, Nova Scotia, for a similar unloading. The ship was part steam and part sail. When the wind was good we used the sails, otherwise the steam. The trip was fairly smooth, but we ran into fog on the coast of America, and proceeded to Baltimore with foghorns blowing almost continuously. After landing there we had to go through the Customs House to have baggage examined. There were no other regulations, and no red tape in those days. They turned you and your baggage loose, and you went your way.

I had a railroad ticket, or order for one, to St. Paul, but in the meantime I heard that all the inhabitants there were Swedes and Danes – no Catholics, as Father thought! I had the ticket changed to Grand Island, and after an uneventful train journey I arrived there on May 16, 1887 – my seventeenth birthday! I went to the Wisconsin Hotel to stay the night, and got my breakfast there the next morning. Then, with a letter in my pocket from our priest in Chester, I started out to find the priest in Grand Island. I found Father Wolfe at the church residence on Second Street. He welcomed me kindly and took me into the house to talk over my plans. Together we went out among the parishioners trying to find a job for me. We finally found one with Mr. Ike Alter, a cattle feeder, who lived on West Second Street. He had some trotting horses on the adjoining lots and some cattle in rented pastures north of town. My job was to take care of the horses, currying and feeding them and cleaning the box stalls, and to mow the lawn, along with other odd jobs. One day his milk cow got balky and refused to go out to pasture, and he wanted me to ride with the other boy to take her there. "Can you ride a horse?" he asked me. I readily said I could, although I had never been on a horse. A Negro boy name Alec helped me to mount Mr. Alter's little black pony – and I immediately fell off on the other side. I won't repeat what Alec said. He jumped on the horse himself, and away he went to take the cow to pasture. That evening Alec put a saddle on the same pony, and told me I'd better learn to ride. This I did. I was to take Alec's place at work while he went to Chicago with some cattle for Mr. Alter, so it was necessary for me to know how. Both Mr. Alter and Alec were kind to me. Mr. Alter put up with so many of my mistakes, teaching me everything he could. He said, "John, you are learning fast."

I stayed with Mr. Alter as long as he needed me; then he told me of a farmer, Mr. Perkins, who needed someone to plough for him. I had never used a plough nor a team of horses. He set me to hooking up the horses. I was nonplussed for a minute, but went at it. He saw that I didn't know how to do it, so help me. After this, I did it myself – but in my own way. One day I would hook one horse on one side, the near side, and the next day I hooked him on the off side. Then I changed them each day. I did not know that the lines should be tied on the outside when I unharnessed them. Mr. Perkins was puzzled, but all he did was ask me why I changed them around. I didn't want to admit that I didn't know how, as there so many things that I didn't know, so I told him, "I think it is better that way, so each horse will learn to work on either side." He let it go without saying more, but I did it right from then on. I worked here a month longer."

So, although we still have not discovered the identity of Lieutenant A.F. Hughes, mentioned in the Parish Magazine, May 1917, we have had an interesting and surprising journey which has shed light on life in Chester at the turn of the 20th century. It has also revealed the extraordinary lives of the family of Francis Augustine Hughes, a benefactor of the Shrewsbury Roman Catholic Diocesan Education Fund, from which some of our own schoolchildren will have benefited.

The author wishes to thank Mrs. Charlotte Hoak of Long Grove, Illinois for supplying the information and letters upon which this essay is based.

John Curtis May 2017

References

1. Charity Commission website, Charity Number 525988-4, Parent Charity Shrewsbury Roman Catholic Diocesan Education Fund Governing Document Will Dated 24 March 1942
2. Western Mail 11 August 1884, South Wales Daily news 11 August 1884, Cardiff Times 16 August 1884

From Shoes to Sparks to Shells

Gunner Charles Henry Creighton

Charles Henry Creighton was born in Chester on 2 October 1889 and baptised at St. Werburgh's on 20 October. His father Patrick was a shoemaker and over the years the family lived in various locations in East Chester. Patrick's business was in Lower Bridge Street, adjacent to Gamul Terrace. Charles attended St. Werburgh's School and later worked in the family business. Sadly Charles' mother Margaret died in 1900 at a relatively young age. By 1911 the family still at home, consisting of father Patrick, elder sister Mary, elder brother Joseph and Charles, were living at 3 Cuppin Street, sometime later moving to number 21.

Gunner Charles Henry Creighton
Reproduced by kind permission of the Creighton family

When conscription was introduced, Charles enlisted at Chester, with the Royal Garrison Artillery, on 1 March 1916 and on 31 August 1916 found himself leaving Southampton for Le Havre, as part of the British Expeditionary Force. On 17 August 1917 he was attached to the Canadian Corps Signal School for instruction in wireless telegraphy.

Charles returned to his unit on 19 September 1917 and spent the remainder of his service as a wireless operator with the 24th Heavy Battery of the Royal Garrison Artillery. He fortunately survived the Great War and was demobbed on 23 September 1919. After returning to Chester he resumed civilian life as a shoemaker, marrying in 1920 his fiancée, Lilian Stanbridge, whom he had first met in Southampton, whilst waiting to be posted abroad.

The newly married couple lived at first with Charles' family at 21 Cuppin Street but later made their own home at Sefton Road, in Hoole. They became stalwarts of St. Werburgh's parish. Charles wrote about his wartime experiences, mainly for his family, in three papers which we have reproduced here. Each paper gives a wonderful picture of a different aspect of army service during the Great War. His family have given us permission to reproduce these papers.

Ann Marie Curtis   July 2017

A Night Ride

"How goes the time Ted? Six o'clock! I must saddle up. I'm last orderly tonight."

Half an hour later I am ready to leave the lines. In my satchel I have the despatches for Headquarters, where I call to collect the orders for the night to take on to the Battery. It is about a couple of miles to Headquarters, so I touch Kitty with my spurs and she breaks into a trot.

At half past six on a January evening there is little daylight left and I am almost on top of any troops that may be on the road before I can discern them. I give a sharp "Look out!" and they scatter to the side, cursing the rider who is in such a hurry on a dark night.

Presently I see the red light of the level crossing and a few yards further on is the narrow lane which brings me to my first calling place. This bye path is in such a bad state of repair that it is useless for anyone to try and guide a horse so as to miss the shell-holes with which it is pitted, so I let the reins loose and leave Kitty to pick her own steps to the sandbagged ruins of the chateau, which is now our Headquarters.

The Corps Despatch was late and I have been kept waiting at Headquarters for an hour, consequently, it is now pitch black. Kitty is tired of waiting and no sooner have I unloosed her than she prances off before I can get my feet in the stirrups. Arriving again at the top of the lane she turns her head to return home but with a tug of the rein and a jab of the spur I turn her head towards the Battery.

There is a lot of heavy traffic on the road tonight. Motor buses having taken troops up the Line as far as they dare go, are returning; and the glare of their headlights as they pass me by, so blinds me that for a second or two I am dazed and only conscious of moving through space. The jingle of chains just in front of me apprises me of the presence of wagons and carefully I draw Kitty out and guide her past them. As I go forward the traffic grows less and less until at last I have become a solitary traveller. I am at the bridge on which in day time is seen the notice "Box Respirators and Steel Helmets must be worn East of this Point." I un-strap mine, put it on my head, stow my soft cap into my pocket and swing my Gas Respirator into the "Alert" position. This is the firing line. The boom of the guns has grown louder and louder as I came along and now the roar is terrific. The hideous scenery is lit up by their flashes as though by lightning, then swallowed once more into darkness.

The last mile of my journey is over a sheer track, traversing a stretch of country which is a regular quagmire. The water sets the sleepers afloat, making great gaps between, in which horses often get their legs trapped and broken. One is lucky to cross it without casting a shoe and hundreds of these are strewn on either side. From one end to the other there is not the slightest protection from shells or splinters and so if Fritz is crumping, stumbling across this nightmare of a track is an hour of agony.

Five minutes more and I shall be across. A shell whistles overhead and bursts in the mud and I hear the rattle of the splinters as they fall on the road. Still I crawl along. The road seems interminable. Another shell! Thank goodness Fritz is lengthening. Hello! The hard road. Behind the traffic man's hut at the cross roads, I tie my horse, then take a hundred steps further along, take a half turn to the left and count fifty. My destination is reached.

To reach the sap I descend forty feet underground. The pumps which are manned night and day, to prevent the bunks from being flooded, are grunting away. In the bunks along the passages the gunners are reading, writing or chatting before going to sleep. I have only to leave my despatches at the office and I'm ready to return.

The rising moon, making the avenue of trees through which I rode look like an aisle of some great cathedral, has lit me back to the horse lines once more. "Are you there Picket?" I cry. A lamp moves forward and when it is near me, the man raises it above his head, turning the light on my face. "It's you, Orderly is it? Right oh! Leave the mare to me and I'll put her rug on. You'll find a drink of tea on the stove." "Thanks. Goodnight!"

My night ride is finished.

C. H. Creighton

The Ears of the Guns

The airmen have been dubbed "the eyes of the guns." Few members of the general public have heard of "the ears of the guns" and yet the title might be bestowed with equal appropriateness on the wireless operator, popularly known to the gunners as "Sparks", whose office is one of the most essential, exacting and responsible in the battery. He is the connecting link between the aeroplane and the artillery. If the airman deserves the encomium of being the eyes of the artillery, equally then does the wireless operator, deserve the title of being the artillery's ears.

While there is light, he is on duty and from dawn till dusk he sits at his instrument, with the phones fastened to his ears, listening to the persistent buzzing of the planes hovering over Fritz's lines, sending down their observations, thus keeping the guns busy firing on hostile batteries, transports and moving troops.

Gunner Charles Henry Creighton
Reproduced by kind permission of the Creighton family

One of the chief difficulties of an operator is to discriminate between the various calls of the numerous machines – all sending their observations at the same time – and from them to select only those which refer to targets which come within range of his own battery's guns. If one imagines a crowded meeting in which everybody is trying to speak at once, the difficulty of this task will be appreciated.

To obviate this difficulty he adjusts his condenser – or, as it is technically called – "tunes in to the wavelength" until the particular machine he wishes to listen to sounds the predominant note in his ears. There are two types of call which an operator has to listen for:- a zone or general call, and a battery or particular call. The former applies to all batteries in the zone, the latter to one battery only.

The R.A.F. is divided into squadrons, each squadron being responsible for a certain part of the line, or zone, which according to its' importance is allotted so many batteries. A pilot on patrol duty will report anything he sees:- trains, activity of batteries etc. He gives the map coordinates and every battery within range fires a stipulated number of rounds on the target.

But it is the special call which is most interesting to an operator, when he transmits a shoot exclusively for his own battery.

An observer has some particular object he wishes to destroy, so he engages a battery and marks each shot that is fired, sending down after each one, the exact distance, and direction it falls from the target, until the guns are trained dead onto it.

This is done in a very simple way. On the map with the target as centre, circles are drawn at regular intervals, and each circle is given a letter. The circumferences of these circles are divided like the face of a clock, thus by merely quoting the letter of the circle and the figure on the circumference, the exact relation of the shot to the target is known.

Although there is little excitement in an operator's life, he has a very trying occupation, requiring the greatest concentration of mind and patience. The deeds of the flying men have justly made their names famous but we mustn't neglect to honour also, the silent indefatigable worker hidden away in a lonely dugout – "Sparks".

C. H. Creighton

The Sky Pilot

The Padre is one of the most popular officers at the front. You are always certain of him acknowledging your salute with a pleasant smile and a cheery "Good-day." If he happens to be going your way he will fall in with you and chat on any conceivable subject like a chum. On these occasions he uses infinite tact; he never preaches and but for the black edging on his epaulets you wouldn't know you were conversing with a parson. He has an instinct for knowing something that will interest you. There is an unfailing topic of conversation to anybody who has been to the front – the different parts of the line they have visited – and many of the places you know, the Padre is sure to know, and probably he has participated in the same "stunts".

Whenever the Battalion goes into the trenches the Padre goes also and follows it over the top in an attack, to minister to the wounded. I know of one Battalion which lost a Padre each time it went into the trenches for three successive times.

Among the Padres of the different denominations there is a spirit of comradeship. They have forgotten their old prejudices; bigotry and rancour are dead. If you don't know where to find a minister of your own persuasion, ask any Padre you meet and he will do all he can to put you in communication with one. In a dugout in the Ypres Sector, two chaplains – one an R. C. the other a C. of E. lived together and held their services.

The Padre needs no church. He plants his altar anywhere. I have attended Divine worship in a barn, having for an altar a broken door supported on some cartridge boxes, with the dull boom of the distant guns for organ music. I have knelt in the ruins of a chateau where the wind sighed through as though in lamentation for those who were gone. Often I have listened to the Padre in the open air.

"I was with your boy in his last moments." After the stab of the fatal telegram – "Your son has been killed" what a balm to the wounded heart is the letter of the Padre. Not lying uncared for on the battle field but with a Padre by his side assuaging his agony by words of heavenly consolation and hope. What a link between you and the one you loved is he who caught that loved one's dying words.

This war has taught us many lessons. It has brought the parson and his flock together under common circumstances, perhaps from it may evolve the solution of the problem of the empty churches.

Gunner C. H. Creighton, 72012,
24th Heavy Battery, Royal Garrison Artillery, B. E. F. France.

Two Brothers and Two Wars

Martin and Bridget Gorman (nee Brown) lived at 50 Steven Street with their two children, Johnny and George. Both parents were Irish immigrants – Martin was from Ballaghaderreen, Co. Roscommon and Bridget (nee Brown) from Hollymount, Co. Mayo. Originally called O'Gorman, they changed their surname to Gorman at some time between the births of their sons John Ambrose and George.

John Ambrose O'Gorman was born on 27 March 1898 and was baptised the same day, as he was ill and thought to be in danger of death. He survived and was brought to St. Werburgh's on 10 April so that ancillary baptismal rites could be performed. On 1 December 1916 he enlisted with the Royal Army Medical Corps and was sent to France, where he had the harrowing task of getting the badly injured soldiers back to the field hospital under extreme conditions. He was later transferred to the 4th Battalion Cheshire Regiment, Army number 5632, and was demobbed on 27 February 1920. He married his wife Lucy on 4 August 1930. He later served in World War II, with the Royal Artillery during the Blitz in Liverpool and then later fought in France and Belgium. He received shrapnel wounds whilst in France and was transferred to the Rehabilitation Centre in Crabwall Manor, Chester.

His brother George Gorman was born on 22 May 1900 and was baptised at St. Werburgh's on 3 June the same year. Information from George's family indicates that, although too young to be called up at the start of the war, George lied about his age to enlist and was stationed abroad. He served with the 51st Battalion, Welsh Regiment, Army number 79798. In 1920 he was still in the army, serving with the 55th Battalion, Welsh Regiment but had left the army by the time of the 1921 census. He and his wife Emmeline were married on Christmas Eve 1923 at St. Antony's RC Church, Saltney. They went on to have 12 children. Like his brother, George also served during World War II. He was stationed at the Mersey forts manning the Bofors guns, where he was injured and taken to the Dale Hospital.

George Gorman

Etty Thompson, George's daughter, wearing her British Empire Medal

Following in their father's footsteps George's sons, Terence (Mick) and Martin both enlisted during World War II, into the Royal Air Force and the British Army respectively.

George's family carried on the connection to service in the two world wars. His daughters, Etty, Dolly and Pat, were stalwarts of the women's section of the Royal British Legion. Etty, who joined in the mid-1960s was the recipient of many awards, including the Royal British Legion gold award and poppy award, and in 2013 she received the British Empire Medal from the Queen in recognition of her many years of service.

Stella Pleass   **August 2017**

The author gratefully acknowledges the contributions of Julie Holmes and Karen Phillips, both George Gorman's granddaughters. Julie is Etty Thompson's daughter. Karen is Jimmy Gorman's daughter.

The Duke's Dash through the Desert

The land upon which St. Werburgh's Church is built, has always been regarded as having been sold to St. Werburgh's by the 1st Duke of Westminster. If so, then the 1st Duke continued to take an interest in the parish, after the church had been built. During the 1890's he donated £5 annually to the St. Werburgh's Schools Fund[1]. He also visited the school on a regularly spasmodic basis and usually left a bounty to be spent on sweets or other treats for the children[2]. He was a very welcome visitor, especially as far as the children were concerned.

The 2nd Duke of Westminster was his grandson, Hugh Richard Arthur Grosvenor, born in 1879 and mainly raised by his grandfather, as his father had died in 1884. The 2nd Duke was usually addressed by his nickname Ben d'or, as his hair had a red tinge, similar to that of one of his grandfather's race horses of the same name. Bendor served with the Royal Horse Guards and saw active service during the Boer War. His grandfather died in December 1899 and Bendor then succeeded to the title and estates. After a brief visit back home, he returned to South Africa in February 1900 to serve with the Imperial Yeomanry as an ADC to Lord Roberts and Lord Milner. Bendor married Constance Edwina Cornwallis-West in February 1901 and he resigned his commission in December of that year. The couple had two children, Ursula born in 1902 and Edward born 1904, who would inherit the family title and estates. Sadly Edward died in 1909. His death was a personal tragedy for the family and was the subject of a eulogy in the March edition of St. Werburgh's Parish Magazine. Another daughter, Mary was born to the couple in 1910 but later the Duke and Duchess became estranged.

2nd Duke of Westminster, Major Hugh Richard Arthur Grosvenor, during his service in South Africa

In 1914 the Duke volunteered for active war service and was given a temporary commission in the Royal Naval Volunteer Reserve, assigned to the Motor Boats Section, patrolling home waters. This was terminated on 21 April 1915. A more active role was granted to him after he had designed and had manufactured 10 armoured motor cars. They were made by Rolls Royce at Crewe and delivered to the Westminster Coach and Motor Car Works in Chester Town Hall Square, until recently the site of Chester Library. The cars were fitted out to the Duke's specifications and he had them sent to Egypt, all at his own expense. The Duke then joined the Motor Machine Gun Corps in Egypt on 26 September 1915[3].

British Empire forces had been in place at Suez since the beginning of the war, in order to safeguard this essential seaway. The Senussi were an Arab religious sect resident in Libya and Egypt, who were courted by the Ottoman and the German Empires. In the summer of 1915, the Ottomans persuaded the Grand Senussi, Ahmed Sharif es Senussi, to raise jihad, attack British-occupied Egypt from the west and encourage insurrection in Egypt. This was to divert British forces from an Ottoman Raid on the Suez Canal, from Palestine.

The Senussi crossed the Libyan-Egyptian border in November 1915 and fought a campaign along the Egyptian coast, where British Empire forces at first withdrew. They later defeated the Senussi in several engagements, culminating in the Action of Agagia and the re-capture of the coast in March 1916.

It is during the campaign in March 1916 that the Duke of Westminster showed considerable initiative, heading the Light Armoured Car Brigade. At first there had been little opportunity for service but in the exploit on 14 March 1916 the armoured cars proved their value in desert warfare. They were able to move quickly in the desert, provided that there was no deep sand, and so counteract the natural mobility of the desert tribes.

Mediterranean Coast of North Africa

Rolls Royce armoured car, Palestine 1918

After an enemy camp had been discovered at Bir Asiso, some 23 miles from the British positions, the Light Armoured Car Brigade – 9 armoured and 1 open, with a total crew of 32 men – captured all of the enemy's 40 guns and machine guns, took 3 Turkish officers and about 40 other men as prisoners, killed 50 men and wounded many more[4].

Using information gained from prisoners, it was ascertained that the crews of the torpedoed "Moorina" and "Tara" were being held some 75 miles west of Sollum. All of the three armoured car batteries spent 16 March servicing their vehicles and at 3.00am on 17 March, 42 cars then dashed off to Bir el Hakim (Bir Hakkim), covering 120 miles of hostile territory, without support and rescued the prisoners, without loss of life. The prisoners, who had been close to death by starvation, included Captain Rupert Gwatkin-Williams and crew of the "Tara" which had been torpedoed in the Mediterranean in Nov. 1915.

The exploits of the Duke were given prominence both by national and local newspapers and Major Hugh Richard Arthur, Duke of Westminster, Cheshire Yeomanry, was awarded the DSO for this action, as well as being promoted to Colonel. The action did however mark the end of his somewhat ad hoc approach on the battlefield and his conduct during the remainder of the war was less spectacular. The cars subsequently proved not really suitable for desert warfare because they easily became sand clogged and were always in need of servicing. However, they did prefigure both the armoured car and the tank, which were to be introduced somewhat later.

Violet Mary Geraldine Nelson

The Duke returned to England after the war and he and his wife were soon divorced. Then the Duke's eye fell upon another prospective bride, Violet Nelson, daughter of Sir William Nelson of Acton Hall, Wrexham and niece of Thomas Cormac Nelson, who had donated the Nelson Cup to St. Francis' and St. Werburgh's parishes. The fact that Violet was already married to Major Francis Rowley and had a small son, did not seem to perturb him. In fact it proved that Violet could become the mother of sons and a marriage to her might solve his inheritance problems. Violet succumbed to his charm offensive, obtained a divorce and married Bendor in 1920. The couple had no children and the Duke took several mistresses. The couple divorced in 1926. Bendor married twice more but neither union produced any children. However, the Duke did seem to enjoy a very contented final marriage, until his death in 1953. The title then passed via several cousins, until Lt. Colonel Robert Grosvenor, grandfather of the present 7th Duke, succeeded in 1967.

Ann Marie Curtis **November 2016**

Bibliography

Field, L. Bendor *The Golden Duke of Westminster*, CALS ISBN 0-297-78046-8
Bendor – Duke of Westminster, A personal memoire by George Ridley with Frank Welsh with a forward by Anne, Duchess of Westminster held at CALS ISBN 0-86072-096-9

References

1. Sturman, M.W. *Catholicism in Chester, A Double Centenary, 1875–1975*, pp84, 86
2. Log books of St. Werburgh's Boys' and St. Werburgh's Girls' Schools Z DES 46/2 and Z DES 47/3 held at Cheshire Archives and Local Studies (CALS)
3. WW1 Record of Hugh Richard Arthur Grosvenor ADM/337/117 National Archives
4. Chester Chronicle Saturday, 25 March 1916, held at CALS

Third Time Lucky at St. Werburgh's

In the 13 March edition of the Cheshire Observer, 1915 there was a short piece about 10 wounded soldiers who had arrived at Hoole Bank Auxiliary Hospital in Chester. One of those listed was Lance Corporal Frederick Walters 4599, of the Connaught Rangers.

Frederick was a former regular army soldier and enlisted with the 3rd Battalion, Special Reserve, Connaught Rangers, on 12 October 1914[1]. He arrived in France on New Year's Day 1915, just in time to prepare for the spring offensive[2]. Those troops who had survived the horrors of 1914 had dug in and carried out a defensive strategy throughout the winter. Now, an offensive was being planned for spring 1915. An attack on the German positions around Neuve Chapelle, on 10 March 1915 was to be the first of several offensives which would hopefully re-take territory north east of the Allied trenches. Though

Sister Harriette McNulty

well-planned, as always, unforeseen events and responses muddied the waters and only 2km. of extra territory around Neuve Chapelle was captured. It was probably during the first day, of what was later called the Battle of Neuve Chapelle, that Frederick Walters was injured and evacuated to this country for treatment.

At the same time, Sister Harriette McNulty was nursing Indian Army patients at the Brighton Pavilion Hospital. Harriette had been born in Londonderry on 29 December 1975. By 1901 her parents had died and she was living with her elder sisters Caroline and Brigid in William Street. Sometime after this, Harriette moved from Londonderry to London, where her sisters Marguerite and Charlotte, who were now both married, were living. Their address was 113 Chesterton Road, Kensington and later 133 Chesterton Road. By 1911 Harriette was working as a nurse at the Central London Sick Asylum Poor Law Infirmary, in Cleveland Street[3]. When war broke out, Harriette volunteered for duty with the British Red Cross and would doubtless have been snapped up immediately, as trained nurses were in extremely short supply. She served in France from 1 November 1914 but later she was sent to the Brighton Pavilion Hospital, where she nursed Indian troops. This hospital was taken over by the War Office in January 1915 and Harriette then became part of Queen Alexandra's Imperial Military Nursing Service Reserve. On 12 February 1915 Harriette renewed her contract as a QAIMNSR for another 12 months[4].

Somehow, Walters and McNulty had made each other's acquaintance before the Great War and had become engaged. Twice they had planned to get married but on each occasion, though banns had been called, one or the other had been posted away and their plans had had to be cancelled. However, when Harriette heard of her fiancé's evacuation to a hospital in Chester, she set plans in motion for a third attempted wedding. She applied for a special licence, which would enable her and Frederick to marry at any licensed building in this country. The licence was expensive but that was of no consequence at this stage. Harriette had already received a posting to Egypt but there was apparently some delay in sailing. The licence was obtained just in the nick of time and Harriette and her sister Mrs. Charlotte McVeigh made the journey by train to Chester. Then they went to Hoole Bank Hospital and conveyed Frederick, who was wheel chair bound, to St. Werburgh's Church[5].

Canon Chambers was willing to carry out the ceremony but the ladies had not thought to bring another witness with them and so Fr. Maurice Hayes was commissioned to be best man. The wedding occurred on Tuesday 8 June at 11.00am. No doubt the two clerics wished the couple the best of good luck and then the two ladies pushed Frederick back to Hoole Bank.

Royal Red Cross Medal

The matron of Hoole Bank Hospital, Mrs. Smith, had prepared a celebration tea for the patients and newly-weds, though it may not have been possible for the ladies to stay and partake. They had to catch a train back to London, and Harriette from thence to Brighton, as she was due to leave for Egypt the following day!

Harriette then worked in the Anglo-American Hospital in Cairo, where she herself later succumbed to health problems. She was repatriated to this country in late 1916 and was granted sick leave until 22 February 1917. On 27 February 1917 her service was terminated. She had returned to her sister, Mrs. Marguerite Clarke's house, at 133 Chesterton Road in Kensington, from where she conducted a campaign to be granted a pension which took account of her service at Brighton. Eventually this was granted in 1919[6]. Harriette's war service was recognised when she was awarded the 1914–15 Star, the British War Medal and the Allied Victory Medal. She was also awarded the Royal Red Cross Medal for exceptional services in military nursing. She was presented with this medal, by King George V at Buckingham Palace and the event was recorded in the British Journal of Nursing, issue 21 April 1917.

After their wedding, Frederick continued to be treated at Hoole Bank Hospital but it has proved impossible to find any records concerning his discharge. He was eligible for the 1914–15 Star, the British War Medal and the Allied Victory Medal. It is possible that he may have died soon after the end of the war. His wife, Harriette died in London, in 1924.

Hoole Bank House today

Hoole Bank House was used as an Auxiliary Hospital throughout the Great War and was closed as such in 1919. The owners of the House, Mr. and Mrs. Hayes, had been devastated by the death of their son Harry, during the Great War. They never wished to return to the house where he had grown up and so, in 1920 Hoole Bank House was donated to the National Institute for the Blind, which organisation used it as a holiday home. After passing through a series of several different owners, from 1969 it has been the home of The Hammond School.

Though over a hundred years have passed, St. Werburgh's is still there on Grosvenor Park Road, and it's Marriage Register still contains the details of the June day in 1916 when Frederick Walters of Hoole Bank Hospital and Harriette McNulty of London, were eventually married, at the third time of trying.

Ann Marie Curtis **July 2017**

The author wishes to acknowledge the contribution of David Rees, of Hoole History Society, in the cross referencing of material concerning Harriette McNulty.

References

1. Great War Forum, mhifle July 2017
2. WW1 Medal Rolls Index Card for Frederick J. Walters accessed via Ancestry
3. Census for 1901 accessed via Ancestry
4. QAIMS file for Harriette McNulty WO/399/5310 National Archives
5. Cheshire Observer 12 June 1915
6. QAIMS file for Harriette McNulty WO/399/5310 National Archives

The History and Mystery of the War Memorial Chapel St. Werburgh's Catholic Church, Chester

As early as December 1917 Canon Chambers, the rector of St. Werburgh's since 1903, proposed in the Parish Magazine the building of a memorial to the parishioners who had given their lives in the Great War. At this time the outcome of the war was by no means certain but whichever way events were to play out, Canon Chambers was convinced that the parish of St. Werburgh, which had already made so many sacrifices during this war (and was to make still more) should have a memorial to commemorate them. In his opinion the memorial should be a side altar portraying Our Lady of Sorrows and in this chapel should be placed a plaque carrying the names of the fallen men.

Canon Chambers felt that only persons who had lived in the parish or been benefactors of it should be named on the plaque and that the family proposing a name should donate a sum of perhaps £1. I feel sure that this subscription idea was not strictly adhered to in the ensuing years. There were persons named on the memorial whose families could not possibly have afforded such a sum. On the other hand there were generous donors who probably paid more than the quoted £1.

After 1917 no more magazines were published, probably due to paper rationing. Newspapers also were curtailed e.g. Cheshire Observer fell from around eighteen pages to around four during this period. However, we can surely imagine without written evidence, the rejoicing which was experienced in the parish when the guns fell silent on 11 November 1918 as the Armistice was signed and when the Peace Treaty of Versailles was signed on 28 June 1919. Perhaps those celebrating most were the children, who were given a day off school on each occasion[1]!

We can also imagine the mixed feelings of those families to whom a father or son was not to return. There must have been much planning and fundraising within the parish during the next few years, so that the Memorial Chapel and Plaque to the fallen, could be realised. These activities culminated in a letter sent from Canon Chambers to the architectural firm of Edmund Kirby and Sons of Liverpool, on 5 April 1921. Edmund Kirby was the architect who had originally designed St. Werburgh's Church. Kirby died in 1920 and his son Edmund Bertram Kirby was the recipient of this letter. In it, Canon Chambers asks Bertram Kirby to design an altar for the Great War Memorial Chapel. He wishes the altar to be in red sandstone, with a Pieta relief in white stone or plaster. He also mentions that Hardman's of Birmingham have received a commission to make a plaque, with the names of 96 fallen parishioners upon it. He expected the plaque to arrive in another two months and it had certainly been placed on the wall of what was to become the War Memorial Chapel, by October 1922.

War Memorial Chapel, St. Werburgh's Catholic Church, Chester

A letter sent by Canon Chambers to Bertram Kirby on 11 October 1922 asks Kirby to now design a cavity in the altar. The cavity should be large enough to contain a bottle enclosing a scroll listing the 96 names. Apparently he had promised this to the families who wanted their loved ones named. He said that the 96 names represented 96 grieving mothers and was most insistent that Kirby should include a cavity in the design of the altar. Kirby apparently completed this extra task and Canon Chambers congratulated him later, saying that the whole church of St. Werburgh was a tribute to both his father and himself[2].

The altar and plaque having been installed, on 15 September 1923 the Great War Memorial Chapel was dedicated at a High Mass celebrated by Hugh Singleton, Roman Catholic Bishop of Shrewsbury. The Cheshire Observer of 22 September 1923 carried a lovely picture of the Memorial Chapel and an article about the dedication. It was apparently the first Great War Memorial to be placed within a Chester Church. The Chester Chronicle carried a description of the Memorial Chapel and almost the full text of the sermon preached at the dedication ceremony! The Memorial Chapel was described in glowing terms and the altar as a whole was said to be an exquisite sculpture and an asset to the City of Chester[3].

However, the fate of the memorial plaque has not been so fortunate. It was wrought by Hardman and Co. of Birmingham, the premier metal workers of the day, who had also produced most of the stained glass and metalwork within St. Werburgh's Church. Sadly, during some restructuring work in the church post WW2, the plaque was lost. This was a tragedy for the parishioners of St. Werburgh's.

In the 1980's Fr. Lloyd, an assistant priest at St. Werburgh's tried to reconstitute the list of names which had been on the plaque. This was a complex and extremely difficult task. It involved trying to contact living relatives of past parishioners and asking help from the Cheshire Military Museum and any other bodies who might have information. Internet access to some records was not as freely available as it is today but Fr. Lloyd and his team eventually compiled a list of 68 names. (They probably did not know the story of the 96 names in the altar cavity.) The 68 names were written in illuminated text on card and placed in a frame in the Memorial Chapel. Joseph Gray, Roman Catholic Bishop of Shrewsbury officiated at the dedication ceremony in 1990[4].

We now fast forward to 2013. Many citizens and Government officials felt that in the year of the centenary of the start of the Great War, commemorative events or activities should take place. Local History Societies were asked to promote these and many chose to undertake research into the names on the memorials in different parts of the country. It seemed as though this could be feasible for St. Werburgh's, if a group of interested people could get together to engage in the work. 68 are a great many names to research! Fr. Paul Shaw was very supportive of the idea and a group of interested parishioners started work. Their efforts were rewarded when the biographical details of the 68 parishioners who died in the Great War were placed on our parish website. Seven more persons were discovered whose names should have been on the list but were not placed there in 1990. This brought the total to 75.

During the research phase, two of the study group went to visit the Liverpool Records Office, where the papers of Edmund Kirby and Sons have been deposited. They were delighted to find there, the letters previously described, between Canon Chambers and Bertram Kirby, about the War Memorial Chapel and the scroll of 96 names. Unfortunately this meant that they now had at least 21 more names to find and research! It also meant that the full original list of fallen men was buried within the altar but there was no way of reaching it and discovering the names. So near and yet so far!

More new names for the memorial were suggested and checked out but there seemed no way that the mystery of the full list of original names on the plaque could ever be solved. Then internet research revealed that the Hardman archives had been deposited in the Wolfson Archive Centre of Birmingham Library. Much of the firm's archive material had been destroyed by a fire in Hardman's premises but the remainder was in Birmingham Library. It seemed too much to hope that records of the St. Werburgh's items would be preserved. Against all the odds however, it was found that the order form for the original St. Werburgh's Great War Memorial Plaque was intact. On the order form was a list of the 96 names which Canon Chambers had mentioned. There was also a description of the plaque and its inscriptions[5]. What a bonanza!

In a separate file there was discovered a letter from Canon Chambers to Hardman's, yet again requesting an alteration. Apparently the rather frail mother of a fallen soldier had not been able to get down to St. Werburgh's in time to put her son's name on the list. Canon Chambers was concerned that it should be added. By this time the plaque was complete and had been hung in St. Werburgh's. Hardman's agreed to make an additional piece of bronze with the name of James Francis Kelly inscribed, which could be added to the original plaque. The plaque had cost £100 for the 96 names, roughly £1 per name. The name of James Francis Kelly cost over £3[6]!

The discovery of what we came to call the Hardman List allowed us to compare the names listed on the original memorial, the 1990 memorial and those gathered during the 2014 research period. As had been suspected, a few names on the 1990 memorial were not valid, most of the newly gathered names were and 36 completely new names had been found on the original memorial. This brings the total number of names for the new WW1 memorial plaque in St. Werburgh's, to 121.

Today in the War Memorial Chapel there are also lists of parishioners who died in WW2, Korea, Northern Ireland and Afghanistan. The altar of red sandstone, with its contrasting white Pieta, is still stunning and provides a place where parishioners can remember and pray for service personnel lost in all wars and their families. It is special in many ways but particularly in the way that the names of its original Great War dead were first gathered, then lost and then, after two attempts, found again.

Ann Marie Curtis April 2014

References

1. Log Book of St. Werburgh's Girls' School, ZDES 47 Cheshire and Chester Archives and Local Studies, Duke Street, Chester (CALS)
2. Deposit of Edmund Kirby and Sons, 720KIR/872 Liverpool Records Office, St. George's Square
3. Chester Chronicle, 21 September 1923 CALS
4. Leaflet re. Dedication of WW1 Memorial 1990 held at St. Werburgh's, Chester
5. Order 181, Hardman Order Book for 1920–1922, MS 175/A/4/3/9/10 Archives, Birmingham Library
6. Miscellaneous letters in Hardman Archives, MS 175/A/4/3/9/10 Birmingham Library